Fiscal Years
2020 - 2029

Community

Legislation

Judicial

Academics

Production

Distribution

Advancian
Systemic Reform Solutions
Global Economic Security Initiative

Real Solutions

ECONOMIC SECURITY AND SOCIAL STABILITY INITIATIVE

Advancian is a global initiative to prevent poverty, unjust economic disparity, human rights violations and abuses with use of data compiled with global political, monetary, production, distribution, academic, and social system application technology.

QUICK FACTS:

To evolve, global societies require global solutions. Plan 360 includes:

- The solution for 100 percent global employment
- A standardized global compensation system to ensure the payment of fair wages for all members of society, and to accurately determine the true cost of production for the stabilization of prices
- A dual monetary and earned equity economic systems will ensure money has true value and will prevent financial collapses
- Global debt settlement plans ensure the fair repayment of investments to all stakeholders and prevents enslavement of future generations that would have been burdened with our debts
- Ends the dependency on corporations for the payment of wages and the provision of health and retirement benefits
- Methods and tools to end political and social corruption and that serve to build and preserve social alliances
- Truly free open and fair markets
- The inclusion of global and local labor unions and trade guilds that protect the rights of the labor force without the worry of fair compensation arguments that hinder corporate and labor relations
- A system that upholds the rights of the individual and sets those rights as a primary focus to ensure equality for all people

Your donation helps spread awareness about the Systemic Reform Movement

BOOK

Title:	Advancian - Systemic Reform Solutions
ISBN:	978-1-7337740-3-1
Version:	3.2020

PUBLISHER

Published By:	AdvanCN
Offices:	Chicago, IL USA
Website:	AdvanCN.org
Phone:	+1 (312) 274-5055

INITIATIVE

Advancian is a global Systemic Reform Movement and the developer of the plans for the System Core – and subsidiary of AdvanCN. Your donation is needed and appreciated. To support systemic reform initiatives donate at http://Advancian.org or send your gift to:

> Advancian
> *Mail Center of Chicago*
> 332 South Michigan Ave., Lower Level - A67
> Chicago, IL 60604-4434
> +1 (312) 274-5055

AUTHOR

Author:	Wrina Iamwe – Chief Trustee
Author Contact:	iamwe@AdvanCN.org
Editorial Assistant:	Mark Hirmer – Chief of the Board of Directors

TABLE OF CONTENTS

PART I – AMEN CODE

CONFIRMATION OF THE PLAN FOR MANKIND AND THE DIVINE RIGHT OF THE PEOPLE

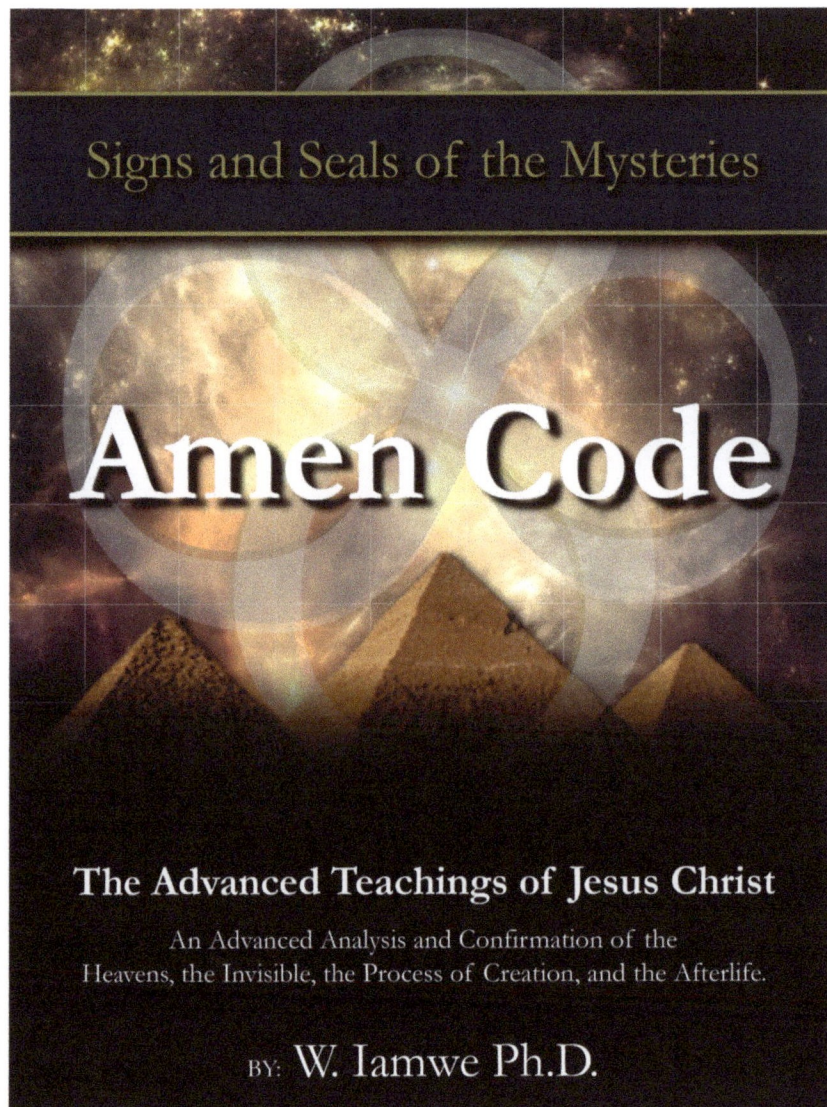

Signs and Seals of the Mysteries

Amen Code

The Advanced Teachings of Jesus Christ

An Advanced Analysis and Confirmation of the
Heavens, the Invisible, the Process of Creation, and the Afterlife.

BY: W. Iamwe Ph.D.

Note: This document is gender-neutral, unless specified.
The words man and men are used interchangeably and refer to
humankind as a whole, which is inclusive of both males and females.

Our goal is not to shut down systems, nor needed processes, nor administrations. Governance is required to ensure we have the basic necessities of life such as food, shelter, heat, electricity, transportation and communication systems, as well as laws of agreement, security, and peace of mind.

Our goal is to perfect that which our forefathers, with limited knowledge and technology, could not achieve; that which men who hold and have held power have not accomplish – the perfection of our social and economic systems; a perfection that ensures access to what is required, so each man and woman can achieve their full potential.

There must be peace and security if we are to advance. Therefore, we must develop the systems required to yield it. Which, in turn, will enable us to forgive and Love each other.

I am not an idealist, nor a utopian. I understand hatred, corruption, and the ignorance that leads to man's greed.

I understand how easy it is to speak of justice and righteousness, and how difficult it is to enact those sincere beliefs, especially, when so much pain has been inflicted.

To build the systems we propose herein, will require the building of trust and a pledge of nonviolence in an atmosphere of anger, in an age of lying and corrupt men. Men who are motivated for resources and profit; men, who thirst for war and dominance of a global empire they are not capable of ruling.

Creating a global system and convincing the world to join hands for a peaceful resolution will not be an easy task. I believe in God but suffer no delusions.

What I propose can only be achieved by great men:

Men who do not flee with fear.
Men who take on the unknown.
Men who believe in themselves and their visions.
Men who believe anything is possible.
Men who do not yield.
Heroes.
The called, chosen, and faithful.

Continued…

To change our world we must jointly will it.

The things mankind creates are willed from the core of our being. Our core is the force of creation, and, our link to our creator.

If you desire to make the world a better place; if you desire to end hunger, poverty, job loss, exploitation and abuses that have led to economic and social dysfunction; if you sincerely believe this world can be saved; if you wish to mend wounds and heal hearts; if you desire to end corruption; if you desire to effect law and have a vote that truly matters; if you will take up the pledge of peace, I request not that you follow us, but the union of our wills.

Wrina Iamwe
email: iamwe@AdvanCN.org

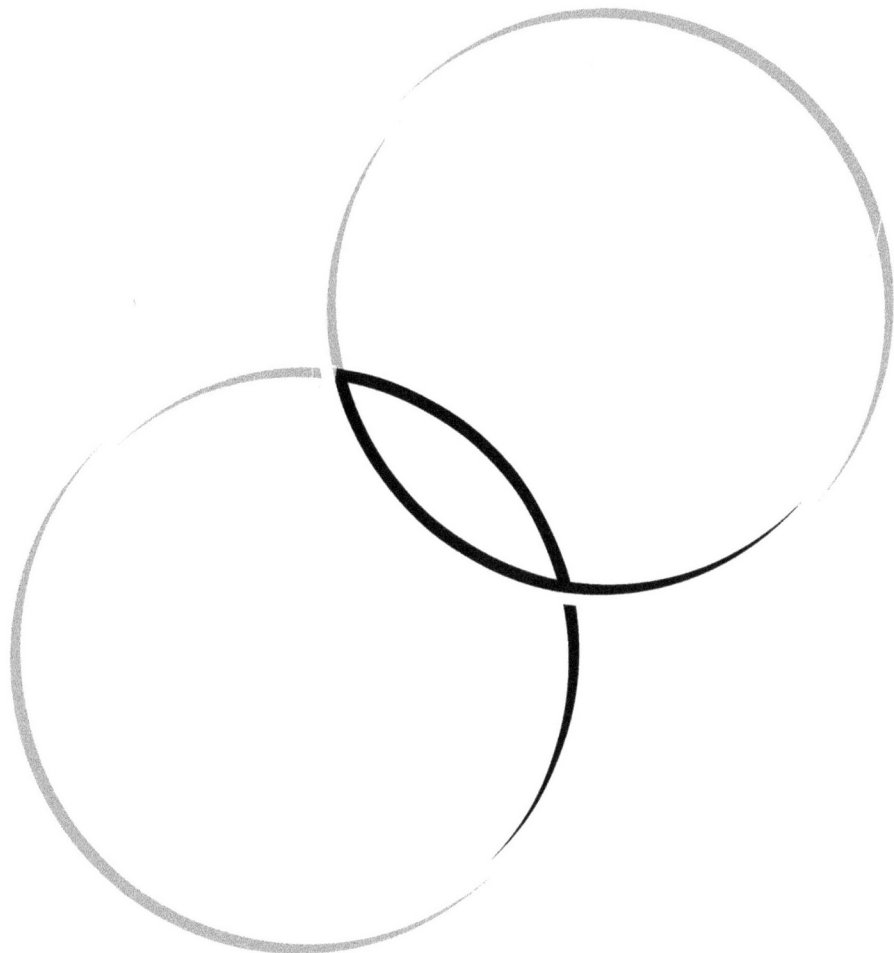

INTRODUCTION

Advancian is a systemic reform movement focused on 1) the development of social and economic software applications and integration systems termed the System Core, 2) human rights, and 3) legislation for constructive social and economic reform.

The premise of *Advancian* is that by merging the best aspects, ideologies, and processes of capitalism, democracy, and socialism we can create a world that is equitable and just for the permanent end of poverty for all people.

The System Core is a solution to address the dysfunctional aspects of our social and economic systems. It is a comprehensive, multifaceted, non-fractional education, policy, social and economic development, human services access program, and computer/online/mobile application. Specifically, *Advancian's* systemic reforms focuses on the creation of technological applications for: monetary stability, need assessment analysis and provision, production efficiency and ecological effect tracking and analysis, resource provision tracking and access, democracy elevation; education equality, affordability, and motivation; job creation and employment stability; fiscal transparency and accountability; and local and international debt settlement for the prevention of domestic and international violence, which has propagated religious, ethnic, political, and national conflicts.

Your commitment of support will aid in the construction of real social and economic technological systems that can be implemented locally, nationally, and internationally, enabling the people of the world to conceive that we can create and that they should expect superior social and economic systems.

THE NEED

The dicode effects (constructive versus destructive) of natural Law which determines the proper functionality of a system or process has, by merit of empirical evidence, revealed that our social and economic systems do not function properly – if they did function properly, there would be no need for charitable organizations or foundations. Based on natural Law, the predictive result for mankind, without infusion of constructive actions and processes, is not favorable.

There are aspects of capitalism, democracy, and social ideology that have proven to function well. If properly implemented and the rights of all people secured, these systems can function more efficiently; serve a broader percentage of the population without abuses; and make significant improvements in the quality of life of all people.

The current systems we make use of have been corrupted by individuals whose purposes and intentions do not honor the potential of mankind. Our systems are without proper checks and balances, and without applications that yield transparency, which serves to embolden corruption in our political and economic systems.

What Advancian is not

Advancian is not a prescriptive plan for imposing an Orwellian New World Order. Advancian is the antithesis of Orwell's vision of the New World Order, as secrecy is not embraced – our mission and preparations are not and will not be concealed. Rights are outlined to protect the people from censorship and intimidation. Our plans were chartered to ensure: human life, equality of vote, freedom of choice, full transparency, justice, freedom of speech and religion; to ensure the will of the people can abolish unjust laws, and individuals can propose and amend law; to ensure individuals and groups are protected from arrest and incarceration for offenses that have not resulted in physical injuries or death; and to ensure the people's grievances are resolved.

Advancian is not a regime that can be imposed, but a way of living that can be adopted. It is not a pipe dream, but a vision that can be accomplished. It is not a set of rules, but a way of thinking about how we solve problems. The software solutions we propose are not implementation-ready, but plans to create working system prototypes that can be implemented and utilized to explore the complex relationships between needs, abilities, resources and possibilities. The systems we describe are what we think will work. We do not pretend to have all the answers – it will take a global effort to refine and improve the systems and tools that we propose. Advancian is an invitation to the world to create the ultimate solution.

What the System Core is and Who it Serves
The technological applications, which are outlined in detail as we proceed, make use of constructive outcome logic. For example, the interlacing system design for our economic system interrelates with the policies and various systems we have conceived to ensure social and economic stability.

1. The Dual Monetary System makes use of Earned Equity for standard needs provision and money for Capital Markets.

2. Our global monetary standards make use of thirteen factors to stabilize the creation of money, and ensure the value of money globally without need of monetary policy manipulation. Through interlinked National and Global Compensation and Transaction Administrations (GCTA), the equitable payment of compensation is ensured regardless of gender, nationality, or ethnicity/race (see http://Advancian.org/model-1).

3. The Earned Equity System interlaces with Labor Management Systems to ensure one-hundred percent employment of all able-bodied persons, and also secures an individual's retirement through the Standard Needs Earned Equity System, to prevent the debt burden of retirement accounts upon states and governments.

4. Our Dual Monetary System interlaces with our Political and Production Systems, and our 60/30/10 Resource Partition Plan and Systems to provide manpower. Proper provision of manpower ensures that the products society determines (by vote) to be required, are provided for all people, based on indigenous materials, resources, de-production and recycling, and will be tracked by Production and Resource Inventory applications, and components.

5. Our local and global 60/30/10 Resource Partition Systems will interlace with Production Systems to ensure resources are available for Standard Needs and Capital Markets (Capital Markets - require monetary exchange), to prevent resource based wars and conflicts.

6. In-turn, the Standard Needs Earned Equity System and Capital Market Systems interlace with our Employment Systems and use the Global Compensation Standards to determine compensation based on skill level, education level, and position hierarchy, ect., to ensure price stability.

7. Capital Markets Systems are utilized and allow an individual to purchase goods and services, which are not available in the Standard Needs Earned Equity System, and thereby ensures innovation.

8. Our Legislative System is interlaced with our Production System and the Standard Needs System so citizens can determine what products are needed, the availability of resources, and grant resource acquisition rights to corporations.

9. Corporations are interlaced within the system without having the expense of resource or labor procurement, creating open and fair markets, and securing labor rights, unions, and independence. Also, ecological devastation can be minimized based on de-production (labor will be committed to the de-production process through the Earned Equity System) and mutual consensus, which will be tracked by Resource Warning Systems.

10. Our Education System is also interlaced with the Earned Equity and Monetary Systems as the rate of one's compensation is directly linked to an individual's education and skill level, and serves as a natural incentive for higher education pursuits. This will also help to prevent job discrimination, which helps to diminish social stresses that provoke protectionism and intolerance.

11. Our Debt Settlement Plans (see Advancian.org/model-3) and currency conversion (See Advancian.org/model-2) systems ensure a peaceful transition for all global markets.

The vast scope of Advancian will require a conglomerate of individuals from numerous industries, professions, institutions, and nations, individuals who are currently being sought out to aid this project. Creation of the applications we term "The System Core", will be a project of mass undertaking – and a legacy and monument comparable to the pyramids of Egypt.

For the last ten years we have worked to develop the initiatives for Advancian – created the Methodology and Calculations for Global Economic and Social Security; created the Global Compensation Standards, Implementation Plans, and Online Interactive Calculators; and conceived the Global Debt Settlement Plan and Online Interactive Calculator – without compensation. We have a sincere and earnest need to dedicate our energy towards endeavors that help to heal and educate the world.

Social and economic systems are dynamic and intricate, and must, if they are to function correctly, embrace the micro and macro functionality of its various parts and interrelated systems. They must constructively balance the rights of the individual and society. To ensure stability for the end of poverty, we must peel back, account for, and analyze all the layers of our social and economic systems to ensure the needs of the people can be met. If needs cannot be met with the constructs at hand, we must develop innovative technology and systems and ensure they function correctly, and determine viable cooperative solutions.

The systems we currently embrace are not befitting of conscious beings with the ability to mold their environments and perceptions. The end of poverty, fear, and need are concepts embraced and ardently pursued by advanced societies and conscious beings. Within us is a vibrant light that is diminished by injustice, inequality, and pain, which limits potential.

The system applications we propose are innovative, yet, many of the components already exist under private systems. These separate systems do not interface nor interlace to yield the dynamic information required to motivate social and economic change, nor to ensure the proper management of social and economic systems.

With your assistance we can build the dynamic social-economic systems required to unify mankind for the permanent and peaceful end of poverty. This will motivate people to pursue knowledge and education with a new found hope of earned rewards for their labor and a renewed belief in liberty and justice. The systems, services, and knowledge The System Core will produce will help to end the hypocrisy of a system that promotes the inalienable rights of all people, yet cunningly destroys the spirit of hope, belief in freedom, and the attainment of justice.

OPENING STATEMENT

THE PROBLEM

The social and economic systems we envision are interdependent and intricately woven together with the societies of each nation through the earth's vast ecological systems. Time and trials have revealed that though we speak different languages, and the hues of our skin differ, we are emphatically one and inseparably linked (regardless if we wish to acknowledge this truth or not). All people require the same basic necessities: food, shelter, water, clothing, medical care, and education.

The actions of one affect the whole, and our cumulative actions produce worldwide effects – some good, some bad. Typically, however, our actions are unmeasured, which allows us to ignore or to deny our destructive effects, and to disassociate the root cause. In a macro sense, we excuse our actions through legislated rights, use the excuse of tradition, and report our abuses as necessary acts for the interest of our nations. In a micro sense, we indulge our desires to the point of obesity, purchase items we do not need, made by forced labor or low wage slaves which set idle in our closets, in storage, or on display shelves.

The 1.5 million nonprofit charities [1] and social service agencies in the United States and the vast number of charities throughout the world have yet to solve the cause of poverty, political and economic instability, and social stresses that lead to poor parenting, intolerance, the mass killing of civilians, and premature death due to disease, famine, suicide, revolution, and war.

Trillions in today's dollars have been invested and donated in an attempt to end the various strains of man's afflictions and suffering. Thousands of people have been helped, yet the struggle of poverty, hunger, disease, educational inequality, clean water, affordable housing, and economic stability still persists in this, the twenty-first century.

Are we doing something wrong? Are the social and economic systems and policies we make use of designed to fail? The answer to both questions is yes.

Our current condition is directly and ascertainably linked to the policies, laws, systems, processes, and ideologies we devise, use, and enforce. Thus, the cause is man.

The majority of our problems are caused by our lack of love for self, other beings, and the earth; which results from:

---

[1] According to the National Center for Charitable Statistics (NCCS)

- Our lack of understanding of what is right
  (If an action results in a destructive physical outcome for self or another, the action is not right (positive/good), it is destructive (negative/evil).
- Our belief that we have the right to inflict physical or mental harm upon those who are of different: religious faiths, political beliefs, nationalities, races, colors, gender, economic classes; education, skill, or knowledge levels; or those who have homosexual preferences.
- Our lack of acknowledgement of the cause of an effect.
- Our allowance of social, political, and judicial corruption.
- Our fear of the damage other men can inflict upon us and our families and friends.
- Our desire for unearned wealth, and the belief of entitlement for that which we have not expended energy to produce.
- Our need for resources, the limited supply of resources, and our inability to collaborate to equitably distribute resources.
- Our inability to accurately calculate needs and account for resources.
- Our greed and the elevation of self above others.

The systems controlled by the men who have maneuvered themselves into power, lack the ability to compute resource availability compared to needs, and promote the wasteful use of resources. And we, the people, are unable (or unwilling) to collaborate to determine the proper processes to undertake to improve our systems, which inhibits the engagement of appropriate plans and actions.

Thus, the appropriate social agenda to encourage need provision and conservation is not promoted nor adopted. Instead, a destructive agenda of continuous unsustainable growth that ensures our extinction is believed and embraced.

Yet, most of us either love the system as it is (rather, we love our status, convenience, and ego, and ignore the negative effects that result from our actions); or, we fear, hate or are indifferent to the systems we are told we democratically control.

To truly end poverty, hunger, unemployment and the various ailments that plague our world a systemic cure is required. A systemic cure also requires the ascendance of consciousness of all human beings, especially those who create money, control access to natural resources, and legislate laws, the people who initiate conflict and those who support it, and those who enforce man made laws.

The policies and schemes created by established intellectuals and reputed best economists have proven not to work well. The use of Federal Reserve System, Central Banks, and International Monetary Fund policies have created unemployment, world-wide poverty and abuse, inflation, recessions, market collapses, housing bubbles, unnatural monetary creation, insolvent banking systems, and indebted generations yet to be born – their concepts are based on old world oligarchies, false theories, and skewed ideologies.

Many of these intellectuals and economists acknowledge the systems they have created cannot be fixed, and are based on flawed theories that are not adequate in concept for a global economy with billions of participants. They have synthesized fractional banking and quantitative easing policies which fictitiously increase the money supply and thereby demand. High demand raises the prices of goods and services for the poor, which slowly festers rebellion, results in war – and is a system of culling.

The fear of equitable distribution of natural resources would diminish if people were taught, recognized, and acted constructively based on real outcomes. Individuals could recognize these real outcomes if they were provided with fully disclosed information that revealed both positive and negative effects. Truth can only be determined with accurate reporting systems.

THE PROBLEM IS SYSTEMIC

The systems we make use of are not compliant with Natural Law, and thus fail to ensure the needs of the people are met. Our current systems are inadequate for:

- Analyzing the true state of production and capacity
- Determining the true state and percentage of unemployment
- Determining the true will and desire of the people
- Assessing the true effects of legislation and production
- Ensuring and enforcing resource conservation
- Ensuring innovation and open markets
- Ensuring the proper education of all citizens
- Ensuring efficiency, justice, and deterring crime and corruption
- Ensuring people can develop their full potential

Further, governing administrative bodies are inadequately educated for solutions, and often are cruel and corrupt beyond logic and reason.

Many nations suffer the effects of prescribed poverty, ill health, are exploited, and lack the technical education and skills to properly make use of the land's resources for the benefit of its native population.

Even though our systems as well as the individuals we have placed our faith and trust in to administer our systems have failed us, there is fear and reluctance to abandon old ideas that do not work. To do so would further erode confidence in a system people must believe in because there is no alternative.

The American Dream was publicly defined in 1931 by James Truslow Adams in *Epic of America*. Adam's often-repeated quote states, "*The American Dream is that dream of a land in which life should be better and richer and fuller for everyone, with opportunity for each according to ability or achievement.*" Adam further adds, that the American Dream is not, "... *a dream of motor cars and high wages merely, but a dream of social order in which each man and each woman shall be able to attain to the fullest stature of which they are innately capable, and be recognized by others for what they are, regardless of the fortuitous circumstances of birth or position.*"

Every human is entitled to the basic requirement of life, which many have termed the "American Dream." Achievement of the "American Dream" which we term "Standard Needs", for the vast majority of people is impossible. The potential to achieve "the ideal life" for most has broken under weight of a swollen welfare state of entitlements and subsidies that many rich men benefit from by means of government grants, contracts, policies, and institutionally sanctioned low wage slavery. Greedy individuals (not necessarily rich men, but often the case) lack understanding of the effects their ill conceived concept of the "ideal life" has on other people and our environment.

Greed is a dissociative mental illness that allows the afflicted to act compulsively to fulfill perceived short-term or long-term needs and compulsions without thought of the long-term effects their actions play upon others, society, and the ecological systems we all require. Greed is destructive, and acceptable only to those who have yet to elevate their level of consciousness.

Our problems are numerous yet rooted in the same cause— the violation of human rights:

Political (Legislative) and Judicial Injustice

- The inability to effectively participate in or change political policy and legislation.
- The threat of imprisonment and physical violence to force obedience to unjust laws.
- The use of misleading information to enforce man-made laws and political or resource acquisition agendas.
- The inability to submit grievances and receive justice.

Production and Distribution of Injustice

- The inequitable distribution of resources because of monetary inequity.
- Artificial cost and arbitrary price concepts for need based resources.
- Barriers to entry (closed markets with high cost capital investment requirements to gain access).

Compensation Inequality

- Arbitrary determination of labor value, which determines one's social class, the availability of resources, and the education one can afford.
- Slavery whether low wage, induced, or forced because of the concentration or the disparity of wealth.

Academic and Information Inequity

- Inadequately informed and uneducated members of society.
- Limited, manipulated, and inaccessible information that prevents proper decision making.
- The high price of higher education.

We, as a society, have not confirmed the rights and standard needs for all people, and there is no system accurately tracking the fulfillment of all needs to ensure they are met. Because people lack accurate information, they are not conscious of the true scale of need, nor the need for resource conservation. We require a root cure to reverse these negative effects.

THE SOLUTION

Though many achievements have been made, and numerous people assisted, the war against poverty, exploitation, and corruption has been fought unsuccessfully for centuries. The war has not been lost, only slow to utter the victory cry, awaiting the ideals and constructs of an awakened generation.

The initiative, Advancian, is not a fractional approach to solve our challenges, nor is Advancian a request for a small stipend to place a bandage on a festering wound, because, what is required is a systemic cure.

Advancian is a complete solution proposal to remedy the dysfunction of process and policy that has led to: monetary instability, unemployment, labor and human rights violations, welfare dependency, poverty; and unaffordable healthcare, housing, healthy food, medicine, education, and training.

To solve our challenges what is required is a centralized system that:

1. Accurately conveys information that details needs
2. Accounts for all material resources and human resources
3. Determines the true cost of providing needs
4. Ensures adequate compensation and stabilizes costs

5. Allows people to actively participate in the construction and approval of legislation, and to control the judicial process and outcomes to ensure justice for all people.

Advancian is the proposal of a systemic solution based on a global vision that can end social and economic injustice.

The task of creating a compassionate and just society seems daunting. Yet, the causes of poverty and inequity will continue to exist without international collaborative action and the building of a Global Information System (GIS), that is able to intake and disseminate accurate data – knowledge of both good and evil.

THE SYSTEM CORE

The concepts the System Core makes use of are based on logic, and the effects derived from the observance of natural laws, that unlike the laws of man, are unalterable; and truth which reveals the positive and negative effects of actions.

The proposal we submit to you is indeed no small task, and yet it is a task that must be undertaken if mankind is to unite, if war is to be prevented, if poverty is to claim no further victims – as poverty was contrived in the minds of evil men and prospers because of the absence of love, because destructive men and women have prevailed.

The System Core is necessary and plausible
We must advance jointly, to ensure that:

- An open system that takes all actions into account is created
- The system tracks all needs, the distribution of all resources, and details all compensation and exchanges
- The data is accessible to all people
- Every individual contributes to the formation of agreements that govern their interactions
- The people have the right to amend the system, should corruption occur

As we proceed, the System Core will be outlined in context of how it will enable achievement of the concepts proposed and as a solution to the problems addressed in this opening statement.

Due to the international climate of distrust and the failures and corruption of current administrative bodies, the initiative we are proposing requires an unbiased, honest, effective, and independent leadership to establish international communication and to inspire global cooperation to ensure the System Core's development. Further, the vast scope of this initiative requires a conglomerate of individuals from numerous industries.

Advancian was formed to coordinate this challenge, and will serve as an advisor for the benefit of all people regardless of nationality, religion, race, gender, or class, and will ensure the interest of the individual is balanced with macro-economic, social, and international needs.

The world has changed and is changing. Millions are awake and ready to soar. The systems we propose will prepare and awaken billions.

We ask that you do not limit us. Endow us with a new legacy, one that will allow us and the generations that are to be born to achieve our full potential – a legacy and monument that will be greater than the pyramids of Egypt.

We all stand on the shoulders of the great men and women that came before us; those who laid our foundation and laws, and those who built our infrastructure and developed technology. Thus, those aspects of our current systems that function positively are embraced and will be retained.

> **The Lord said, "If as one people speaking the same language they have begun to do this, then nothing they plan to do will be impossible for them…"**
>
> **Genesis 11:6**

Meaning: If the people of the world are <u>united</u>, in clear understanding and in agreement about what we need to do, then act – it will be.

SOLUTION SUMMARY

INNOVATION

The System Core is an innovative solution that ensures global stability of monetary systems; the equitable settlement of all debt; global price stability; secures employment for all able-bodied persons; and is a method to prevent social and economic collapse.

The System Core is a tool to stabilize democratic societies. Currently, there are no comparable all inclusive solutions, nor are there viable monetary creation models, nor debt settlement alternatives that are equitable and have proven to function correctly to mitigate financial, economic, and social collapse.

Currently, people must make use of the systems in place which are rife with corruption and abuses. There are no alternatives because alternate methods for governance, monetary creation, and resource acquisition are considered treasonous by the conglomerate of governments, banks, industry, media, and learning institutions which all serve as one impenetrable monopoly that exacts control over people to the point of exploitation and abuse, and are the root cause of poverty, social decay, and economic collapse.

NETWORK COLLABORATION

Collaboration with all countries, industries, and organizations is vital to the success of the System Core. Thus, all organizations and persons are welcome for the planning and development process, and their input will help to ensure the needs of all people, corporations, and organizations are considered, and will enhance our global initiative.

LONG-TERM VISION

Our vision is to ensure every man and woman has an equitable social and economic system that allows them to achieve success without abuses and exploitation of other beings.

Advancian will help shape the System Core's ideology and methodologies to ensure all stakeholders receive equitable access to resources and services. Upon completion of the System Core, we will be an Independent Advisor; without official appointment of legislative rights; nor will we have control over the System Core. The System Core will have a globally elected administrative oversight board of directors who will be completely answerable to the people of all nations, and their joint powers restrained by the policies suggested and detailed herein – which will require enactment by the people of every nation of the Global Alliance.

The System Core will be the property of the people of all nations. AdvanCN, does not seek to rule, nor to govern the people of any nation, but to ensure they are endowed with the rights and tools to govern themselves.

Many obstacles will need to be overcome to achieve our vision of an equitable world. The first challenge is invalidating the ideology that people have the right to inflict physical and mental harm on other men; so that we may end physical conflict to encourage trust among all nations. Overcoming this initial challenge is essential to ending abuses, which all nations must agree to, to begin the process of collaboration to build the System Core.

The System Core is a major global undertaking with collaborative elements, and will be a closed system with checks and balances to ensure proper functionality for global data input with advanced system processing and intelligent algorithms for every process and industry. We envision a system where individual programmers will be able to submit core application enhancements and components.

The initial framework for the System Core is outlined in this proposal, and may be modified as various participants provide insight into the requirements needed for successful operation.

EVALUATION OF SUCCESS

We have outlined a complete list of benchmarks that will indicate the success of the System Core. The benchmarks can be viewed in the section titled, Highlights Benchmarks and Benefits of Success, page 24.

RISK AND CHALLENGES

Informing the world about, and developing the System Core, will be a challenge because many governments and nations are nationalist in nature, protective of their national interest (which they should be) and may perceive the System Core as a challenge to their independent authority and sovereignty.

Others may view the System Core as a New World Order with schemes of global social and economic conquest. This is not our intent, which will be evident as one reads the proposal. If the safeguards written into the proposal are not adhered to, abuses could occur, as they have with our Constitutions and Bills and laws for human rights.

Distrust can only be overcome with complete transparency of all programming code and data, and open access to the technology and hardware required for the System Core.

Establishing trust will be a long process that will be built over the duration of system planning, development, and the integration process; and must be maintained during implementation. Therefore, the System Core must be a global initiative without exclusion.

The System Core must be accepted as independent, unbiased, and non-exclusive.
Just as nature provides food for all people and beings to ensure their existence; the System Core must be legally classified by all nations as a force similar to nature, which is to be unbiased in time of war or national conflicts.

All nations will have access to system technology, and will be educated about every aspect of programming and technology for their own peace of mind and security.

We estimate within 20 years of global system integration, mankind will learn to work together peacefully and mend our world.

Many challenges will occur. With any relationship that requires healing, open communication, complete transparency, patience, and forgiveness will be required.

SCALABILITY

We can begin planning, development, and initial system testing. Full implementation will commence when the people of each major nation agree on its capability to ensure justice and equality. Individual nations will be able to adopt the System Core when the people are ready and meet infrastructure requirements.

If we do nothing; if we do not begin to explore what is required to perfect our social and economic systems; if we continue down the same path, if we continue to lack checks and balances, fairness, and stability, we move the world closer to its destruction.

There is a point at which, due to preexisting conditions, old systems cannot be fixed, regardless of the measures taken. Thus, proactive actions are required. If we do not create a system that functions properly, we will destroy each other and our world.

The construction of the System Core may seem daunting, yet, without the attempt our destruction is inevitable. This is said not to cause fear, nor panic, nor to prompt your gift, but because it is a fact. There are natural laws all, no matter how great, must bow to.

IMPACT

The System Core will impact the lives of every nation, of every man and woman throughout the world, and all corporations, and governments.

The System Core will aid in analysis to compile accurate data to mitigate poverty; will help to end hunger that does not derive from nature (i.e. extreme drought versus sanctioned induced hunger), and will aid us in the best use of our resources.

The Human Development Report (Date: 7.8.2014) estimates:

- Total percentage of world population that lives on less than $2.50 a day is 50%
  Total number of people that live on less than $2.50 a day is three billion
- Total percentage of people that live on less than $10 a day is 80%
- Total percent of world populations that live where income differentials are widening is 80%
- Total percentage of world Income the richest 20% account for is 75%
- Total number of children that die each day due to poverty is 22,000
- Total number of people in developing countries with inadequate access to water is 1.1 billion
- Number of children in the world is 2.2 billion, of which one billion live in poverty
- Total number of children that live without adequate shelter is 640 million (one in three)
- Total number of children without access to safe water is 400 million (one in five)
- Total number of children with no access to health services is 270 million (one in seven)
- Total number of children who die annually from lack of access to safe drinking water and adequate sanitation is 1.4 million

In addition, thousands of people die each year due to resource, political, or social conflicts; most are the result of rights violations.

The System Core will help each community determine the cause of deficiencies and conflicts so we can solve them.

PROJECT DURATION

We estimate the System Core can be planned and developed within four years, and implemented globally thereafter within three to five years.

With your support the planning process can begin in 2020, and international implementation achieved by 2026.

PROJECT RISK

Awareness is required to ensure the people of every nation are informed about the System Core, and to ensure it is fully funded. Funds are required to build the System Core, however prior to planning and development it is essential to obtain consensus. Thus, the distribution of publications, the production of information videos, and the building of a collaboration portal so all people can input their ideas about the functionality of the system and the various components they will require, in addition to the systems outlined in this proposal, will be necessary. Thus, disinformation and a lack of communication, participation, and consensus pose the greatest risks.

The online communication and project management portal for Advancian is located at http://SoAct.org.

SYSTEM CORE COST

Cost estimates for the planning and development of the System Core are estimated at $627, 306,022 for Phase I - Planning, through Phase V - Testing. With an estimated 144,000 foundation members contributing $622 per year (on average), for seven years, the cost is roughly $51.86 per month, or $1.73 per day per foundation member. The project will require a commitment by a joint commission of foundations, private donors, governments, corporations, education institutions, and the people of every nation.

The System Core is financially sustainable based on implementation of the monetary models used for the operation of the System Core, which is explained in detail within the proposal.

SYSTEMIC REFORM MOVEMENT

Centralized Groups. Forums. Events. Communication. News. Project Management. and Transparent Funding System

Collaborate with people who are actively working to heal the world through non-violent, constructive effect driven plans and initiatives.

Together, we can create the world we envision.

| LOGIN | REGISTER | Code for Liberty |

Believe we can right the world - Act

Hello, We are live online.

LEADERSHIP - INTRODUCTION

NFP Initiatives is the oversight organization for Advancian to ensure participation by a broad spectrum of individuals, financial transparency, and mission fulfillment.

AdvanCN is the founder and designer of Advancian. AdvanCN is a religious organization, established in 2008, to bring about global peace. The religious influence and inspiration serves to ensure that AdvanCN can build the System Core without government interference, as the first amendment rights within the constitution of the United States, allows a religious organization and the people to bring about societal advancement without it being considered treasonous, as it states:

Amendment I - Congress shall make no law respecting an establishment of religion, or prohibiting the free exercise thereof; or abridging the freedom of speech, or of the press; or the right of the people peaceably to assemble, and to petition the Government for a redress of grievances.

The religious foundations of AdvanCN is detailed in the book Amen Code. Advancian – Systemic Reform Solutions is the second part of the Amen Code and fulfillment of the order's religious mission.

PROJECT CREATOR

Wrina Iamwe is the founder of AdvanCN and Advancian, author, the visionary of the System Core and the developer of the plans, methodology, and system calculations:

- Global compensation standards, calculations, and implementation plans
    - Hierarchy
    - Maximum Compensation standards
    - Consumer Credit
    - RP Tax Grant
    - Residual Income
    - APEC – Accurate Past Earnings Calculator
    - Student Compensation
- Global debt settlement plan, calculations, and processes
- 60/30/10 Resource partition plan
- Resource usage efficiency calculations

Ms. Iamwe was born in the United States in 1970, grew up in San Diego, California, and migrated to Chicago, Illinois in 1995.

Ms. Iamwe received her Master's in Social Economics and a Ph.D. in Theology from the Ordination Institute – Chicago Seminary, a subsidiary of the Order AdvanCN.

Her doctoral research focused on understanding the common ideological goals of religious, social, and political groups to determine the requirements for the creation of mutually beneficial standards that result in the achievement of global social and economic security, equitable practices and processes, and political policies for the prevention of violence and poverty.

LEADERSHIP

AdvanCN is creating public awareness of systemic solutions for poverty, economic and monetary instability, and inequality through: 1) publication of the *Advancian - Systemic Reform Solutions - Strategic Plan; 2)* videos, workshops, and live online question and answer sessions; and 3) the submission of our global economic solution to organizations, corporations, and governments.

Advancian will inspire the citizens of every nation to address local and global political, social, and economic challenges so that we may end exploitation and abuses, ideological killing (social, political, and religious), to empower people with the means to achieve their full potential.

The vast scope of Advancian will require a conglomerate of advisors and consultants from numerous industries, professions, institutions, and nations.

Advancian welcomes their insight and aid, and will be open to collaborate with all elements of society to ensure their interests are understood and taken into account when planning the development of the System Core.

STRATEGIC PLAN SUMMARY

The strategic plan delineates the process of how we can achieve global social and economic security and stability, and is a global initiative to secure the people's commitment for the development of the System Core.

Advancian is also a proposal of policies, standards, and best practices, as well as the construction of the software applications to perfect our social and economic systems, to mitigate the theories, policies, principles, practices, and methods that have caused, encouraged, and legitimized the greatest harms. Advancian is composed of global concepts, processes, ideologies, as well as the physical hardware and computerized system applications that will be required to ensure economic security and social stability worldwide. It will also stimulate advances in technology, computing, and large database research that will enable solution of Complex Global Challenges:

- Water Sustainability
- Complex Biological System Analysis
- Replenishable Energy
- Clean Production and Manufacturing Systems
- Efficient Production and Distribution Systems

- Dynamic Cause and Effect Analysis Systems:
  - Policy
  - Disease
  - Food Consumption
  - Drug Research
  - Environmental Impact

Advancian makes use of right-minded logic that is constructive of the individual as well as each nation. The concepts within the strategic plan:

- Ensure true democracy
- Stabilize the value of every nations' currency (to prevent economic and social collapse)
- Ensure the just settlement of debt caused by flawed economic policy
- Ensure the individual can positively affect the outcomes produced by their society
- Ensure individuals are provided with the opportunities and education required to solve the challenges that may endanger our long-term existence.

Some of the concepts introduced within this proposal are innovative; some are common sense solutions that would not be effective if implemented fractionally.

Advancian uses *Constructive Outcome Measures*:

1. Must ensure freedoms and the right of life regardless of an individual's classification (nationality, religion, race, economic class, gender, etc.) to ensure true security; and may not cause, nor promote physical harm.
2. Must produce constructive outcomes for every aspect of the social and economic systems they affect.

3. Must aid in the accomplishment of global peace.

Advancian's concepts are actualized with use of the System Core. The System Core is composed of integrated computer applications and global system networks that enable input and tracking of the effects produced by the concepts, policies, and theories within the strategic plan to ensure the proper functioning of social and economic system segments.

Willit Ideology

Willit ideology is the driving force and belief that each man and woman is endowed, by our creator, with the force of will to design and create the world they desire (with joint consensus, collaboration, and fairness) that they might achieve their full potential, and that such actions should be in alignment with the constructive effects of natural Law. Willit is also a social and political movement for the advancement of mankind. For this reason Willit is the term we use for the creation of money with global standards that ensure a stable and fair monetary system.

System Core

The System Core is the mechanical construct, technology, and software required to create an equitable and sustainable world-wide economic system. It is an independent Global Exchange and Transaction Network governed by Willit ideology and the people of every nation.

PRESENTATION ORDER

First, the benchmarks of success will be highlighted so you can ascertain the benefits of the solutions we propose, versus the damage caused by the failed systemic theories currently in place.

Second, the major applications, processes, concepts, reforms, and ideology required to achieve economic security and social stability (peace and security) will be outlined in context of how they will be integrated into the Global Application Network of the System Core to ensure interrelated data cohesion for strategic analysis, planning, and action, based on the frontend user's vantage.

The outline will include and define the following major concepts:

ECONOMIC AND SOCIAL REORGANIZATION

- **Willit Monetary System**
  The global standards for the creation of Money
- **Standard Needs Earned Equity**
  The standards to replace antiquated taxation
  ideology and system processes

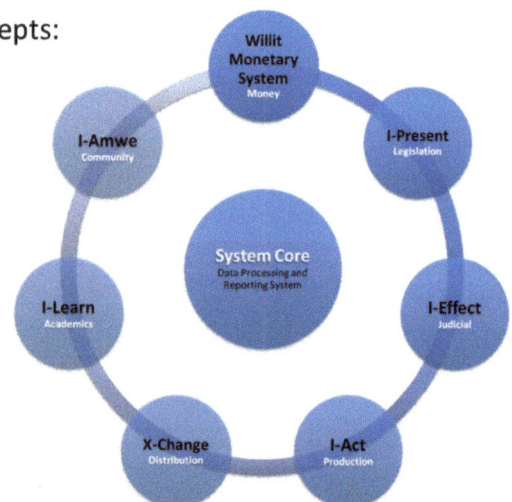

- **Debt Settlement Plan**

  The standards and processes to secure repayment of
  a nation's debt obligation, to rebuild international trust
  and to foster symbiosis

- **60/30/10 Resource Partition Plan**

  The standards for access to resources and International Trade

- **Resource Usage Efficiency**

  The standards to ensure resource usage efficiency

Third, the effects of, and requirements for *Advancian* will be presented:

- Envisionments – An outline of how the systems will affect everyday life
- The Foundational Laws required to secure individual freedoms and the functionality of the System Core
- Technological and infrastructure requirements
- Plans for the System Core's development and global implementation
- Development Budget - Financial and resource requirements based on current system processes

HIGHLIGHTS BENCHMARKS AND BENEFITS OF SUCCESS

New concepts are indicated by an underline. An explanation of the concept is listed in the Terminology Section, following the Highlights Benchmarks and Benefits of Success, or are expanded upon throughout the proposal.

The following is a summary outline of the concepts (C), processes (P), proposed laws (L), and Goals (G), incorporated within the strategic plan *Advancian*:

MERGER OF MAJOR SYSTEM CONCEPTS

Goal: To ensure the Perfection of our Social and Economic Systems

The best aspects of Capitalism, Socialism, and Democracy are merged to ensure the rights of the individual and the cumulative rights of society, so the best elements of all systems are used to solve our social and economic challenges.

DUAL MONETARY SYSTEM

Goal: To ensure Economic Stability, needs are met, and every person is adequately compensated for their energy investment to prevent slavery and monetary inequity.

1) **The Willit Monetary System**

   Money (which we term Willits) is created with use of global compensation standards and issued by the Global Compensation and Transaction Administration (GCTA).

   View the Interactive Calculator at: Advancian.org/model-1

   - Payment of all wages/compensation and confirmation of Earned Equity which allows one to access Standard Needs is issued by the Global Compensation and Transaction Administration (GCTA).
   - All wages issued are audited and viewable by all members of society so the people of every nation may ensure the financial stability of their nation and the stability of other participating nations, and to discourage corruption.
   - Willits are protected from theft, fraud, and divorce.
   - Willit compensation (money) issued to an individual for production and service provision is termed: Base Energy Expense/Rate (BEE or BEER).
     Cumulative BEE is used to determine production cost of a product or service and is termed the True Cost and takes into account all compensation issued for the production of a product and/or the provision of a service, to ensure price stability, and establishes the financial stability and production health of a nation.

- Money creation (Willits) is standardized, centralized, stable, and ensures equality of value between all nations. Willits are literally backed by the energy expensed by individual People.
- Full disclosure of compensation, and the fact that Willits can only be exchanged for goods and services guards against political corruption and bribery, and is a deterrent to illicit commerce.

Process Highlights:

- Willits are created when an individual works in either a Standard Needs Earned Equity position, or a Capital Market position.
- Willits are created based on thirteen standard factors:
    1. Age
    2. Life expectancy
    3. Hours worked
    4. Work hardship levels
    5. Skill level or task
    6. Position hierarchy
    7. Shift differential
    8. Travel compensation
    9. Over-time
    10. Economic and Social Adjustment standards
    11. Conservation Incentives

    Bonus structure

    12. Good health and social interactions
    13. Production efficiency
- Willits are used exclusively for the procurement of goods and for the payment of compensation to individuals for services rendered.
- To prevent the dead from affecting material existence and limiting the potential of new generations through taxation and debt, Willits cease to exist upon the death of the individual and their spouse (or the adulthood of minor child/ren), as well as any debt owed to the deceased.

The Willit Monetary System ensures money and work have true value, and is preventive of unearned compensation and entitlements, and wealth concentration.

Every individual will have the choice of participating in the Standard Needs Earned Equity System or payment of the True Cost for all goods, services, and social benefits. Every individual may also participate in the Capital System to earn Willits for the goods they desire.

Price Stability

- Price Stability is achieved for Goods and Services based on the Global Compensation Standard for the creation of Willits (real money).
  Disclaimer: Each Nation's production efficiency rate may differ. Thus the price of their products may vary from other nations. However, the value of each nation's Willits (money) will be equivalent based on compensation standards.

2) <u>Standard Needs Earned Equity System</u> -- in Lieu of Taxation
   Goal: To ensure the basic needs of all people are met and that the will of the people is known and able to affect policy, economic, and social outcomes.

   We estimate one-hundred percent employment will be achieved, and individuals will work no more than 16 hours per week to ensure their basic necessities are provided. This is based on shortening our current 40-hour work week, and the assumption that nearly 60 percent of each nation's population pool has able-bodied persons who will require employment due to the elimination of unneeded jobs after the System Core is implemented. We also assume that young adults 16 years of age and older will need to gain work experience. Thus, the higher the population, the fewer hours one is required to work.

   - (G/L) The Standard Needs Earned Equity System is assurance of Basic Necessities (food, housing, education, utilities, medicine, technology...) as part of the Standard Needs Earned Equity System Agreement approved by the people of each nation.
   - (C) Insurance and health benefits are provided through the Standard Needs Earned Equity System.
   - The refusal to Earn Equity for the procurement of Standard Needs, or abuse of the Standard Needs system, is an offense for which a community may request the removal of a citizen. Information regarding offenses that result in exile and mandatory removal are outlined in the I-EFFECT section.
     Example: A citizen has five children, and the parent/s refuse to work the required equity hours for the care of their household would result in either removal or temporary exile (Level 4, see page 139 - Re-Admission).

FOUR-TIER ECONOMIC EXCHANGE SYSTEM

The System Core will make use of four markets for the exchange of goods and services. The complete plan is provided in the full proposal – see pages starting at 121.

1. The Standard Needs Market System (Payment Type: Earned Equity)
2. Administrative and Governance Procurement System
   (Payment Type: Legislative Enactments approved by the people, based on Standard Needs Earned Equity – Example: National Defense Enactments are fully funded as protection against roué nations is a Standard Need)
3. I-WAUT Capitalist Consumer Market System - (Payment Type: Willits)
   I-WAUT is the acronym for "I Will Accept Universal Tender".
4. Black Market System (Payment Type: Willits)
   Goal: To ensure those who participate in or exploit what is referred to as the Black Market (goods or services deemed destructive to the individual), have a system of ethics and a means of resolving disputes without engaging in violent actions. Black Market concepts are reviewed in the xChange section.

60/30/10 RESOURCE PARTITION PLAN

Our proposed Material Resource Allocation is partitioned based on the following percentages: 60 percent for Standard Needs Earned Equity, 30 percent for Capital Markets, and 10 percent for International Trade (for debt settlement, needed resource procurement, and to prevent corruption). The Partition Plan is activated once all Standard Needs are met - with agreed upon Standard Needs retaining allocation priority.

The Resource Partition Plan ensures resources are distributed fairly, and the fair balance of social, corporate, and international needs and for the prevention of corruption.

CORPORATE INTERLACING

Corporations are phenomena that infect societies with the ideology of acceptable destruction. Corporations have convinced people to accept the most egregious offenses: labor abuses; waste, ecological damage – the list of corporate offenses is long. Corporations and governments have been able to commit atrocities because they hold and dangle the carrot – products (resources) and money (access to products) – the ability to buy and sell.

For centuries billions of people have been convinced money is valuable, when what is truly valuable is one's labor and skills, as well as innovative thinking.

Within our current system, to receive money, you must alter your perception (create a business persona), and justify the acceptance of destructive behavior.

The very essence and nature of a corporation is destructive. Destruction is required if we are to make products that are foreign to the natural processes of the earth.

Corporations have a systemic effect. Their actions affect lives, and ecological and environmental systems because they make use of the resources every person needs (water, energy, raw and recycled materials and minerals), and currently, they are allowed to affect policy and law.

Corporations have proven themselves to be destructive anomalies, without the natural Law of consequences for their actions and are akin to ravenous beasts if they are protected by political policies and not limited by laws to force constructive effects.

The act of modern day production for provision is literally the destruction of the environment because it ignores the laws of nature, the balance of creation and destruction. By human design, corporations are destructive, therefore by natural Law they must be restrained, if they are to be productive members of society. To civilize corporations, they will be interlaced with society, to ensure they act in the best interest of all stakeholders.

To ensure corporations and businesses are compliant with their initial inception and enterprise (the provision of goods and services), they are given no more reign than what is required for efficient functioning.

Goals – to ensure corporations function efficiently and to prevent corporate exploitation we will:

- Free corporations, small businesses, and administrative units from the payment of wages, insurance and health benefits; and free them from the payment of resource acquisition, maintenance, and development cost, so they can focus their efforts on efficient production and service provision – with use of compensation and earned equity issued by the GCTA, based on i-Present Production Enactment approval.
- (G) Financial, resources, and labor procurement barriers that prevent the establishment of needed businesses or services will be removed with use of iPresent's production enactment system (For details see: I-Present Legislation and Production Systems details):
  - Products are proposed to the people through submission of a legislative production enactment.
  - Upon approval of the enactment, resource allocation is granted (based on priority levels):
    - The processing of compensation for Human Resources is approved and administered.
    - If the proposal is submitted by a private corporation, escrow accounts for management team payments are established.

- Resources are granted for facilities, upgrades, and for production or service provision.
    - (Private Corporations) If production approval is not procured from the people, the right of enterprise is granted based on attainment of pre-purchase orders in the Capital Market Place I-WAUT.
- (G) Assurance of technological, medical, and social advancement through the removal of financial barriers for research, development, and production (also based on iPresent concepts and the Standard Needs system).
- (C/G) Open markets for entrepreneurs with use of the iPresent Production Enactment Process
- (L) Corporations, businesses, and administrative production units will be granted the right to produce products or to provide services, and will be limited to their stated mission and allotted no further rights. Thus, corporations will have no means to contribute to political campaigns, nor the right to influence policy (nor will any contribution be required or needed based on the iPresent Legislation Process). They, however, will have the right to establish processes in alignment with their production or service provision mission and goals.
- (C) Research and development will be an industry unto itself. Logic:
    - To ensure inventors are properly compensated for their inventions.
    - To prevent the hoarding of intelligence by corporate/profit motivated interests.
    - To ensure global technological and scientific advancement.
- (G) Achievement of no less than 85% recycling; and the use of Maximum Use Efficiency Standards to prevent waste (see page 111).

IAMWE SYSTEM IDEOLOGY

The "i-am-we" concepts firmly establish the rights of the individual and the people of every nation to prevent exploitation of their labor and their lands, yet embraces symbiosis to ensure trade and the exchange of resources, knowledge, and technology.

Goal: To secure human rights and the right of employment for all people.

- (P/L) Establishment of global and localized labor unions and training guilds for all trades and professions, including managers and supervisors.
- (C/L) The Centralization and Automation of the Hiring Process and Employee Placement (with exception to creative, executive management, and elected positions).
Goal: 100% employment of able-bodied persons

- (G/L) Assurance of basic necessities (food, housing, education, utilities, medicine, technology, etc.) as part of the Standard Needs Earned Equity System Agreements approved by the people
- (G/L) Assurance of Justice and Physical, Resource, Financial, and Social security for all people:
  - (P) Legislation and judicial outcomes, production rights, and resource allocation will be proposed, investigated, reviewed, and approved by the People; with each individual having equality of vote, and job and rights protection, regardless of gender, race, color, origin, class, religion, sexual gender preference, physical handicap, or age.
- (G) The end of imprisonment and fines for victimless crimes; the incorporation of Cause and Affect Training for minor transgressions; and the use of exile in-lieu-of the death penalty or imprisonment.
- (C) Complete corporate, administrative, household (inner family members only), and governmental transparency (with exception to military intelligence).

ECONOMIC SECURITY AND SOCIAL STABILITY

The strategic plan is comprised of the plans for the software applications that enable the actualization of the concepts, theories, policies, and goals within *Advancian*, and cumulatively termed Willitism. The software applications and hardware are cumulatively termed the System Core.

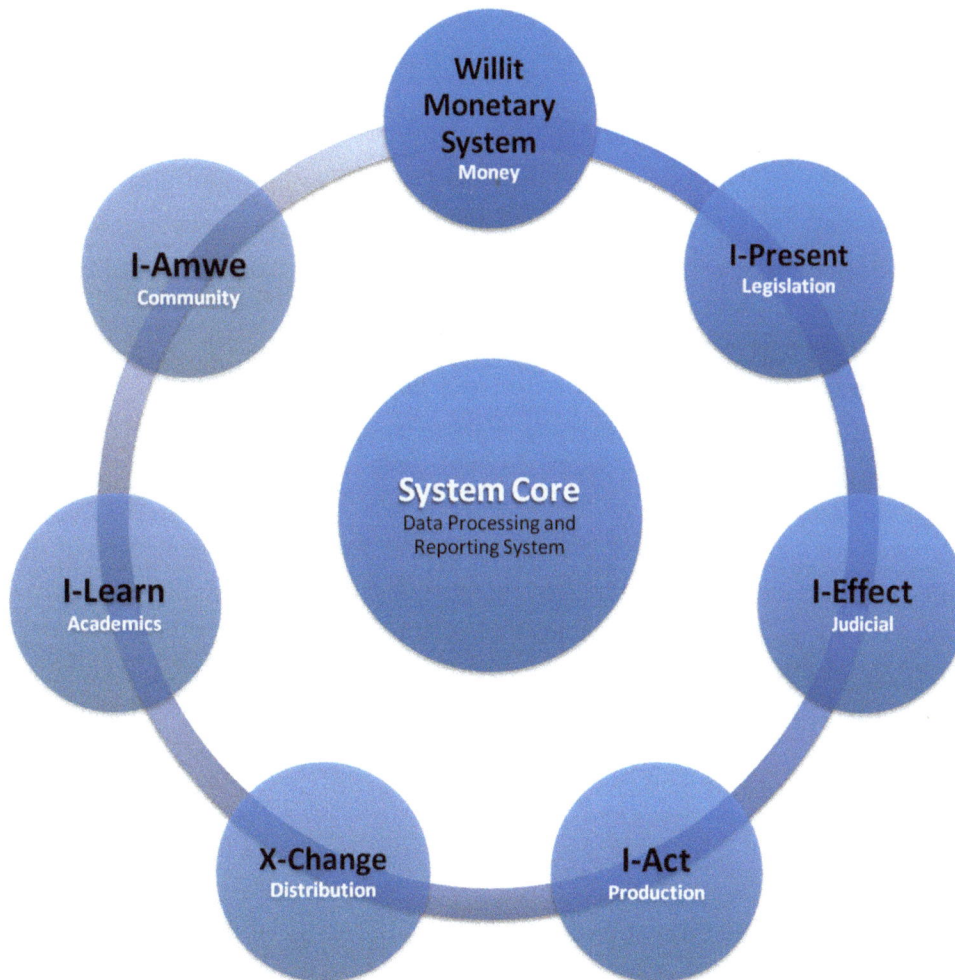

Information yields knowledge. Information allows us to determine what works so we can determine constructive solutions. Information has the power to alter action and opinion. Actions make use of force, and force is power. Thus, if one controls information, one controls the source that yields power – the minds and thus the will of people.

With use of the System Core, individuals will have the means to input and process accurate information to ensure the people are in full knowledge, and thus, in control of the systems they require for an advanced society.

First, we will introduce and define the System Core, after which, terminology and concepts for Advancian will be introduced. Then, the plans processes, applications and concepts will be detailed.

THE SYSTEM CORE SUMMARY
The Centralization of Information, Not Power

The System Core is the centralization of information to ensure everyone has access and the ability to ensure their effects are constructive, or to correct their action. The System Core is not the concentration nor the centralization of power.

The individual is fundamental and vital to the System Core. The needs and desires of the individual are used to compile data for strategic action and processes, to meet needs and desires, and to warn of resource declines and production inefficiencies; and to ensure economic and monetary equality, based on sound global standards.

The System Core is not a New World Order where the people are kept in submission with Orwellian means of control with use of propaganda, surveillance, misinformation, denial of truth, manipulation of the history and historical records, physical abuse, or fear.

Nor, is the System Core a system of theocracy, where priests or clergy claim right of knowledge of God's rules and laws, and subjugate the will of the people through guilt and mind control.

The System Core is not the replacement of old regimes for equally abusive and self-serving administrations, but a system that aids in the negation of the root cause of human errors and ensures the option of choice, while adopting the best of man's achievements.

WHAT IS THE SYSTEM CORE?

The System Core is a completely transparent, multi-national social and economic integrated global computer system for the creation of money, open communication, accurate data collection and processing for effect analysis, strategic planning, and process efficiency, to ensure the needs of every person are met.

The System Core is a system to track all things, so we can view and analyze the effects that derive from varied and diverse activities and the effects derived from the proper enforcement of laws.

Our world will be a different place; one that not necessarily lacks corruption, but makes it viewable for all to see, so we can make better decisions to negate corruption and error.

The System Core will enable all People to receive real-time and accurate information regarding every aspect of social and economic activity that affect their nations, regions, communities, and lives, so that the people can make sound decisions regarding processes, policy, and law.

The System Core will integrate the technology and data of our current systems to ensure that every individual can reach their full potential by ensuring they have the resources and support they require.

The equality, security, and justice resulting from the implementation of the System Core will ensure good people will no longer be compelled to serve corrupt men.

Tunisia's once-feared police, who carried out President Zine El Abidine Ben Ali's repressive policies, join hands with protesters. A man holds a sign that reads "Police with the people." [Photo: AP]

Source: The Hindu (thehindu.com) - February 13th 2011; "Middle East rises up for democracy"

God (creation, the universe, or if one prefers, life), allows free will. God will not correct that which man has caused in error. Nor, will the corrupt men who benefit from the system reform it.

The end effects and outcomes a system or process produces determines its effectiveness. Thus, how our policies, laws, and social and economic systems affect all people, especially the individuals considered to be of the lower class, is confirmation of how well or how poorly our social economic systems function. Based on the cumulative state of our current global economic outcomes, our systems have failed.

If the System Core ever deviates from its mission, the people will have the constitutional right to amend or disable it. However, corrupt systems are a reflection of the individuals who control the governance of its laws, policies, practices, and precedents.

We all require financial and physical security to ensure our basic necessities. We also require access to propose our ideas to determine if what we wish to create is valuable and desired by our community, and the world.

Under the current systems of governance, most people are without access to resources to achieve their potential. Many are without basic human requirements to ensure their life.

The system proposed herein ensures basic needs can be obtained, and that if our basic needs cannot be met, it will give us factual evidence to determine the causes, so we can take appropriate action. It ensures opportunities are accessible not only for those born into wealth, but also available to each person with talent, intelligence, and earnest desire.

Hearts and MINDs Working together
to create the Right Systems

M.I.N.Ds - My Independent Needs and Desires

TERMINOLOGY DEFINITIONS AND GENERAL INFORMATION

STANDARD NEEDS

Standard Needs are products and services the people agree to contribute their skills and energy to produce or provide, which yields Earned Equity.

Standard Needs are products or services all members of society receive because the product and or service is a basic necessity, or requirement, that if one were denied, would cause negative physical effects, or that could endanger the life of the individual.

The goods and services required for the existence of a community are also Standard Needs.

Examples: Food, shelter, medicine and medical procedures, utilities, administration and communication systems.

Cold climate communities would also require heating. Thus, the Standard Needs of communities will vary, yet resource allocation for communities of similar size would be equivalent and based on the region's resources, which will necessitate inter-regional and international trade.

EARNED EQUITY

Earned Equity is the right of access to the products and services the people have agreed are Standard Needs for all people – with exception to individuals who are permanently exiled for crimes against humanity or human rights violations.

To place orders for Standard Needs, one's Work Equity Requirement (quota) must be in good standing, or Willits are required to purchase Standard Needs items at True Cost.

Earned Equity cannot be transferred, nor exchanged.

WORK EQUITY REQUIREMENT- STANDARD NEEDS SYSTEM

To obtain access to Standard Need items for Earned Equity, one must complete the monthly work equity requirement. The work equity requirement is determined by taking all the man hours required to produce all Goods and Services the people have determined are Standard Needs for society. The total "Man Hours" are then divided by the total able-bodied citizens, and fractioned based on household size.

A community will be able to quickly ascertain its viability, and, if additional citizens are required, or the community should be absorbed, or deconstructed.

Thus, Earned Equity is equal to the total energy output required to produce or provide all agreed upon Standard Needs, divided by all willing and able body members of society and proportioned based on household size. Earned Equity and Standard Needs ends the need for taxation.

We estimate average work equity requirements, per individual, will be 16 hours per week.

WILLITS (MONETARY COMPENSATION)

Willits derive their name from that which is required for the creation process – will. Will is the desire to achieve a goal or outcome, which requires the exertion of an individual's force. Force in terms of the Willit process is the control of one's energy for the extraction, movement, or assembly of resources for the production of a product; the completion of a task to provide a service, or the de-construction of material for the recycling process.

Within the System Core, Willits (money) determines wealth, and directly correlates to the effort expended by an individual, their education, knowledge level, ingenuity, and creativity.

The payment of Willits (compensation/money) for the energy output for production or service provision is issued by the Global Compensation and Transaction Administration (GCTA) and based on thirteen global compensation standards:

1) Age (none discriminatory, used to determine the use of one's life force in minutes)
2) Life expectancy (standard), which equate to one's life force
3) Hours worked
4) Work hardship levels
5) Skill level or task, which equates to one's energy expense
6) Position hierarchy
7) Shift differential
8) Travel Compensation
9) Over-time
10) Economic and Social Adjustment Calibration Levels
11) National Resource Conservation and Population Incentives

Bonus Structure
A bonus structure that is based on good citizenship and production efficiency, as shown in the following figures:

12) Health and Good Citizenship
13) Production Efficiency

The Willit creation process is detailed in the Willit Monetary System section, see page 54.

Model 1	Model 2	Model 3	Model 4	Model 5	Model 6
Willit Monetary System	Currency Conversion	Global Debt Reconciliation	Local Debt Reconciliation	Resource Usage Efficiency	National & Global Exchanges
Full Frame	Full Frame	Full Frame	Full Frame	Full Frame	Full Frame

Tabs: Welcome | Compensation Standards | Hierarchy | Max. Compensation | Consumer Credit | Tax Grant | APEC | Residual Income | Inventors Production Units | Household Ledger | Student Time Sheet | Student Compensation | Working Youth

Willit

Your True Value has never been more clear

Real Money - Backed by the Will of The People

A Systemic Reform Movement Solution - Created by: AdvanCN.org - W Iamwe, Trustee

BENEFITS

1. Willits calculate an individual's energy output and ensures fair compensation regardless of nationality, race, or gender.

2. You can never lose Willits nor have them stolen from you.

3. Willits never deflate or inflate in value and ensure price stability for all products. Groceries, gas, clothing, luxury goods, and services.

4. Willits are naturally produced and only exist as long as you do. Thus, wealth concentration and unfair advantage is prevented.

5. Willits are backed by your energy output and the energy output of all members of society, and cannot be arbitrarily created and distributed, and thus ends fiat money.

6. Willits have an auditable trail to ensure accurate accounting and reporting on the true state of our economic output and efficiencies.

7. Not taxable!!! All the Standard Needs of society, including the needs for administration and governance are provided by the People through Standard Needs Agreements and tax grants; your Willits will not be stolen by means of taxation. See Tab : Tax Grant - for the tax plan and calculations.

8. Prevents slave labor, wage slaves, and unfair trade practices.

INSTRUCTIONS

WILLIT - GLOBAL COMPENSATION STANDARDS CALCULATION

Willit Monetary System Compensation Calculation

Update the sample data (1-13) with your data to determine your true value

After you update the data with your own information, select "UPDATE" to view your base Willit compensation rate.

The following fields help to calculate your base Willit Compensation - i.e., the minimum you will be paid.

STEPS

		Today's Date:	9/27/2019
1 of 13	Date of Birth		11/23/1970
		Current Age:	48.88
2 of 13	Life Span Expectancy / Productive Age / or Retirement Age		86

Vote Required to establish or to modify "Life Span Expectancy"

	Potential Life Force: Will / Power / Energy - in minutes		45,201,600
Minutes in days		Days - used to date	17,840
1440		Minutes - used to date	25,689,600
Days in Year		Estimated Remaining years (productivity)	37.12
365		Estimated Remaining minutes	19,512,000

	Estimate of Willit energy to be used for production		
3 of 13	40	Weekly Hours	2400
3b	0	Minutes	0
	40.00	**Total Production Minutes:**	2,400

Does not include Travel Time (See: Step 8)
Max. 40 hours (See: Step 9 - to calculate Over-time (OT))

CALIBRATION POINT LEVELS (CPL)

Work Hardship Level

Easy Labor	Medium Labor	Normal Labor	Hard Labor	Hazard Pay
1	5	8	12	15

WHL to be set by member vote of independent labor unions and guilds for each industry

	Work Hardship Level *(also consider desirability of the position - See Step 10)*	CPL: Level 1 to 15	
4 of 13	8		8
			19,200

Select Knowledge/Skill Level or Task Level:

	Knowledge / Skill Level of Member	CPL: Level 1 to 35	
5 of 13	16		16
	OR		307,200
	Task - Level	CPL: Level 6 to 26	
5b	0		0
	Either 5a or 5b must be set to zero (0)		0

Education Range or Skill Equivalency

				Bachelors	Masters	Ph.D.	CMS
Elementary	Pre Junior High	Junior High	Advanced	College	College 2	College 3	Production
Level 1-3	Level 4-6	Level 7-9	Level 10-12	Level 13-16	Level 17-20	Level 21-24	Level 25-35

Standards for certification to be set by production and service Units, education institutes.

					Expert		
					Local to 26		
					State to 29		
					Nation to 32		
					Global to 35		

Task Level

General	Specific	Technical	Advanced	Mastery	Master Work
Level 6-8	Level 9-11	Level 12-15	Level 16-19	Level 20-23	Level 24-26

	Hierarchy	CPL: Level 8 to 1	
6 of 13	6.0		6.0
	Select Hierarchy Standards, go to tab: "Hierarchy Status CPL"		1,843,200

Hierarchy

Student	Apprentice	Staff Member	Supervisor	Manager	Director	Executive	President
8	7	6	5	4	3	2	1

How many people do you directly supervise?

	If Level 5.9 through Level 1.0, select:			up to 10	11 to 20	21 to 30	31 to 40	41 to 50	51 to 60	61 to 70	71 to 80	81
	Resources or Units under your direct supervision		4.44%	8.88%	13.32%	17.76%	22.20%	26.64%	31.08%	35.52%	
6b	No. of Direct Supervisees	0		
6c	Supervision Percentage:	4.44%	0.0000
	Supervision CPL:	4.44%	

Vote required

Willits

Compensation Rate (Base / BEE)

Your Weekly Willit Compensation - Based on Production Minutes:	**$1,379.19**	
Hourly Rate:	34.48	
Per Minute Rate:	0.57	

Base Compensation Rate (BCR) - The Minimum Compensation Standard

Additional Benefits & Compensation (ABC):

Weekly

Weekly Rate w/ ABC	**$1,379.19**	
Hourly Rate:	34.48	
Per Minute Rate:	0.57	

Total Min	Total Hours
2400	40.00

Option SD	Shift Differential: Evenings, Weekends, and Holidays	CPL 1 to 2
7 of 13	1	1.0
	Willits Compensation with Shift Differential:	$1,379.19
	Hourly Rate:	34.48
	Per Minute Rate:	0.57

Shift	Standard	Evenings	Overnight	Weekends	Holidays
0	1	1.5	2	1.5	2

Supervisory Benefits:	$0.00	
Travel Compensation:	$0.00	
8 of 13	Days Worked	0
	Travel Time	90	Minutes
	Travel Allowance: 45-minutes to or from work per day (1.5-hours per work day)	

From Step 6b - c; for supervision of over 24 individuals

Travel Rate	Days Worked			Travel Days			
50%	0	1	2	3	4	5	6

Over-time Minutes:	$0.00	
9 of 13	OT - Rate	0	$0.00
9b of 13	Hours	0	
9c of 13	Minutes	0	
	Total OT Minutes	0	

Overtime Time	Standard OT	Holidays
0	1.5	2

Annual

Annual Wage - Weekly Rate x 52 weeks:	**$71,717.79**
with Max. Performance Bonus:	$86,061.34
Weekly Rate with: ABC (x) 52 weeks:	$71,717.79
Tax Grant - 0.2% of Base Compensation:	$14,343.56
Bonus Standard Needs Work/Performance Bonus	$14,343.56

Based on Base Compensation Rate

Bonuses are included in Lifetime Maximum Compensation Calculation only for Standard Needs Work

Link

Tax Grant to be issued to Governance Solos see RP-Tax Grant

ESAO Economic and Social Adjustment Options - CPL

PVHD	Differential: Perceived Value and High Demand	
10 of 13	0	0.0
	Annual Willits Compensation with: Shift Differential:	$0.00
	Hourly Rate:	0.00

"Perceived Value" is an optional factor for those who request compensation above the standard base rate. The High Demand "premium factor" is declared by a nation. If one feels they should be compensated to a higher degree, one can, when submitting their skills for employment consideration demand a higher rate. Nonstandard rate request can be honored by Global Compensation and Transaction Administration - upon National Acceptance (just as for CMS) either per individual or Class Action. And simply means one reaches their earning caps and thus retirement earlier than others.

RCPRI National Resource Conservation and Population Reduction Incentive

11 of 13	Conservation Incentive	Select: Yes or No	Incentive
	Percentage Increase or decrease	0.00%
	Annual Wage - Weekly Rate x 52 weeks	N/A
	with Max. Performance Bonus:	N/A
	Weekly Rate with: ABC (x) 52 weeks:	N/A
	Tax Grant - % of Base Compensation:	N/A

With various System Core components, we will be able to detect when resource requirements are insufficient to meet needs of the population. If required, a nation can enact the conservation incentives.

* Population Reduction Incentive percentage can be enacted by national vote, with a percentage range of: 0% to 100%.
* Resource Conservation will use a negative percentage range from (-1%) to (-65%), and be enacted by national vote. Non-punishment, benefit based incentives for population reduction.

The population reduction incentive is issued for households and individual who commit to not having children.

The Willit rate an individual is paid for the provision of labor is the Base Energy they have expensed.

True Cost for all products and services can be accurately determined with use of BEE (Base Energy Expense) rates issued for the production of a good or service.

BEE is also used to determine global efficiency rates, and reveals the level of technological advancement of a nation, and thus can be used to accurately determine a nation's Gross Domestic Production (GDP).

TRUE COST

True cost is determined by the Willits issued by the GCTA for goods produced and services rendered.

True Cost is determined by the Willit Rate of Compensation paid out to all production and service members for the provision of a service and/or the creation of a product; from the extraction of raw resources to the delivery of the final product/service to the market place. If applicable, the total Willit Compensation paid/payable is divided by the production yield (the number of items produced), which determines the True Cost rate for each unit.

Both Price and True Cost (TC), will be listed for all goods and services to ensure full disclosure. The Price of an item is the asking rate for a good or service in excess of the True Cost and only applicable for Capital Markets (iWAUT and Black Market).

TRUE COST PRINCIPLES & LOGIC

The true cost of production, may vary per nation and district because of man hour cost due to a lack of technological development and innovation. Thus, requiring more man-hours in-lieu-of machine hours.

Why is it important to pay the True Cost if one does not participate in the Earned Equity System?
Until all people pay the True Cost we will not understand that we need each other, nor how valuable resources are, nor how important each person is and the necessity to work together, and to share the natural resources provided to all freely by God.

Example: If a property cannot be maintained at True Cost levels; if a private business fails underweight of True Cost; if products are not affordable because one must pay the True cost; if a private farm is not sustainable because it must pay people their True Cost, the un-affordability is evidence that the product should be shared, or of social inequity and abuses. It is also an indication of flawed perception of truth, illogical thinking, inadequate leadership or management, or misconceived social system structure, processes, and laws.

For far too long, people have benefitted by exploiting other people's labor, while the people that do the work receive little benefit, live in poverty, and are inadequately cared for, nurtured, and educated. To exploit other people's labor is seen by some to be savvy business practices, instead of what it truly is, theft.

WILLIT COMPENSATION USAGE

Willits can be used in the capital market or the Standard Needs Earned Equity Market to pay for Standard Need items. Or, if one selects not to participate as a Standard Needs worker, Willits are required to pay the true cost for all social benefits (Standard Needs).

I-WAUT MARKET

i-WAUT is the acronym for: I Will Accept Universal Tender (Willits)
Similar to current capital acquisition markets, the i-WAUT market is where one can purchase Goods or Services that are not available in the Standard Needs Market. One gains access to the iWAUT markets with Willits.

GCTA - Administrative Body

The Global Compensation and Transaction Administration (GCTA) is the oversight body and auditor of Willit Compensation distribution; oversees the transactions for the exchange of Willits for goods and services; and facilitates the conversion of a Nation's Willits for international exchange of goods and services by individuals.

The GCTA ends the need for fractional and reserve banking, and eliminates the fees and interest banks charge individuals, businesses, and nations, thus eliminating future debt obligation.

The GCTA is composed of a global body of Willit Administrators consisting of: analysts, auditors, accountants, payroll clerks, and governance compliance officers.

Willit Administrators will be located onsite at production and service facilities, business offices, and will be randomly selected from a pool of qualified individuals.

All administrators will be sworn into office, are legally liable and subject to exile for theft, acceptance of bribes, falsification of documentation, or the illegal transfer of Willits; and will be rotated to different facilities to ensure integrity and as a fraud prevention measure.

All transactions by Administrators are viewable by the people to ensure the people have final oversight of audits and analysis to prevent corruption and malfeasance.

The GCTA will **_not_** have legal authorization to charge interest for the creation of money, nor for the provision of oversight services. The performance of the responsibilities of the Global Compensation and Transaction Administration is a Global Standard Need, for which administrators receive Earned Equity, and Willit compensation.

Current banking system technology and data will be integrated into the System Core's Willit Monetary System. Mobile and internet devices will have access to process, review, and audit transactions, and to convert money, investments, stock and commodities into Willits; for which the calculations for the Bond/Investment/Debt Calculator will be used. Details are provided in the i-Willit section, and the factors involved in the calculation provided on the following pages.

APEC

APEC is the acronym for Accurate Past Earnings Compensation. APEC ensures that compensation is paid to individuals who have been exploited: low wages, those who were actual victims of slavery, lawsuits that were won and were not paid, and victims of embezzlement and theft.

APEC Calculation – (Accurate Past Earning Compensation Calculation)

WillitCompensationCalcu... ×

advancn.org/spreadsheets/willit_calculation/WillitCompensationCalculator%20Final/WillitCompensationCalculator%20Final.htm

Your True Value | Maximum Compensation | APEC Past Earning Calculator | Inventors Production Units | Student Time Sheet | Student Compensation Calculator | Working Youth

Accurate Past Earnings Compensation Calculations (APEC)

Past Earning Compensation: **$424,795.22**
APEC Calculation agreed upon year: **2007**
Enter Current Year: **2015**

Note:
A foundation agreement is required to determine the date we will begin calculating wage deficiencies and abuses of the labor force.
Documentation of the wages you were paid are required to make an accurate determination of the energy investment you should have been compensated to determine your separation amount.

Global Standards	Current Calculation Standards
Date of Birth	11/23/1970
Retirement Age	86
Hours Per Week	40
Weeks Per Year	52
Production Minutes	2400
Work Level	8
At the time of Exchange	16
Knowledge Skill Level	
Hierarchy	4

Year		Work Level	Knowledge Skill Level	Hierarchy	Weekly Rate	Weeks Worked	Annual
1	2014	8	16	4	1,846	52	$95,981
2	2013	8	15	4	1,690	52	$87,870
3	2012	7	14	5	1,079	52	$56,092
4	2011	7	13	5	979	52	$50,918
5	2010	6	12	5	758	52	$39,403
6	2009	6	11	5	680	52	$35,345
7	2008	6	10	5	605	52	$31,457
8	2007	6	9	5	533	52	$27,729
9		0	8	5	77	52	$0
10		0	1	5	9	52	$0

Total: (APEC) Transferable to Willit Account: **$424,795**

Work Level

Easy Labor	Medium Labor	Hard Labor	Hazard Pay
1	5	10	20

Knowledge Skill Level
Education and Skill Levels:

None	Graduate	Advanced	Professional	Dr	Master
1	5	10	15	20	25

Hierarchy

Student	Staff Member	Supervisor Manager	Director	Executive	President
8	5	4	3	2	1

Debt Settlement Calculator

International Debt Reconciliation - Bonds Stocks Loans and Investments

	INPUT FIELDS	Afghanistan	Argentina	Brazil	Iran	Mexico	United States (1)	Luxembourg (2)	Switzerland (3)	Australia (4)	Netherlands (5)	Ireland (6)	Norway (7)	United Kingdom (8)	Denmark (9)	Belgium (10)	Austria (11)	Germany (12)	France (13)	Sweden (14)	Finland (15)	Spain (16)
			Low Income Countries Example																			
STEP 1: Debtor Country's Compensation Avrg (US Dollars) As of 2011	42,983	84.88 mth	546.97 mth	348.39 mth	303 mth	4.8563 hr	51,495	50,610	47,810	45,385	45,161	45,160	43,607	43,250	42,173	41,923	41,421	37,544	37,269	35,582	34,903	32,957
STEP 2: Enter the amount you paid for the Bond (not face value)	100	100	100	100	100	100	100	100	100	100	100	100	100	100	100	100	100	100	100	100	100	100
Debtor Country Hourly Rate: Average Hourly Rate (based on 40 hr work week)	20.66	0.49	3.14	2.00	1.74	4.86	24.76	24.33	22.99	21.82	21.71	21.71	20.96	20.79	20.28	20.16	19.91	18.05	17.92	17.11	16.78	15.84
STEP 3: Debt Holders' Annual Rate: Average Hourly Rate (based on 40 hr work week)	51,000 / 24.52	24.52	24.52	24.52	24.52	24.52	24.52	24.52	24.52	24.52	24.52	24.52	24.52	24.52	24.52	24.52	24.52	24.52	24.52	24.52	24.52	24.52
Differential Percentage % (Debtor Debt Holder)		0.84	0.13	0.08	0.07	0.20	1.01	0.99	0.94	0.89	0.89	0.89	0.86	0.85	0.83	0.82	0.81	0.74	0.73	0.70	0.68	0.65
STEP 3b: Debt Holder's work hours to purchase bond	4.08	4.08	4.08	4.08	4.08	4.08	4.08	4.08	4.08	4.08	4.08	4.08	4.08	4.08	4.08	4.08	4.08	4.08	4.08	4.08	4.08	4.08
Debtor Nation's Average Citizen would have had to work the following hrs:	4.84	204.90	31.90	49.92	57.40	20.59	4.04	4.11	4.35	4.58	4.61	4.61	4.77	4.81	4.93	4.96	5.02	5.54	5.58	5.85	5.96	6.31
Work Percentage Difference for Debtor Citizen	15.73%	98.01%	87.17%	91.83%	92.89%	80.19%	-0.97%	0.76%	6.25%	11.01%	11.45%	11.45%	14.50%	15.20%	17.31%	17.80%	18.78%	26.38%	26.92%	30.23%	31.56%	35.38%
Percentage of Work Hours counted for Debt Holder	84.27%	1.99%	12.83%	8.17%	7.11%	19.81%	100.97%	99.24%	93.75%	88.99%	88.55%	88.55%	85.50%	84.80%	82.69%	82.20%	81.22%	73.62%	73.08%	69.77%	68.44%	64.62%
	100.00%	100.00%	100.00%	100.00%	100.00%	100.00%	100.00%	100.00%	100.00%	100.00%	100.00%	100.00%	100.00%	100.00%	100.00%	100.00%	100.00%	100.00%	100.00%	100.00%	100.00%	100.00%
STEP 3c: Hours (to be compensated (x) % Difference)	3.44	3.44	0.52	0.33	0.29	0.81	4.12	4.05	3.82	3.63	3.61	3.61	3.49	3.46	3.37	3.35	3.31	3.00	2.98	2.85	2.79	2.64
Rate of Debt Compensation (RDC) or Minutes Per Hour	206.22	206.22	31.39	19.99	17.39	48.47	247.07	242.83	229.40	217.76	216.69	216.68	209.23	207.52	202.35	201.15	198.74	180.14	178.82	170.73	167.47	158.13

STEP 4..8 Complete Field to determine your Willie Compensation

	Input	Afghanistan	Argentina	Brazil	Iran	Mexico	United States	Luxembourg	Switzerland	Australia	Netherlands	Ireland	Norway	United Kingdom	Denmark	Belgium	Austria	Germany	France	Sweden	Finland	Spain
Today's Date	11/23/19	4/4/2015	4/4/2015	4/4/2015	4/4/2015	4/4/2015	4/4/2015	4/4/2015	4/4/2015	4/4/2015	4/4/2015	4/4/2015	4/4/2015	4/4/2015	4/4/2015	4/4/2015	4/4/2015	4/4/2015	4/4/2015	4/4/2015	4/4/2015	4/4/2015
Date of Birth	11/23/1970	11/23/1970	11/23/1970	11/23/1970	11/23/1970	11/23/1970	11/23/1970	11/23/1970	11/23/1970	11/23/1970	11/23/1970	11/23/1970	11/23/1970	11/23/1970	11/23/1970	11/23/1970	11/23/1970	11/23/1970	11/23/1970	11/23/1970	11/23/1970	11/23/1970
Life Span Expectancy Productive Age or Retirement Age	44.39	44.39	44.39	44.39	44.39	44.39	44.39	44.39	44.39	44.39	44.39	44.39	44.39	44.39	44.39	44.39	44.39	44.39	44.39	44.39	44.39	44.39
Age	86	86	86	86	86	86	86	86	86	86	86	86	86	86	86	86	86	86	86	86	86	86
Work Level (also consider desirability of the position)	2,681	631	408	260	226	630	3,212	3,157	2,992	2,831	2,817	2,817	2,720	2,698	2,631	2,615	2,584	2,342	2,325	2,219	2,177	2,056
Knowledge/Skill Level of Member	34,852	8,25	5,304	3,379	2,936	8,101	41,755	41,039	38,769	36,803	36,621	36,620	35,360	35,071	34,198	33,995	33,588	30,444	30,221	28,853	28,302	26,724
Hierarchy	139,408	3,295	21,216	13,514	11,755	32,763	167,020	164,156	155,074	147,209	146,482	146,479	141,442	140,284	136,790	135,979	134,351	121,776	120,834	115,412	113,210	106,898
Divided by Remaining Years	41.61	41.61	41.61	41.61	41.61	41.61	41.61	41.61	41.61	41.61	41.61	41.61	41.61	41.61	41.61	41.61	41.61	41.61	41.61	41.61	41.61	41.61
FINAL Willie Compensation for Your Bonds, Stocks, Loans and Investments	$209.41	$4.95	$31.87	$20.30	$17.65	$49.21	$250.88	$246.58	$232.94	$221.12	$220.03	$220.03	$212.46	$210.72	$205.47	$204.26	$201.81	$182.92	$181.58	$173.36	$170.05	$160.57

Enlarged View: Debt Settlement Calculator

International Debt Reconciliation - Bonds Stocks Loans and Investmer

		INPUT FIELDS	Low Income Countries Exan	
		Enter Annual Rate:	Afghanistan	Argentina
STEP 1:	Debtor Country's Compensation Avrg (US Dollars) As of 2011	42,980	84.88 mth	546.97 mth
STEP 2:	Enter the amount you paid for the Bond (not face value):	100	100	100
	Debtor Country Hourly Rate: Average Hourly Rate (based on 40 hr work week)	20.66	0.49	3.14
STEP 3:	**Debt Holders' Annual Rate :** Average Hourly Rate (based on 40 hr work week)	51,000	24.52	24.52	24.52
			24.52	24.52	24.52
	Differential Percentage % (Debtor / Debt Holder)		0.84	0.02	0.13
STEP 3b:	Debt Holder's work hours to purchase bond:		4.08	4.08	4.08
	Debtor Nation's Average Citizen would have had to work the following hrs:		4.84	204.90	31.80
	Work Percentage Difference for Debtor Citizen:		15.73%	98.01%	87.17%
	Percentage of Work Hours counted for Debt Holder:		84.27%	1.99%	12.83%
			100.00%	100.00%	100.00%
STEP 3c:	Hours (to be compensated (x) % Difference) :		3.44	0.08	0.52
	Rate of Debt Compensation (RDC) or Minutes Per Hour		206.22	4.87	31.39

STEP 4. - 8. Complete Field to determine your Willit Compensation Rate:

Today's Date		4/4/2015	4/4/2015	4/4/2015
Date of Birth		11/23/19	11/23/1970	11/23/1970
Age		44.39	44.39	44.39
Life Span Expectancy/ Productive Age / or Retirement Age		86	86	86

See: Compensation Rate Level (Select Next Tab Below)

Work Level (also consider desirability of the position)			
Easy Labor — Hazard Pay	2.681	63	408

Knowledge/Skill Level of Member	Skill Level 1 - 25		
Elementary — PhD	34.852	823	5.304

Hierarchy			
President — Student	139.408	3.293	21.217
Divided by Remaining Years	41.61	41.61	41.61

FINAL	Willit Compensation for Your Bonds, Stocks, Loans and Investments	$209.41	$4.95	$31.87

Social Economics is the process of merging the best aspects of capitalism with true democracy for the benefit of both the individual and society; which yields the term "social capitalism" or "cooperative capitalism."

Within the capitalist scheme, the principle means of production (material resources), are owned by private individuals who can monopolize and adversely affect the availability and cost of products and services; who can manipulate markets as well as the legislative process for unfair advantage; and, who can abuse the labor force required to create the products capitalists profit from.

Profit and money have the ability to motivate positive or negative outcomes. However, money is not the cause of social and economic inequity – inequity is due to corruption of individuals. The use of money to influence destructive actions; the exploitation and atrocities committed by individuals and corporations to obtain money; and the dysfunctional economic processes individuals must maneuver to obtain money, pose the greatest threats to society.

Labor and materials are required if one is to create wealth, thus the theft of, and exploitation of, land, and abuse of the labor force by corporations and business-people will continue until their greed is contained. Greed is a mental illness.

LOGIC

All the resources of the earth belong to all people and not exclusively to those who have selfishly exploited resources and labor for profit, which has compromised our ecological systems.

A well-designed social-economic system ensures inventors, entrepreneurs, production and service units, and private corporations have access to the resources required for production and service provision, and that appropriate oversight is administered to prevent fraud, inefficiency, waste, and theft to ensure the needs of all people are met.

The people jointly manage and grant _Usery Rights_ (see definition within this section) of resources required for production and distribution based on established allocation priority levels and recommended conservation measures, if applicable.

The people of every nation determine allocation rights for their natural resources and recycled materials; and determine the maximum labor hours an individual works daily for the production of goods and the provision of services.

All requests for the provision of goods and services for the operation of a production or service unit or independent business will be submitted to the people through iPresent's Production and Service Enactment process.

The allocation of resources by the people (in combination with and use of System Core Applications: iPresent, iEffect, Standard Needs Agreements, and with the construction of the Law of Rights and Governance) will end abuses by governments, corporations, and individuals:

- The people vote on resource allocation for production, by approving the products to be manufactured.
- Resources—human labor as well as materials, are allocated at no cost to Corporations and Production Units.
- Resources are granted to Private Corporations based on bulk pre-paid order manufacturing efficiency standards.
- Individuals who own or are the executives of corporations can opt to retain their use of private property – but will be required to pay True Cost, for all _Social Benefits_.
- The people maintain the facilities and mechanics used for production and distribution of all products to ensure corporations can function properly and within required regulations.
- Each production or service unit, and trade Union or Guild will have the final approval over two of the global compensation standards used to determine compensation levels for each job function and task: work level – option 4, and knowledge and task level – option 5. Each member of a union or guild must confirm the levels via vote, to ensure the people of the Union or Guild remain in control of the factors that determines their compensation levels, and thus prevent abuse of the labor force.
- Desires (non-essential goods) are fulfilled, yet retain second level production allocation priority based on the 60/30/10 City/State/National Partition Plan, to ensure the basic needs of all people and sanctioned administrative bodies have the resources required to function efficiently.
- Private businesses/corporations that are not granted rights of production by enactment, may acquire resources through the Right of Production, based on pre-purchase orders, which may be restricted based on resource allocation priority requirements.

USERY RIGHTS

Usery is the right to make use of, but not the right to declare individual or sole ownership of, the material resources provided by nature/God. All resources are controlled by the people of each nation and not by corporations, nor by individuals with monetary advantages or legislated authority, thereby limiting their ability to manipulate and dictate policy and resource usage rights.

Social Benefits are the benefits provided by society, such as Standard Needs, infrastructure, transport systems, global computing and networking systems, and communication systems – that make use of the natural resources provided by God (creation) to all mankind.

The cost of production and facility maintenance for Corporations and Production Units is zero upon Production Enactment approval, and will be added to the nation's Standard Needs.

Allied Corporations and Production Units

Corporations receive what they have always wanted, zero expense for: human labor, maintenance, and material cost. Upper level management is still able to receive fair compensation for their production and management acumen. Within the Willit compensation system, it is possible to make from Ⓦ 300,000 to over Ⓦ 1 million Willits annually, so long as the people are willing to purchase the good or service (see Figure 1 on the following page).

Allied Corporations relinquish private property rights to the people, in exchange for zero expenses. Intellectual property rights remain with the inventor or invention team. The invention is placed in the public domain, and the inventors are compensated monthly based on patent usage percentages.

Willits are granted to inventors so long as the invention or concept is in use (see: Production section).

Private Corporations

Private corporations that have not relinquished private ownership rights incur upfront costs for production, and all iWAUT products must be pre-purchased to prevent waste and idle merchandise.

Materials for production are distributed to private corporations so long as they remain efficient and are not in violation of safety standards. Private corporations incur the true cost of facility maintenance, and social benefits such as infrastructure, transportation costs, and taxes.

Costs are automatically deducted from their Willit escrow accounts upon the sale of goods, and profits transferred to their Management Team escrow accounts to compensate management teams and "owners."

Production inefficiency and violation of Safety Agreements or laws will suspend or terminate resource allocation and a producer's or corporation's production rights.

FIGURE 1

| Your True Value | Maximum Compensation | APEC Past Earning Calculator | Inventors Production Units | Student Time Sheet | Student Compensation Ca |

Maximum Compensation Calculator

Life Time Earnings and Transfer: $20,971,716.27

					$ Willits	Percentage	Weekly Increase By	
		Age	Remaining Yrs YR CNT	Weekly Total	Annual Total	Increase	Year	
Date of Birth	11/23/1970	44.39	41.61	1	1,846	95,981			
Retirement Age	86	45.39	40.61	2	1,891	98,345	2.46%	45.45	2.46%
		46.39	39.61	3	1,939	100,828	2.52%	47.75	0.06%
Hours Per Week (Enter)	40.00	47.39	38.61	4	1,989	103,439	2.59%	50.22	0.07%
Weeks Per Year	52	48.39	37.61	5	2,042	106,190	2.66%	52.89	0.07%
Production Minutes	2400	49.39	36.61	6	2,098	109,090	2.73%	55.78	0.07%
		50.39	35.61	7	2,157	112,154	2.81%	58.92	0.08%
Work Level	8	51.39	34.61	8	2,219	115,395	2.89%	62.32	0.08%
At the time of Exchange		52.39	33.61	9	2,285	118,828	2.98%	66.03	0.09%
Knowledge Skill Level	16	53.39	32.61	10	2,355	122,472	3.07%	70.08	0.09%
Hierarchy	4	54.39	31.61	11	2,430	126,347	3.16%	74.51	0.10%
		55.39	30.61	12	2,509	130,475	3.27%	79.38	0.10%
		56.39	29.61	13	2,594	134,881	3.38%	84.74	0.11%
As you age your value increases naturally		57.39	28.61	14	2,685	139,596	3.50%	90.67	0.12%
As we age, we gain knowledge and experience.		58.39	27.61	15	2,782	144,653	3.62%	97.24	0.13%
As a result, we obtain insight. With insight, one becomes more		59.39	26.61	16	2,886	150,089	3.76%	104.55	0.14%
valuable to society.		60.39	25.61	17	2,999	155,950	3.90%	112.71	0.15%
		61.39	24.61	18	3,121	162,287	4.06%	121.87	0.16%
As one's life on earth is coming to an end, life becomes more		62.39	23.61	19	3,253	169,161	4.24%	132.20	0.17%
precious. One should select what they invest their energy into		63.39	22.61	20	3,397	176,644	4.42%	143.89	0.19%
with care.		64.39	21.61	21	3,554	184,819	4.63%	157.21	0.20%
		65.39	20.61	22	3,727	193,787	4.85%	172.47	0.22%
Thus, Willit Compensation Increases incrementally, naturally.		66.39	19.61	23	3,917	203,670	5.10%	190.06	0.25%
		67.39	18.61	24	4,127	214,615	5.37%	210.48	0.27%
		68.39	17.61	25	4,362	226,803	5.68%	234.39	0.31%
		69.39	16.61	26	4,624	240,459	6.02%	262.62	0.34%
		70.39	15.61	27	4,920	255,865	6.41%	296.27	0.39%
		71.39	14.61	28	5,257	273,380	6.85%	336.83	0.44%
		72.39	13.61	29	5,644	293,470	7.35%	386.33	0.50%
		73.39	12.61	30	6,091	316,746	7.93%	447.62	0.58%
		74.39	11.61	31	6,616	344,032	8.61%	524.74	0.68%
		75.39	10.61	32	7,240	376,463	9.43%	623.67	0.81%
		76.39	9.61	33	7,993	415,644	10.41%	753.49	0.98%
		77.39	8.61	34	8,922	463,929	11.62%	928.55	1.21%
		78.39	7.61	35	10,094	524,906	13.14%	1172.64	1.53%
		79.39	6.61	36	11,622	604,338	15.13%	1527.54	1.99%
		80.39	5.61	37	13,694	712,098	17.83%	2072.30	2.70%
		81.39	4.61	38	16,666	866,625	21.70%	2971.69	3.87%
		82.39	3.61	39	21,285	1,106,806	27.71%	4618.86	6.01%
		83.39	2.61	40	29,445	1,531,160	38.34%	8160.64	10.63%
		84.39	1.61	41	47,755	2,483,244	62.18%	18309.31	23.84%
		85.39	0.61	42	126,270	6,566,054	164.41%	78515.59	102.23%
		86.39	-0.39	43	0	0	-100.00%	-126270.27	-264.41%
		87.39	-1.39	44	0	0	NaN	0.00	NaN
		88.39	-2.39	45	0	0	NaN	0.00	NaN
		89.39	-3.39	46	0	0	NaN	0.00	NaN
		90.39	-4.39	47	0	0	NaN	0.00	NaN
		91.39	-5.39	48	0	0	NaN	0.00	NaN
		92.39	-6.39	49	0	0	NaN	0.00	NaN

Continuous ...

SYSTEMIC REFORM SOLUTIONS

Willit System

The Integration of Complex Economic Systems to ensure needs are met, prices are stable, and fair compensation is issued to all people.

1a. iPresent (module integration)

The production of products or provision of a service is first approved by the People through the iPresent process.

Once a production enactment is confirmed by General Vote of the People, all resources will be allocated: Human Labor as well as raw and recycled resources and materials.

Standard Need products and services have first level production priority.

iPresent is also used for legislation of agreement between all People for the rules and agreements that regulate their community, city, state, or nation.

1b. Request Human Resources

Production Units, Corporations, and Providers work with Labor Unions and Training Guilds to select compensation levels, certification, and training requirements.

Citizens request services from Independent Service Providers through either the Needs Earned Equity or iWAUT market

Willit Currency is issued by the Global Compensation and Transaction Administration (GCTA) based on previous system account holdings and only for the payment of compensation for work performed in the Standard Needs Earned Equity System. based on approved production or service enactments.
The Capital Markets (iWAUT) function by siphoning Willits from the pool of Willits issued by the GCTA.

Every transaction made can be viewed and audited by the people and linked back to the source
of issuance,
production
order,
and
the

Willits

GCTA (Automated)

1. Confirms Receipt of Willit Distribution request.
2. Confirms worked hours with mobile GPS date (if available) if not available human confirmation required (WA's request - will suffice as confirmation for onsite workers).
3. Willits transferred to member's account or their Earned Equity Account is updated.

purchase
order
issued
by a
corporation
or
private
individual.
The Willit Monetary System ensures money has True Value and hinders fraud because of transparency.

Real Money - 1

Member Logs Out:

1. Logout times are confirmed by supervisions, and on location Willit Administrator (WA); or by GPS and Mobile Labor Force Tracking Systems
2. Shift Yields (automated calculation) are confirmed by employees. Work performance is graded, and concerns noted by supervisors.
3. WA submits Work Verification to GCTA and the Resource Allocation and Product and Service Administration (RAPSA). Once compensation is issued RAPSA calculates a product's or service's gross BEE to determine True Cost, and the product is confirmed as available in either the Standard Needs Earned Equity or iWaut Markets. The cost of transporting a product from an Inventory Center to an individual or Pickup Center/Market is an additional cost (Shipping Cost) payable by iWaut Purchasers and those who have over consumed Standard Need Products (determined by voting agreements).

iAct (module integrat
Tracks production yiel
services provision

Work Begins

Workers note everything the
confirm their yields, and rep
production or service agreem
Workers report all violations
Workplace Oversight Adminis
Stop Action Order, if require
The Willit System ensure the
Labor Force are treated as va
and ensures the protection o

Human Resources Administration (HRA):

1) Receives Job/Task Orders: confirms work hardship, education, and hierarchy levels for compensation

2) Certification checked and skills matched (**iLearn**)

3) Job availability notices are sent to all individuals within the region who meet all certification requirements, and the notices are posted for general public review.

Term Definition: BEE

The Base Energy Expense rate is calculated based on the standards of the Willit Compensation Calculator (WCC).
The WCC is a global labor energy expense rate calculation used to determine the true cost of all labor for production and for the provision of services.

The rate of compensation is based on: Job Hardship, Education Level, the Position's Hierarchy, and Lifespan Expectancy factors.

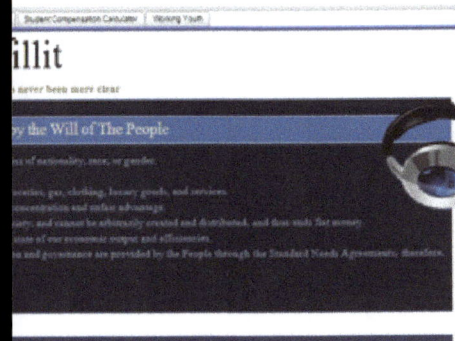

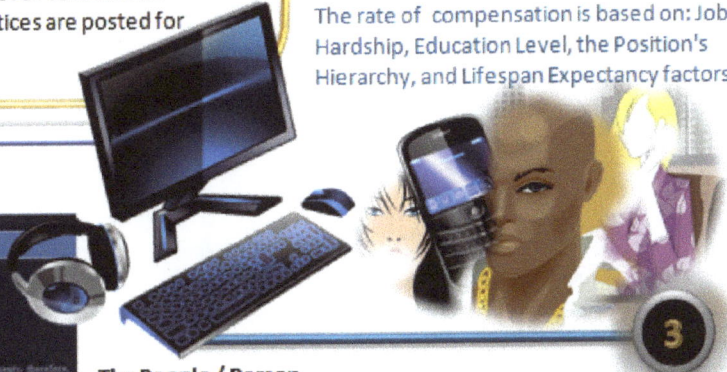

illit

The People / Person

People agree to work (there is no forced labor). One can select to participate as a Standard Needs Earned Equity Member Only, or work in the Capital Markets and earn Willits.

Earned Equity (EE)

Earned Equity is calculated by taking the total man-hours required for the production of all Standard Needs and dividing all man hour requirements by the number of able-bodied persons.
The Earned Equity Energy Expense (E4) requirement is the hours one must contribute to be in good standing;. Those who work in the Standard Needs System, are entitled to access for the agreed upon Standard Need Items and services without additional cost: Food, Housing, medical services, utilities, communication system etc.
Earned Equity workers also earn Willits for efficient production so they can purchase the goods and services they desire from the Capital Markets (iWAUT)

lobal Compensation Standards

r the equitable payment of wages

etermine your rate of compensation at:
tp://willit.ProjectInDivisible.org

Willits for: Earned Equity/Standard Needs Worker

Willits are earned if one is requested to work overtime, and bonuses (Willit Compensation) are paid quarterly to all Standard Needs Earned Equity Members for efficient production
All Citizens whether EE or Capital Markets, receive bonuses for maintaining their health and healthy relationships with other members of society. Bonuses are not included in the True Cost calculation for product pricing. Willits are a living breathing currency that are transferable only for the trade of goods and services. Unused Willit expirer upon an individual's death...

instructed to do,
olations of their
nd hazards.
use of (**iEffect**) so the
on (WOA) may place a

als that make up the
embers of society
n and Labor Rights.

Member Login:

Member logs into the Willit compensation/equity module when they arrive at their employer's work site, to confirm their arrival time. (Computer based, card swipe, and GPS). Offsite workers login to the Mobile Labor Force Tracking System.

Willit System

The Integration of Complex Economic Systems to ensure needs are met, prices are stable, and fair compensation is issued to all people.

1a. iPresent (module integration)

The production of products or provision of a service is first approved by the People through the iPresent process.

Once a production enactment is confirmed by General Vote of the People, all resources will be allocated: Human Labor as well as raw and recycled resources and materials.

Standard Need products and services have first level production priority.

iPresent is also used for legislation of agreement between all People for the rules and agreements that regulate their community, city, state, or nation.

1b. Request Human Resources

Production Units, Corporations, and Service Providers work with Labor Unions and Training Guilds to select compensation factor levels, certification, and training requirements.

Citizens request services from independent Service Providers through either the Standard Needs Earned Equity or iWAUT markets

Human Resources Administration (HRA):

1) Receives Job/Task Orders: confirms work hardship, education, and hierarchy levels for compensation

2) Certification checked and skills matched (iLearn)

3) Job availability notices are sent to all individuals within the region who meet all certification requirements, and the notices are posted for general public review.

Term Definition: BEE

The Base Energy Expense rate is calculated based on the standards of the Willit Compensation Calculator (WCC).

The WCC is a global labor energy expense rate calculation used to determine the true cost of all labor for production and for the provision of services.

The rate of compensation is based on: Job Hardship, Education Level, the Position's Hierarchy, and Lifespan Expectancy factors.

The People / Person

People agree to work (there is no forced labor). One can select to participate as a Standard Needs Earned Equity Member Only, or work in the Capital Markets and earn Willits.

Earned Equity (EE)

Earned Equity is calculated by taking the total man-hours required for the production of all Standard Needs and dividing all man hour requirements by the number of able-bodied persons.

The Earned Equity Energy Expense (E4) requirement is the hours one must contribute to be in good standing. Those who work in the Standard Needs System, are entitled to access for the agreed upon Standard Need items and services without additional cost: Food, Housing, medical services, utilities, communication system etc.

Earned Equity workers also earn Willits for efficient production so they can purchase the goods and services they desire from the Capital Markets (iWAUT)

Willits for: Earned Equity/Standard Needs Worker

Willits are earned if one is requested to work overtime, and bonuses (Willit Compensation) are paid quarterly to all Standard Needs Earned Equity Members for efficient production

All Citizens whether EE or Capital Markets, receive bonuses for maintaining their health and healthy relationships with other members of society. Bonuses are not included in the True Cost calculation for product pricing. Willits are a living breathing currency that are transferable only for the trade of goods and services. Unused Willit expirer upon an individual's death....

Member Login:

Member logs into the Willit compensation/equity module when they arrive at their employer's work site, to confirm their arrival time. (Computer based, card swipe, and GPS).

Offsite workers login to the

Global Compensation Standards

For the equitable payment of wages

Determine your rate of compensation at:
http://willit.ProjectInDivisible.org

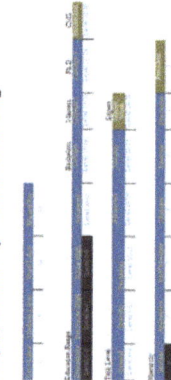

iAct (module integration)

Tracks production yield and services provision

Work Begins

Workers note everything they are instructed to do, confirm their yields, and report violations of their production or service agreement and hazards. Workers report all violations with use of (iEffect) so the Workplace Oversight Administration (WOA) may place a Stop Action Order, if required.
The Willit System ensure the individuals that make up the

Member Logs Out:

1. Logout times are confirmed by supervisions, and on location Willit Administrator (WA); or by GPS and Mobile Labor Force Tracking Systems

2. Shift Yields (automated calculation) are confirmed by employees. Work performance is graded, and concerns noted by supervisors.

3. WA submits Work Verification to GCTA and the Resource Allocation and Product and Service Administration (RAPSA). Once compensation is issued RAPSA calculates a product's or service's gross BEE to determine True Cost, and the product is confirmed as available in either the Standard Needs Earned Equity or iWaut Markets. The cost of transporting a product from an Investory Center to an individual, or Pickup Center/Market is an additional

Willit

Willit Currency is issued by the Global Compensation and Transaction Administration (GCTA) based on previous system account holdings and only for the payment of compensation for work performed in the Standard Needs Earned Equity System.
based on approved production or service enactments.
The Capital Markets (iWAUT) function by siphoning Willits from the pool of Willits issued by the GCTA.

Every transaction made can be viewed and audited by the people and linked back to the source of issuance, production order, and the purchase order issued by a corporation or private individual.

GCTA (Automated)

1. Confirms Receipt of Willit Distribution request.

2. Confirms worked hours with mobile GPS date (if available) if not available human confirmation required (WA's request - will suffice as confirmation for onsite workers).

3. Willits transferred to member's account or their Earned Equity Account is updated.

The Willit Monetary System ensures money has True Value and hinders fraud because of transparency.

Willits

SYSTEM CORE | CONCEPTS PROCESSES AND APPLICATIONS OVERVIEW

The following applications will be detailed as we proceed. We begin with the Willit Monetary System and will conclude with the I-Amwe Community applications.

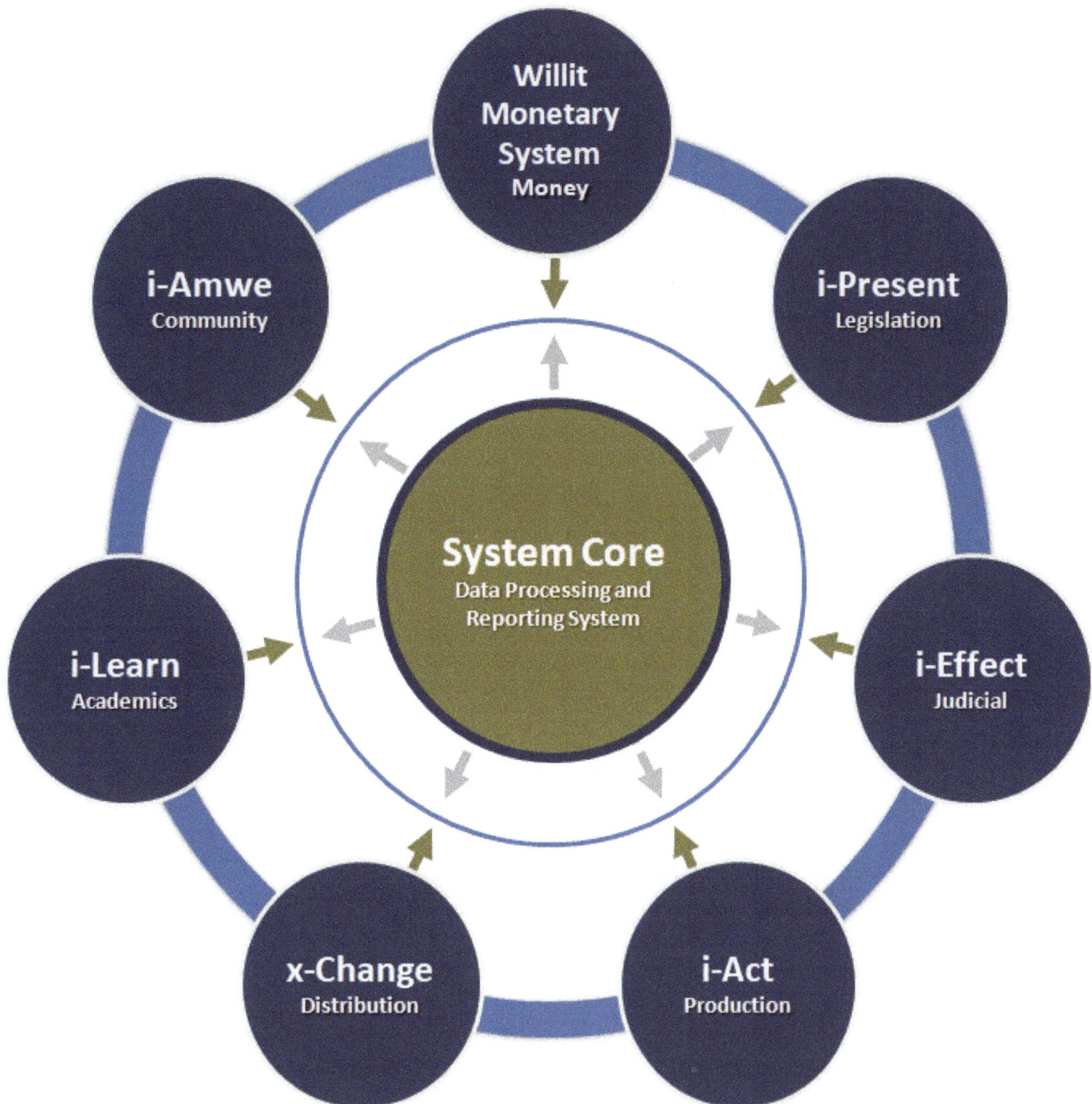

WILLIT MONETARY SYSTEM

The following concepts and departmental system applications will be reviewed:

- Willit Monetary System
- Standard Needs Earned Equity System
- Compensation Caps
- Currency Conversion to Willits

- Reparations
- Global Debt Reconciliation
- Wealth Management

Willit

Your True Value has never been more clear

Real Money - Backed by the Will of the People

BENEFITS OF THE WILLIT MONETARY SYSTEM:

1. Willits calculate an individual's energy output and ensure fair compensation regardless of nationality, race, or gender.
2. You can never lose Willits nor have them stolen from you.
3. Willits never deflate or inflate in value and ensure price stability for all products: Groceries, gas, clothing, luxury goods, and services.
4. Willits are naturally produced and only exist as long as you do, thus preventing cross-generational wealth concentration and unfair advantage.
5. Willits are backed by your energy output and the energy output of all members of society, and cannot be arbitrarily created and distributed, thus ending fiat money.
6. Willits have an auditable trail to ensure accurate accounting and reporting on the true state of our economic output and efficiencies.
7. Not taxable!!! All the Standard Needs of society, including administration and governance are provided by the people through the Standard Needs Agreements; therefore, no taxes will ever be requested of you. The Willits you earn are yours to use for the purchase of goods and services.
8. Willits prevent slave labor, wage slavery, and unfair trade practices.

The current methodology used for monetary creation and valuation has not changed since its inception. Currently, money has value only because of the faith and trust the people have in their systems and administrators, which continues to decline and lingers only because there is no other alternative.

The value and quantity of money fluctuates based on perception, demand, and monetary and political policies which has resulted in economic instability and market collapses, as shown in Figure 2, a history of global monetary declines.

Monetary sabotage alters the perceived value of money to undermine the security and stability of people and their nation, and uses the "standard of living" excuse to rob people in second and third world countries of their labor and material resources.

However, the skills and knowledge used, the energy expensed, and the resources utilized are constants. If money was real and compliant with natural/divine Law, it would reflect this truth.

FIGURE 2

YEAR	COUNTRY	COMMENT
1929-1939	Beggar-thy-neighbor policies in Great Depression	All countries on list devalued their currencies versus gold by more than 10 percent.
1930	Spain	Spain devalues five times between 1929-1937.
1931	Austria, Italy, Spain	Austrian real GDP contracted 24.5% from 1929-1933.
1932	Austria, Denmark, Finland, Greece, Japan, Norway, Sweden, Spain	Japan departs from gold standard in 1931 and devalues yen over next three years.
1933	Canada, Denmark, Greece, Japan, U.S., Yugoslavia	Volatility in Canadian dollar which returned to parity with USD by 1934. Bank of Canada started operations 1935.
1934	Canada, Denmark, Greece, Japan, U.S., Yugoslavia	REER of Danish Krone declined by over 20% from 1929-1939.
1935	Belgium	Belgian franc devalued by 28% in 1935.
1936	Italy, Romania, Spain	Italian lira devalued by over 20% between 1935-1937.
1937	Czechoslovakia, France, Italy, Spain, Switzerland	Switzerland exited gold standard in 1936 and franc devalued by 30% through 1938.
1938	France, Netherlands	France departs gold standard in 1936, 28% depreciation in 1938.
	COLLAPSE OF FIXED DOLLAR RATE TO GOLD AND ERA OF FLOATING EXCHANGE RATES	
1971	U.S. Abrogates Bretton Woods Agreement	Nixon imposes 10% import tax when gold convertibility suspended.
1985	Plaza Accord	G-7 agrees to greater policy coordination to improve function of floating exchange rate system.
1992	EUROPEAN MONETARY SYSTEM CRISIS	
	Italy withdraws from ERM	Lira devalued by 7%.
	U.K. withdraws from ERM	29% adjustment in sterling between 9/92 & 2/11.
1993	TEQUILA CRISIS	
1994	Mexico, Argentina and Brazil	58% depreciation in Mexican peso between 2/94 & 3/95.
1997	ASIAN FINANCIAL CRISIS	
	Hong Kong, Indonesia, Malaysia, Philippines, South Korea	57% depreciation in South Korean won in 1997.
1998	RUSSIAN FINANCIAL CRISIS	
	Russia, Brazil, Hong Kong, Mexico	48% depreciation of the Brazilian Real
2000-2002	Argentina Regime Change	Economic collapse, bank runs, debt default and end of fixed exchange rate to U.S. dollar. Resulted in 80% devaluation of peso.
2007-???	ERA OF COMPETITIVE QUANTITATIVE EASING	
	U.S., euro area, Japan, U.K.	Central bank asset purchases, currency depreciations and volatility.

Source: *Beth Simmons Who Adjusts? Domestic Sources of Foreign Economic Policy During the Inter-War Years, Princeton University Press, Bloomberg*

TIER MONETARY AND EXCHANGE SYSTEM

The Willit Monetary System is composed of a two-tier compensation system, Willits and Earned Equity. Both can be redeemed to acquire goods and services.

- Willits Monetary Compensation
  Redeemable Markets:
  1) I-WAUT
  2) Standard Needs Market (at True Cost)
  3) the Black Market
- The 4th exchange market is for administrative bodies. Requests for Willit allocation is submitted to the people for the production of goods and for the services they require to operate.
- Earned Equity Compensation
  Redeemable Market: Standard Needs Market

REAL MONEY

Willits are a living breathing currency that is literally backed by the will and energy expense of the people. Unlike money, Willits cannot be made from thin air, nor fractioned to create pseudo wealth.

There are thirteen standards used for the creation of and distribution of Willits. Figure 3 displays the standards and the System Core component from which the information is retrieved.

Willits are used to purchase goods and services and help to ensure price stability, and inspire ambition and competition.

If Willits are not used, they cease to exist after the death of the individual. Thus, Willits are compliant with natural laws.

Willits can be used for the purchase of goods and services for one's self, one's spouse, and children under the age of eighteen.

i-Willit

db_1b

Monetary System
Money with Real Value
FAQ

GCTA
Global Compensation and Transaction Administration

Intelligent Automation Systems for Bulk Compensaiton Approval and Audits

Action Order Reviews and Confirmation
Compensation Login Systems
Worker GPS Tracking System
Work Confirmation Systems: Yield and inventory, Service Completion and Order Management Confirmation
Payroll Submission Systems
Willit Account
Willit Issue Order

Equity Issue Order
Willit Escrow Account
Personal Willit Account
National Willit Account
Earned Equity Calculations and Account Confirmations
Consumer Credit System: Interest free for individuals, cities, states and nations
Global Trade Analysis
International Will Exchange
Employee Bonus Compilation Data Systems
Health Citizen Confirmation
Employee Evaluations
Social Systems

FIGURE 3

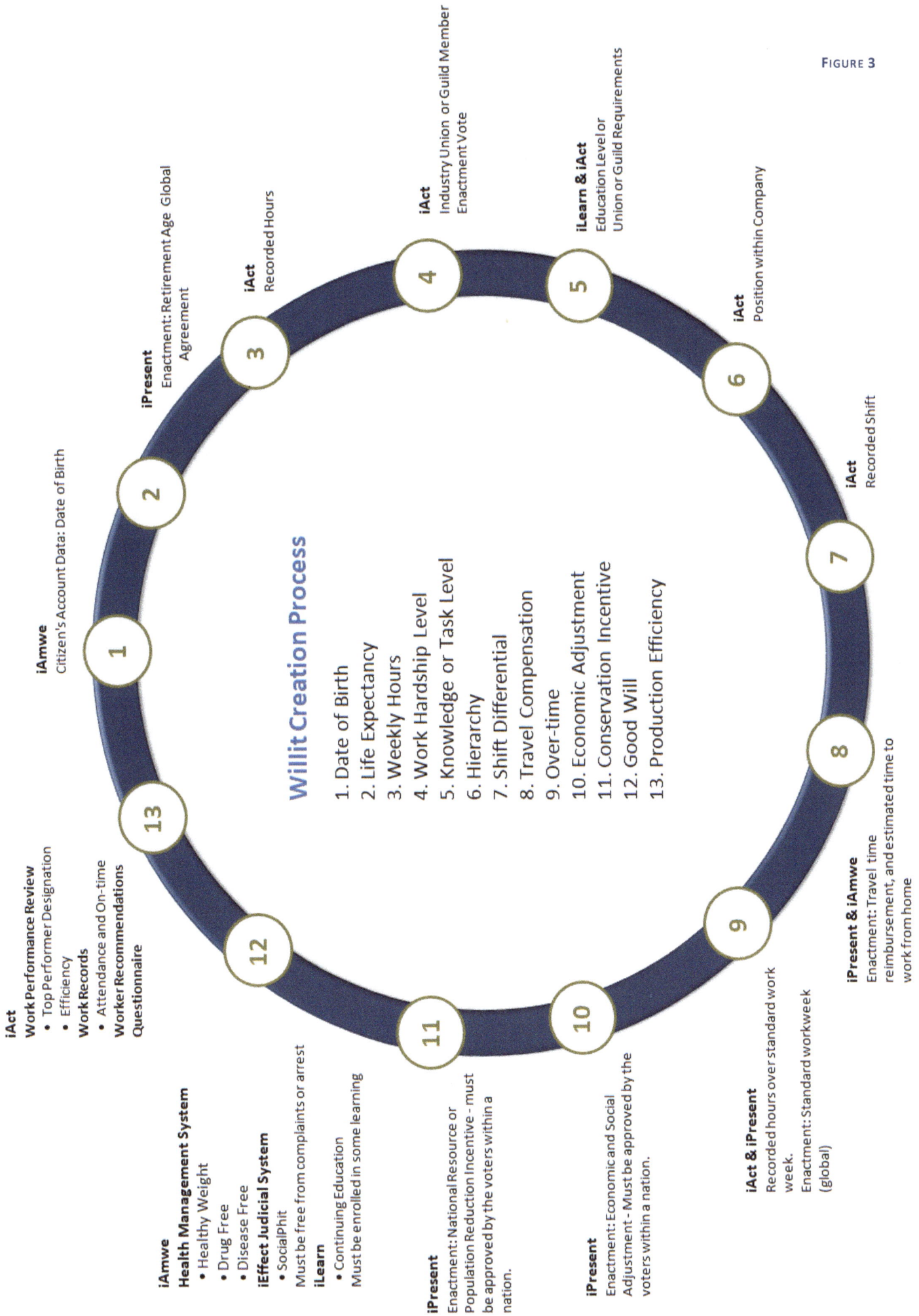

Willit Creation Process

1. Date of Birth
2. Life Expectancy
3. Weekly Hours
4. Work Hardship Level
5. Knowledge or Task Level
6. Hierarchy
7. Shift Differential
8. Travel Compensation
9. Over-time
10. Economic Adjustment
11. Conservation Incentive
12. Good Will
13. Production Efficiency

iAmwe
Citizen's Account Data: Date of Birth

iPresent
Enactment: Retirement Age Global Agreement

iAct
Recorded Hours

iAct
Industry Union or Guild Member
Enactment Vote

iLearn & iAct
Education Level or
Union or Guild Requirements

iAct
Position within Company

iAct
Recorded Shift

iPresent & iAmwe
Enactment: Travel time reimbursement, and estimated time to work from home

iAct & iPresent
Recorded hours over standard work week.
Enactment: Standard workweek (global)

iPresent
Enactment: Economic and Social Adjustment - Must be approved by the voters within a nation.

iPresent
Enactment: National Resource or Population Reduction Incentive - must be approved by the voters within a nation.

iAmwe
Health Management System
• Healthy Weight
• Drug Free
• Disease Free
iEffect Judicial System
• SocialPhit
Must be free from complaints or arrest
iLearn
• Continuing Education
Must be enrolled in some learning

iAct
Work Performance Review
• Top Performer Designation
• Efficiency
Work Records
• Attendance and On-time
Worker Recommendations
Questionnaire

BASE COMPENSATION RATE (BCR)

Willits serve as the base compensation rate (BCR). Thus, Willits also establish the minimum wage one can be paid or compensated for their work. One can earn more than the base rate but will not be compensated for less than the base rate by the Global Compensation and Transaction Administration.

WILLIT CREATION PROCESS

You can access the Willit Compensation Calculator directly at **Advancian.org/model-1**

Select the tab labeled, *'Your True Value'* to calculate your earnings as shown in Figure 4, page 60; or the enlarged image of the calculator following Figure 4.

COMPENSATION PROCESS

1. Enter your date of birth.
2. Leave the life expectancy field at 86.
3. Next, enter the typical number of hours you work in a week.
   - If your hours exceed normal work hours, enter overtime hours and minutes in Overtime fields (Step 9 of 13).
4. Work Levels are pre-assigned for each position when a corporation or production unit requests human resource allocation, and are approved by Global Labor Union and Guild members for each trade or profession – all professions will have a Union or Guild.
5. Next, enter your Knowledge or Skill Level
   - Each member's knowledge level will be accessed from the *iLearn - Academic and Certification System*, and automatically inserted.
   - Task Level Option: If you have a work order that deviates from your usual position, enter it as a task. Tasks will be automatically assigned CPL Levels based on your industry's union agreement.
   - CMS's are Creation Master Specialists. This designation is bestowed upon individuals that a nation deems to be exceptional innovators. The people are responsible for bestowing this special compensation level to individuals requesting or nominated to the designation.

Willit Monetary System Compensation Calculation

Update the sample data (1-13) with your data to determine your true value

After you update the data with your own information, select "UPDATE" to view your base Willit compensation rate.

The following fields help to calculate your base Willit Compensation - i.e., the minimum you will be paid.

STEPS

		Today's Date:	9/27/2019
1 of 13	Date of Birth		11/23/1970
2 of 13	Life Span Expectancy / Productive Age / or Retirement Age	**Current Age:** 48.88	86

Vote Required to establish or to modify "Life Span Expectancy"

Potential Life Force: Will / Power / Energy - in minutes 45,201,600
Minutes in days 1440 | Days - used to date 17,840
Minutes - used to date 25,689,600

Days in Year 365 | Estimated Remaining years (productivity) 37.12
Estimated Remaining minutes 19,512,000

3 of 13	Estimate of Willit energy to be used for production	Weekly Hours 40	2400
3b		Minutes 0	0
	40.00	**Total Production Minutes:**	2,400

| 4 of 13 | Work Hardship Level (also consider desirability of the position - See Step 10) | 8 | CPL Level 1 to 15 | 8 | 19,200 |

Select Knowledge/Skill Level or Task Level:

5 of 13	Knowledge / Skill Level of Member:	16	CPL Level 1 to 35	16	307,200
		OR			
5b	Task - Level	0	CPL Level 6 to 26	0	0

Either 5a or 5b must be set to zero (0)

| 6 of 13 | Hierarchy | 6.0 | CPL Level 8 to 1 | 6.0 | 1,843,200 |

Select Hierarchy Standards, go to tab: "Hierarchy Status CPL"

If Level 5.9 through Level 1.0, select
Resources or Units under your direct supervision | 0

6b	No. of Direct Supervisees	0	0.0000
6c	Supervision Percentage		4.44%
	Supervision CPL		4.44%

CALIBRATION POINT LEVELS (CPL)

Does not include Travel Time (See: Step 8)
Max. 40 hours (See: Step 9 - to calculate Over-time (OT))

Work Hardship Level

Easy Labor	Medium Labor	Normal Labor	Hard Labor	Hazard Pay
1	5	8	12	15

WHL to be set by member vote of independent labor unions and guilds for each industry

Education Range or Skill Equivalency

				Bachelors	Masters	Ph.D.	CMS
Elementary	Pre Junior High	Junior High	Advanced	College	College 2	College 3	Production
Level 1-3	Level 4-6	Level 7-9	Level 10-12	Level 13-16	Level 17-20	Level 21-24	Level 25-35

Production:
Local to 26 CMS
State to 28 CMS
Nation to 32 CMS
Global to 35 CMS

Standards for certification to be set by production and service Units, education institutes.

Task Level

General	Specific	Technical	Advanced	Mastery	Expert Master Work
Level 6-8	Level 9-11	Level 12-15	Level 16-19	Level 20-23	Level 24-26

Hierarchy

Student	Apprentice	Staff Member	Supervisor	Manager	Director	Executive	President
8	7	6	5	4	3	2	1

How many people do you directly supervise?

up to 10	11 to 20	21 to 30	31 to 40	41 to 50	51 to 60	61 to 70	71 to 80	81 or more
4.44%	8.88%	13.32%	17.76%	22.20%	26.64%	31.08%	35.52%	39.96%

Vote required

6. Enter your current position Hierarchy, based on the Hierarchy Status CPL spreadsheet.
   - 6b. If, you supervise other employees enter the number of people you directly supervise.
   - 6c. Leave the supervisor percentage at 4.44 percent. The supervisor percentage will be established by union member vote of each industry.

Hierarchy

STEPS		Options:			Hierarchy CPL:
1 of 3	Employees	0	Select Unit Size (all employees or position)		6.0
2 of 3	Supervisor	N/A	Selection Number of Supervised Employees		0.0
2 of 3	Managers	N/A	Select Number of Managers		0.0
				Average Hierarchy CPL:	6.00
				Applicable options	1.0

Production, Service, or Administrative Unit

			Number of Managers Level 1 to 5	Executives	Directors	Managers	Supervisors	Employees	Hierarchy CPL		Potential
Supervisor Min: 24 (Vote required)		Min Supervised	Min. Under Hierarchy	Min. Supervisors	Min. Supervisors	Min. Supervisors	Supervised	Min.		Max. Years	Achievement
Level 1	President	24	96	24	576	13,824	331,776	7,962,624	1	70	81
			93.60	22	521	12,499	299,981	7,199,539	1.1	69	82
			91.20	19	466	11,174	268,186	6,436,454	1.2	63	79
			88.80	17	410	9,850	236,390	5,673,370	1.3	67	75
	Example:		86.40	14	355	8,525	204,595	4,910,285	1.4	66	72
	Large Corporations, Industry Union leaders,		84.00	12	300	7,200	172,800	4,147,200	1.5	65	76
	Senators, Governors, or Mayors		81.60	10	245	5,875	141,005	3,384,115	1.6	64	75
			79.20	7	190	4,550	109,210	2,621,030	1.7	63	74
			76.80	5	134	3,226	77,414	1,857,946	1.8	62	72
			74.40	2	79	1,901	45,619	1,094,861	1.9	61	72
Level 2	Executive	24	72	0	24	576	13,824	331,776	2	60	71
			69.60		22	521	12,499	299,981	2.1	59	70
			67.20		19	466	11,174	268,186	2.2	55	69
			64.80		17	410	9,850	236,390	2.3	57	68
			62.40		14	355	8,525	204,595	2.4	56	67
			60.00		12	300	7,200	172,800	2.5	55	66
			57.60		10	245	5,875	141,005	2.6	54	65
			55.20		7	190	4,550	109,210	2.7	53	64
			52.80		5	134	3,226	77,414	2.8	52	63
			50.40		2	79	1,901	45,619	2.9	51	62
Level 3	Director	24	48		0	24	576	13,824	3	50	61
			45.60			22	521	12,499	3.1	49	60
			43.20			19	466	11,174	3.2	48	59
			40.80			17	410	9,850	3.3	47	58
			38.40			14	355	8,525	3.4	46	57
			36.00			12	300	7,200	3.5	45	56
			33.60			10	245	5,875	3.6	44	55
			31.20			7	190	4,550	3.7	43	54
			28.80			5	134	3,226	3.8	42	53
			26.40			2	79	1,901	3.9	41	52
Level 4	Manager	24	24			0	24	576	4	40	51
			21.60				22	521	4.1	39	50
			19.20				19	466	4.2	38	49
			16.80				17	410	4.3	37	46
			14.40				14	355	4.4	36	47
			12.00				12	300	4.5	35	45
			9.60				10	245	4.6	34	43
			7.20				7	190	4.7	32	44
			4.80				5	134	4.8	32	43
			2.40				2	79	4.9	31	42
Level 5	Supervisor	24	0.00				0	24	5	30	41
							22	22	5.1	29	40
							19	19	5.2	28	39
							17	17	5.3	27	38
	Example:						14	14	5.4	26	37
	Teacher with a class of students						12	12	5.5	25	36
	Small business owner with up to 24 employees						10	10	5.6	24	35
							7	7	5.7	23	34
							5	5	5.8	22	33
							2	2	5.9	21	32
Level 6	Staff Member	24	0					0	6	20	31
			Favorable Audit 8	Year 2	Year 2	Year 2		Review/Audit 8	6.1	19	30
			Favorable Audit 7	Quarter 3	Quarter 3	Quarter 3		Review/Audit 7	6.2	18	29
			Favorable Audit 6	Quarter 2	Quarter 2	Quarter 2		Review/Audit 6	6.3	17	28
			Favorable Audit 5	Quarter 1	Quarter 1	Quarter 1	Limits industries	Review/Audit 5	6.4	16	27
	Example:										
	Self employed		Favorable Audit 4	Year 1	Year 1	Year 1		Review/Audit 4	6.5	15	26
	or employee without supervisor status		Favorable Audit 3	Quarter 3	Quarter 3	Quarter 3		Review/Audit 3	6.6	14	25
			Favorable Audit 2	Quarter 2	Quarter 2	Quarter 2		Review/Audit 2	6.7	15	24
			Favorable Audit 1	Quarter 1	Quarter 1	Quarter 1		Review/Audit 1	6.8	12	23
			CPL Upon Hire					CPL Upon Hire	6.9	11	22
Level 7	Apprentice	0	0					Apprent. Review 9	7	10	21
			Favorable Review 8					Apprent. Review 8	7.1	9	16
			Favorable Review 7					Apprent. Review 7	7.2	8	19
			Favorable Review 6					Apprent. Review 6	7.3	7	18
			Favorable Review 5					Apprent. Review 5	7.4	6	17
			Favorable Review 4					Apprent. Review 4	7.5	5	16
			Favorable Review 3					Apprent. Review 3	7.6	4	15
			Favorable Review 2					Apprent. Review 2	7.7	3	14
			Favorable Review 1					Apprent. Review 1	7.8	2	13
			CPL Upon Hire					Apprent. Review 0	7.9	1	12
Level 8	Student	0	0					Student	8	0	11
				N/A	N/A	N/A	N/A	N/A	0		
			1,968					47,256,432	72		
									CPL Levels		

Hierarchy

STEPS **Options:** **Hierarchy CPL:**

1 of 3	Employees	Select Unit Size (all employees or position)	0	6.0
2 of 3	Supervisor	Selection Number of Supervised Employees	N/A	0.0
2 of 3	Managers	Select Number of Managers	N/A	0.0

Average Hierarchy CPL: 6.00
Applicable options 1.0

Production, Service, or Administrative Unit

Supervisor Min: 24 — *Vote required*

Example: Large Corporations, Industry Union leaders, Senators, Governors, or Mayors

Level	Min Supervised	Number of Managers Level 1 to 5 (Min. Under Hierarchy)	Executives (Min. Supervisors)	Directors (Min. Supervisors)	Managers (Min. Supervisors)	Supervisors (Supervised)	Employees (Min.)	Hierarchy CPL	Max. Years	Potential Achievement
Level 1 — President	24	96	24	576	13,824	331,776	7,962,624	1	70	81
		93.60	22	521	12,499	299,981	7,199,539	1.1	69	80
		91.20	19	466	11,174	268,186	6,436,454	1.2	68	79
		88.80	17	410	9,850	236,390	5,673,370	1.3	67	78
		86.40	14	355	8,525	204,595	4,910,285	1.4	66	77
		84.00	12	300	7,200	172,800	4,147,200	1.5	65	76
		81.60	10	245	5,875	141,005	3,384,115	1.6	64	75
		79.20	7	190	4,550	109,210	2,621,030	1.7	63	74
		76.80	5	134	3,226	77,414	1,857,946	1.8	62	73
		74.40	2	79	1,901	45,619	1,094,861	1.9	61	72
Level 2 — Executive	24	72	0	24	576	13,824	331,776	2	60	71
		69.60		22	521	12,499	299,981	2.1	59	70
		67.20		19	466	11,174	268,186	2.2	58	69
		64.80		17	410	9,850	236,390	2.3	57	68
		62.40		14	355	8,525	204,595	2.4	56	67
		60.00		12	300	7,200	172,800	2.5	55	66
		57.60		10	245	5,875	141,005	2.6	54	65
		55.20		7	190	4,550	109,210	2.7	53	64
		52.80		5	134	3,226	77,414	2.8	52	63
		50.40		2	79	1,901	45,619	2.9	51	62
Level 3 — Director	24	48		0	24	576	13,824	3	50	61
		45.60			22	521	12,499	3.1	49	60
		43.20			19	466	11,174	3.2	48	59
		40.80			17	410	9,850	3.3	47	58
		38.40			14	355	8,525	3.4	46	57
		36.00			12	300	7,200	3.5	45	56
		33.60			10	245	5,875	3.6	44	55
		31.20			7	190	4,550	3.7	43	54
		28.80			5	134	3,226	3.8	42	53
		26.40			2	79	1,901	3.9	41	52
Level 4 — Manager	24	24			0	24	576	4	40	51
		21.60				22	521	4.1	39	50
		19.20				19	466	4.2	38	49
		16.80				17	410	4.3	37	48
		14.40				14	355	4.4	36	47
		12.00				12	300	4.5	35	46

CPL Levels

CPL Level	Count		Review / Apprentice				Favorable
4.6	245						
4.7	190						
4.8	134						
4.9	79						
5	**24**						
5.1	22						
5.2	19						
5.3	17						
5.4	14						
5.5	12						
5.6	10						
5.7	7						
5.8	5						
5.9	2						
6	**0**						
6.1			Review/Audit 8	Year 2	Year 2		Favorable Audit 8
6.2			Review/Audit 7	Quarter 3	Quarter 3		Favorable Audit 7
6.3			Review/Audit 6	Quarter 2	Quarter 2		Favorable Audit 6
6.4			Review/Audit 5	Quarter 1	Quarter 1		Favorable Audit 5
6.5			Review/Audit 4	Year 1	Year 1		Favorable Audit 4
6.6			Review/Audit 3	Quarter 3	Quarter 3		Favorable Audit 3
6.7			Review/Audit 2	Quarter 2	Quarter 2		Favorable Audit 2
6.8			Review/Audit 1	Quarter 1	Quarter 1		Favorable Audit 1
6.9			CPL Upon Hire				CPL Upon Hire
7			Apprent. Review 9				
7.1			Apprent. Review 8				Favorable Review 8
7.2			Apprent. Review 7				Favorable Review 7
7.3			Apprent. Review 6				Favorable Review 6
7.4			Apprent. Review 5				Favorable Review 5
7.5			Apprent. Review 4				Favorable Review 4
7.6			Apprent. Review 3				Favorable Review 3
7.7			Apprent. Review 2				Favorable Review 2
7.8			Apprent. Review 1				Favorable Review 1
7.9			Apprent. Review 0				CPL Upon Hire
8			CPL Upon Hire				
0			**Student**	N/A	N/A	N/A	**Student**

| | 1,968 | N/A | 47,256,432 | N/A | N/A | N/A | 0 |
| | | | **72** | | | | |

CPL Levels

Level 5 — Supervisor — 24

9.60
7.20
4.80
2.40
0.00

10
7
5
2
0

Example:
Teacher with a class of students
Small business owner with up to 24 employees

Level 6 — Staff Member — 24

Example:
Self employed
or employee without supervisor status

Level 7 — Apprentice — 0

Level 8 — Student — 0

7. Shift Differential
    a. If you work a tradition shift of 9:00 am to 5:59 pm, leave the CPL option at 1
    b. If you work an evening shift from 6:00 pm to 11:59 pm select CPL 1.5
    c. If you work an overnight shift from 12:00 am to 8:59 am select CPL 2
    d. If you work on a holiday select CPL 2

6 Hours	CPL 1	CPL 1.5	CPL2	
	Shift 1	Shift 2	Shift 3	Shift 4 -AM
1	9:00 AM	3:00 PM	9:00 PM	3:00 AM
2	10:00 AM	4:00 PM	10:00 PM	4:00 AM
3	11:00 AM	5:00 PM	11:00 PM	5:00 AM
4	12:00 PM	6:00 PM	12:00 AM	6:00 AM
5	1:00 PM	7:00 PM	1:00 AM	7:00 AM
6	2:00 PM	8:00 PM	2:00 AM	8:00 AM

8 Hours	CPL 1	CPL 1.5	CPL 2
	Shift 1	Shift 2	Shift 3
1	9:00 AM	5:00 PM	1:00 AM
2	10:00 AM	6:00 PM	2:00 AM
3	11:00 AM	7:00 PM	3:00 AM
4	12:00 PM	8:00 PM	4:00 AM
5	1:00 PM	9:00 PM	5:00 AM
6	2:00 PM	10:00 PM	6:00 AM
7	3:00 PM	11:00 PM	7:00 AM
8	4:00 PM	12:00 AM	8:00 AM

8. Travel Compensation
    a. Select the number of days you travel to work. You will be compensated by the GCTA for 90 minutes of travel time each day. The optimal goal is one-way travel of 45-minutes or less to reach your place of employment.
9. Overtime Compensation
    a. Any amount of time (hours or minutes) in excess of the standard work-week (determined by national agreement) should be placed in the Over-time Minutes fields. Hours will be automatically converted to minutes.

Select update to view your base annual compensation.

Selecting the various work hardship, knowledge level, and position hierarchy will allow you to see the variable rates of compensation for your age, and approximate life span.

ECONOMIC AND SOCIAL ADJUSTMENT OPTIONS

10. Economic Adjustment
11. Conservation Incentive

Differential Perceived Value and High Demand (PVHD) and Resource Conservation and Population Reduction Incentive (RCPRI) are optional factors enacted by legislative agreement to increase compensation or Product and Service True Cost to quickly respond to economic factors fairly for all people.

Willits — Compensation Rate (Base / BEE)

Your Weekly Willit Compensation - Based on Production Minutes: **$1,379.19**

Hourly Rate:	34.48
Per Minute Rate:	0.57

Base Compensation Rate (BCR) - The Minimum Compensation Standard

Additional Benefits & Compensation (ABC):

Weekly — Weekly Rate w/ ABC **$1,379.19**

Hourly Rate:	34.48
Per Minute Rate:	0.57

Option SD

Shift Differential: Evenings, Weekends, and Holidays — CPL: 1 to 2

	1	1.0

7 of 13

Willits Compensation with Shift Differential: $1,379.19

Hourly Rate:	34.48
Per Minute Rate:	0.57

Total Min	Total Hours
2400	40.00

Shift	Standard	Evenings	Overnight	Weekends	Holidays
0	1	1.5	2	1.5	2

Supervisory Benefits:

Travel Compensation:		$0.00

From Step 6b - c: for supervision of over 24 individuals

	Travel Rate	Days Worked
	50%	0

		$0.00

8 of 13

Days Worked	0
Travel Time	90

Travel Allowance: 45-minutes to or from work per day (1.5-hours per work day)

Over-time Minutes: — Minutes

	Travel Days
	1 2 3 4 5 6 7

		$0.00

Overtime Time	Standard OT	Holidays
0	1.5	2

		$0.00

9 of 13 — OT - Rate — 0

9b of 13 — Hours — 0

9c of 13 — Minutes — 0

Total OT Minutes — 0

Annual — Annual Wage - Weekly Rate x 52 weeks: **$71,717.79**

Based on Base Compensation Rate

Bonuses are included in Lifetime Maximum Compensation Calculation only for Standard Needs Work

with Max. Performance Bonus:	$86,061.34
Weekly Rate with: ABC (x) 52 weeks:	$71,717.79
Tax Grant - 0.2% of Base Compensation:	$14,343.56
Bonus Standard Needs Work/Performance Bonus	$14,343.56

Link — Tax Grant to be issued to Governance Solos see RP-Tax Grant

ESAO — Economic and Social Adjustment Options - CPL

PVHD

Differential: Perceived Value and High Demand

	0.0

"Perceived Value" is an optional factor for those who request compensation above the standard base rate. The High Demand "premium factor" is declared by a nation. If one feels they should be compensated to a higher degree, one can, when submitting their skills for employment consideration demand a higher rate. Nonstandard rate request can be honored by the Global Compensation and Transaction Administration - upon National Acceptance (just as for CMS) either per individual case or Class Action. And simply means one reaches their earning caps and thus retirement earlier than others

10 of 13

	0

Annual Willits Compensation with Shift Differential	$0.00
Hourly Rate	0.00

RCPRI — National Resource Conservation and Population Reduction Incentive

With various System Core components, we will be able to detect when resource requirements are insufficient to meet the needs of the population. If required, a nation can enact the conservation incentives.

* Population Reduction Incentive percentage can be enacted by national vote, with a percentage range of 0% to 100%.

* Resource Conservation will use a negative percentage range from (-1%) to (-85%), and be enacted by national vote

Non-punishment benefit based incentives for population reduction.

The population reduction incentive is issued for households and individual who commit to not having children

	Incentive
Conservation Incentive — Select Yes or No	N/A
Percentage Increase or decrease	0.00%

11 of 13

Annual Wage – Weekly Rate x 52 weeks:

with Max. Performance Bonus:	N/A
Weekly Rate with: ABC (x) 52 weeks	N/A
Tax Grant - % of Base Compensation	N/A

After you view your compensation, select the Maximum Compensation tab to view the maximum compensation you can potentially earn throughout your lifetime, as shown in Figure 6, page 67.

NOTE: It is important to note that positions in the iAct - Job Allocation System will have various knowledge level requirements. Everyone will be required to meet the minimum knowledge level, and have the appropriate certifications for the position for which they will earn Willits and/or Standard Needs Equity.

Comparable Willit Compensation for various positions is listed in the comparable chart (Figure 5, page 66). Each worker segment has two age variables, and/or a factor within the red box which contributes to different compensation outcomes. For example, in column 1, the variation in age for a President of a production unit will affect the rate of Willit compensation.

MAXIMUM COMPENSATION

The Willit Compensation Calculation Standard is also used to determine the maximum compensation every person will receive over their lifetime.

To view maximum compensation rates, select the Maximum Compensation tab, shown in Figure 6, page 67.

To increase maximum compensation one must work more hours, increase their skills or education level, or obtain a higher position within the production unit they select to contribute their energy to. Individuals may also create their own company or production unit and request human and material resource allocation. Details for production unit approval are provided in the iAct and iPresent segments.

WILLIT PURCHASING POWER

At this point, it is difficult to establish the True Cost of luxury goods because the true cost of production for products, based on current monetary inequalities, prohibits accurate calculations.

Based on True Cost established by Willit Compensation Standards (throughout the production channel), one could estimate products will be more expensive. However, mechanical production should reduce cost, and the high cost of goods will aid in resource conservation and product sharing, which will reduce personal expenses for Standard Needs and products. But more importantly, abuse of the Labor Force will end, and resource conservation/sharing will be commonplace. An example of this would be the car-sharing programs such as Uber and Lift.

FIGURE 5

Comparable Willit Compensation Rates

As of: 12/29/2011

Position Title:	President of Production Unit		Mine Worker		Supervisor		Office Worker		Student/Apprentice	
Age:	60	45	40	25	50	35	45	25	30	18
Days Used:	21900	16425	14600	9125	18250	12775	16425	9125	10950	6570
DBA (Date of Birth):	1/13/1952	1/9/1967	1/8/1972	1/4/1987	1/10/1962	1/6/1977	1/9/1967	1/4/1987	1/5/1982	1/2/1994

Life Expectancy 85 | Energy 40 Hours

Work Level / Hardship:	Medium		Hazard Pay		Medium/Hard		Easy Labor		Easy	Medium
	5	5	15	15	7	7	4	4	3	6
Knowledge Level:	PhD		Junior High	Bachelors	PhD	Masters	Bachelors	High School	Bachelors	
	25	25	7	15	21	16	13	10	15	15
Hierarchy:	President		Staff Member		Manager		Staff Member		Apprentice	
	1	1	5	5	4	4	5	5	8	8
Annual Compensation	**624,000.00**	390,000.00	**93,600.00**	58,240.00	131,040.00	69,888.00	**32,448.00**	16,640.00	12,763.00	**20,955.00**

Major Affects on Lower Wage

FIGURE 6

Maximum Base-Compensation Calculator

Life Time Earnings and Transfer: $32,293,942.71

			$ Willits			Percentage	Weekly Total	Hourly Wage	Year
	Age	Remaining Yrs	YR CNT	Weekly Total	Annual Total	Increase	Increase Per	Step 1	
Date of Birth — 11/23/1970	48.88	37.12	1	1,379	71,718			$34.48	9/27/2019
Retirement Age — 86	49.88	36.12	2	1,417	73,703	2.77%	38.18	$35.43	9/26/2020
	50.88	35.12	3	1,458	75,802	2.85%	40.35	$36.44	9/26/2021
Hours Per Week (From Step 3) — 40.00	51.88	34.12	4	1,500	78,023	2.93%	42.72	$37.51	9/26/2022
Weeks Per Year — 52	52.88	33.12	5	1,546	80,378	3.02%	45.30	$38.64	9/26/2023
Production Minutes — 2400	53.88	32.12	6	1,594	82,881	3.11%	48.12	$39.85	9/25/2024
	54.88	31.12	7	1,645	85,544	3.21%	51.21	$41.13	9/25/2025
Work Level — 8	55.88	30.12	8	1,700	88,383	3.32%	54.61	$42.49	9/25/2026
At the time of Exchange	56.88	29.12	9	1,758	91,418	3.43%	58.36	$43.95	9/25/2027
Knowledge Skill Level — 16	57.88	28.12	10	1,821	94,669	3.56%	62.51	$45.51	9/24/2028
Hierarchy — 6	58.88	27.12	11	1,888	98,159	3.69%	67.12	$47.19	9/24/2029
	59.88	26.12	12	1,960	101,917	3.83%	72.26	$49.00	9/24/2030
	60.88	25.12	13	2,038	105,973	3.98%	78.01	$50.95	9/24/2031
As you age your value increases naturally	61.88	24.12	14	2,122	110,366	4.15%	84.48	$53.06	9/23/2032
LOGIC	62.88	23.12	15	2,214	115,139	4.32%	91.79	$55.36	9/23/2033
As we age, we gain knowledge and experience.	63.88	22.12	16	2,314	120,344	4.52%	100.09	$57.86	9/23/2034
As a result, we obtain insight. With insight, one becomes more	64.88	21.12	17	2,424	126,041	4.73%	109.56	$60.60	9/23/2035
valuable to society.	65.88	20.12	18	2,544	132,304	4.97%	120.45	$63.61	9/22/2036
	66.88	19.12	19	2,677	139,223	5.23%	133.05	$66.93	9/22/2037
As one's life on earth is coming to an end, life becomes more	67.88	18.12	20	2,825	146,905	5.52%	147.73	$70.63	9/22/2038
precious. One should select what they invest their energy into	68.88	17.12	21	2,990	155,484	5.84%	164.99	$74.75	9/22/2039
with care.	69.88	16.12	22	3,176	165,128	6.20%	185.45	$79.39	9/21/2040
	70.88	15.12	23	3,386	176,046	6.61%	209.98	$84.64	9/21/2041
Thus, Willit Compensation incrementally increases	71.88	14.12	24	3,625	188,511	7.08%	239.71	$90.63	9/21/2042
naturally.	72.88	13.12	25	3,901	202,876	7.62%	276.24	$97.54	9/21/2043
	73.88	12.12	26	4,223	219,610	8.25%	321.82	$105.58	9/20/2044
	74.88	11.12	27	4,603	239,354	8.99%	379.68	$115.07	9/20/2045
	75.88	10.12	28	5,058	262,998	9.88%	454.69	$126.44	9/20/2046
	76.88	9.12	29	5,612	291,825	10.96%	554.37	$140.30	9/20/2047
	77.88	8.12	30	6,303	327,749	12.31%	690.85	$157.57	9/19/2048
	78.88	7.12	31	7,188	373,760	14.04%	884.83	$179.69	9/19/2049
	79.88	6.12	32	8,362	434,799	16.33%	1173.83	$209.04	9/19/2050
	80.88	5.12	33	9,994	519,666	19.52%	1632.06	$249.84	9/19/2051
	81.88	4.12	34	12,417	645,698	24.25%	2423.69	$310.43	9/18/2052
	82.88	3.12	35	16,393	852,435	32.02%	3975.71	$409.82	9/18/2053
	83.88	2.12	36	24,114	1,253,905	47.10%	7720.57	$602.84	9/18/2054
	84.88	1.12	37	45,580	2,370,185	89.02%	21466.94	$1,139.51	9/18/2055
	85.88	0.12	38	415,289	21,595,022	811.11%	369708.40	$10,382.22	9/17/2056
	86.88	-0.88	39	0	0	-100.00%	-415288.89	$0.00	9/17/2057
	87.88	-1.88	40	0	0	#DIV/0!	0.00	$0.00	9/17/2058
	88.88	-2.88	41	0	0	#DIV/0!	0.00	$0.00	9/17/2059

BONUSES - Standard Needs Earned Equity

At the end of the production quarters, bonuses are allotted (not included in the BEE (Basic Energy Expense) calculation for the cost of goods). If all needs are met within the quarter and there is "minimal" waste, quarterly bonuses are distributed (Standard Needs Agreement required).

Your quarterly bonus calculation:

Quarterly Bonus = Quarterly Earnings X (Good Will Points + Production Efficiency Points). Bonuses are held in escrow for any citizens with an active complaint against them within the bonus quarter, and may not be issued if the complaint is confirmed as legitimate.

Bonus Percentage

			Promoting Good Health and Social Interaction				
	Healthy Weight	Drug Free	Disease Free	Social Pkit	Continuing Education	Total
12 of 13	GOOD WILL - iAmwe	5 Points Possible	4				
	Health System	0	1	1	1	1	4
		Health System	Health System	Justice System	Education System	

Production Efficiency

		Score	I.Act Production and Distribution Systems
13 of 13	2	4	Top performer designation
		3	Efficient (Work, was completed on time and within standard energy investment criteria)
		3	Attendance and On time
		2	Report Accuracy
		2	Made recommendations for production efficiencies and/or safety standards improvement
		1	Completion of Work Relations Questionnaire (Rate Supervisors and Coworkers)
	15 Points Possible	15	
	15		

20 Bonus Points Possible	
Total Applicable Points:	19
Quarterly Wage:	$17,929.45
Possible to achieve 20% wage rate bonus	
Quarterly Bonus:	$3,406.59
Weekly Bonus for PWAS:	$252.34

View your Maximum Lifetime Willit Distribution based on your current calculation. Select The Maximum Compensation Tab

Bonus Dates	Quarter 1	Quarter 2	Quarter 3	Quarter 4
	January February March	April May June	July August September	October November December
Month End Closing	Last day	Last day	Last day	Last day
Performance Review Deadline	April 7th	July 7th	October 7th	January 7th
Bonus Awarded	April 14th	July 14th	October 14th	January 14th

BONUSES

Bonuses up to 20 percent of an individual's compensation are paid each quarter for: efficient production, providing excellent service, good health, and acceptable social interaction for those who work in the Standard Needs Earned Equity System.

Bonus Willits are <u>not</u> used to determine a products true value nor Base Energy Expense (BEE).

Taking the time to interact with the Willit Calculator will give you a better understanding of how compensation is determined, and the variable factors that affect rates of compensation.

NATURAL ANNUAL COMPENSATION RATE INCREASE

You will notice when viewing the Maximum Compensation Calculator shown in Figure 6, each year the compensation rate increases.

The logic behind the calculation method is, as we grow older, we have less expendable life force and our work experience increases our level of expertise. The Willit Compensation Calculation ensures life force usage and experience is taken into consideration.

FIGURE 7

Consumer Credit Calculation

Also, see: legislative enactment process for production or service unit resource procurement process

First, complete the "Your True Value" tab.

	Product Cost Per:		Month	Quarter	Annual	Input & Assumptions:	Instructions:
Step 1	Cost of Product		433.33	1,300.00	5,200.00	$52,000.00	1. Enter Product Cost
Step 2	Estimated percentage of upkeep					38%	2. Estimate the upkeep of the product based on its useful life duration
	Upkeep and maintenance cost		164.67	494.00	1,976.00	Will be based on actual upkeep cost	
	Total Procurement Cost of Good:		598.00	1,794.00	7,176.00	$71,760.00	
Step 3	Useful Life of Product (ULP)			Months:		120	3. Enter the useful life of the product you wish to purchase (months only)
	ULP must be greater than PBP			Years:		10	
	Procurement Credit Terms:						
Step 4	Payback period (PBP)			Months:		120	4. Enter the number of monthly payments
	PBP must be less than ULP			Years:		10.00	
Auto	Your Life Expectancy (LE)					37.12	
	Life Expectancy must be greater than the Useful life/Payback period of the product					From: Your True Value	
Auto	Credit Term Acceptability				1		0 = Unacceptable Term
	Useful/Payback Period Check				1		1 = Acceptable Term
	Payback/Life Expectancy Check				1		
	Met Criteria Total:				2		Must equal 2 to receive credit

	Credit Determination (automatic)						
Step 5	Employment status:	Select if:				3	5. Select your employment status
Link	Standard Needs = 1 (Equity Bonus)	you work in the Standard Needs Market for				Calculation based on bonus	If you work SN and will rely on Equity Bonus = 1
	WAUT = 2 (Capital)	you accept Willit Compensation for all work				Calculation based on income	If you work in the Capital Markets full-time or contract work = 2
	Both = 3	you work in both the equity and capital marke				Info Link	If you work in both Capital and Equity Markets = 3
Step 6	Employment Terms:	Select if:				At Will	6. Select employment type
	At Will	Leave blank					
Step 7	Contract			Beginning date:		6/18/2019	7. Select contract start date
Step 8				End date:		6/18/2022	8. Select contract end date
			your employment has a limited term (months)			0.00	Employment contract remaining months
				Years:		0.00	Contract Years
Step 9				Monthly Rate:		3,000.00	9. Enter Contract Montly Rate
				Contract Compensation:		0.00	Remaining Compensation

	Revenue	Weekly	Monthly	Quarterly	Annual	
	Standard or/and Bonus Compensati	1,655.15	6,620.59	19,861.78	86,067.70	
	Contract Compensation	0.00	0.00	0.00	0.00	
	Total Revenue	1,655.15	6,620.59	19,861.78	86,067.70	

	Obligation - Debt					62%	10. Percentage of income already obligated to expenses
Step 10	Obligations	1,026.19	4,104.77	12,314.30	53,361.97		From Central Account
	New Procurement	149.50	598.00	1,794.00	7,176.00	29.66%	% Remaining Ann. Income
	Total Obligations:	1,175.69	4,702.77	14,108.30	60,537.97	25,529.72	$ Remaining Ann. Income

	Credit	Weekly	Monthly	Quarterly	Annual		
	Pre-Willit Allocation Scope (PWAS):					PWAS based on PBP years	
	Available PWAS Credit (*Term):	628.96	2,515.82	7,547.47	32,705.72	327,057.24	32,705.72
Step 11	Savings: Select Savings Account					Household Saving Accounts	11. Optional, Select your household savings account
						0.00	Auto Detect Saving Account - Household Ledger
	Total Funds & Credit					327,057.24	
	New Procurement	149.50	598.00	1,794.00	7,176.00	71,760.00	
	Differential PWAS	479.46	1,917.82	5,753.47	25,529.72	Remaining Credit	

CREDIT DETERMINATION

Final

Yes, you are eligible for PWAS Credit

There is no interest for Willit credit. If eligible for the PWAS credit, the monthly amount will be automatically deducted from your Willit account by the GCTA.

The Willit Credit and Financing system ensures interest will no longer be charged for any purchase. Everyone will have access to the goods or services they need based solely on their ability to repay the funds pre-allocated to them, regardless of gender, race, ethnicity or nationality.

Credit Funds will be issued by the Global Compensation and Transaction Administration through your local Consumer Credit Administration and will be accessible online.

See the Consumer Credit Calculator on the following page or login to http://Advancian.org/model-1 and select the Consumer Credit tab.

The following steps are utilized to determine if an individual will be granted non-interest credit, see Figure 7:

1. **Cost of Product**
   Enter the cost of the product.
   We will use the purchase of a vehicle at the Willit rate of $52,000 Willits.
2. **Estimate Percentage of Upkeep**
   The upkeep of the product is determined by the cost of maintenance and repair to maintain the product in usable condition.
3. **Useful Life**
   The useful life of the product is used to ensure the price of the product is worth the cost charged and to ensure the product lasts for the payment duration. Products that do not meet their useful life may be removed from production. Useful life also ensures all resources are utilized for the best possible use.
4. **Payback Period**
   The payback period (PBP) is determined by you or your Consumer Credit Counselor
5. **Employment Status** – Credit determination is based on your employment status.
   The calculation will be determined by
   a. Standard Needs and or your Bonus
   b. Capital Market work in the iWaut Market
   c. or Both
6. **Employment Terms** – Select if you are an at-will employee or if you are under contract.
7. Enter your contract beginning date
8. Enter your contract ending date
9. **Compensation** is calculated based on all Revenue streams
10. **Obligation of Debt** ensures you are fully aware of your repayments obligations for all financial contracts you have agreed to pay
11. Select the Willit Account that will be deducted. You will have the option to select:
    a. Your household account
    b. Personal savings account

c. Or your spouse's account (if you are authorized).

Selection of the Willit Account ensures the purchaser is established in case of divorce or separation.

If your household account is selected each party will have equal rights and access to the item purchased. If you select your personal account, only you will have the right to recover the asset should a separation or divorce occur.

Consumer Credit Calculation

Also, see: legislative enactment process for production or service unit resource procurement process

First, complete the "Your True Value" tab.

Step		Month	Quarter	Annual	Input & Assumptions:	Instructions:
	Product Cost Per:					1. Enter Product Cost
Step 1	Cost of Product	433.33	1,300.00	5,200.00	$52,000.00	
						2. Estimate the upkeep of the product based on its useful life duration
Step 2	**Estimated percentage of upkeep.**				38%	
	Upkeep and maintenance cost	164.67	494.00	1,976.00	Will be based on actual upkeep cost	
	Total Procurement Cost of Good:	598.00	1,794.00	7,176.00	$71,760.00	
						3. Enter the useful life of the product you wish to purchase (months only)
Step 3	**Useful Life of Product (ULP)**			Months:	120	
	ULP must be greater than PBP			Years:	10	
	Procurement Credit Terms:					4. Enter the number of monthly payments
Step 4	**Payback period (PBP)**			Months:	120	
	PBP must be less than ULP			Years:	10.00	
Auto	**Your Life Expectancy (LE)**				37.12	
	Life Expectancy must be greater than the Useful life/Payback period of the product.				From Your True Value	
Auto	**Credit Term Acceptability**				1	0 = Unacceptable Term
	Useful/Payback Period Check			1		1 = Acceptable Term
	Payback/Life Expectancy Check			1		
	Met Criteria Total:			2		**Must equal 2 to receive credit**
	Credit Determination (automatic)					5. Select your employment status
Step 5	Employment status:	Select if:			3	If you work SN and will rely on Equity Bonus = 1
Link	Standard Needs = 1 (Equity Bonus)	you work in the Standard Needs Market for			Calculation based on bonus	If you work in the Capital Markets full-time or contract work = 2
	WAUT = 2 (Capital)	you accept Willit Compensation for all work			Calculation based on income	If you work in both Capital and Equity Markets = 3
	Both = 3	you work in both the equity and capital marke			Info Link	

Employment Terms:	Select if.		6. Select employment type
At Will		At Will	
Contract	Leave blank		

Beginning date:		6/18/2019	7. Select contract start date
End date:		6/18/2022	8. Select contract end date
your employment has a limited term (months)		0.00	Employment contract remaining months
Years:		0.00	Contract Years

Monthly Rate:		3,000.00	9. Enter Contract Montly Rate
Contract Compensation:		0.00	Remaining Compensation

Revenue	Weekly	Monthly	Quarterly	Annual
Standard or/and Bonus Compensati	1,655.15	6,620.59	19,861.78	86,067.70
Contract Compensation	0.00	0.00	0.00	0.00
Total Revenue	1,655.15	6,620.59	19,861.78	86,067.70

Obligation - Debt					
					10. Percentage of income already obligated to expenses
Obligations	1,026.19	4,104.77	12,314.30	53,361.97	62% From Central Account
New Procurement	149.50	598.00	1,794.00	7,176.00	29.66% % Remaining Ann. Income
Total Obligations:	1,175.69	4,702.77	14,108.30	60,537.97	25,529.72 $ Remaining Ann. Income

Credit	Weekly	Monthly	Quarterly	Annual
Pre-Willit Allocation Scope (PWAS):				PWAS based on PBP years
Available PWAS Credit ("Term):	628.96	2,515.82	7,547.47	32,705.72 327,057.24
Savings: Select Savings Account				Household Saving Accounts

11. Optional, Select your household savings account
Auto Detect Saving Account - Household Ledger

32,705.72

0.00

Total Funds & Credit				327,057.24
New Procurement	149.50	598.00	1,794.00	7,176.00
Differential PWAS	479.46	1,917.82	5,753.47	25,529.72

71,760.00 Remaining Credit

CREDIT DETERMINATION

Yes, you are eligible for PWAS Credit

There is no interest for Willit credit. If eligible for the PWAS credit, the monthly amount will be automatically deducted from your Willit account by the GCTA.

Unlimited Potential Realized

Payment and Receipt of Services and Products

(iWaut) Member's requesting service must have Willits available in their account for the work they have agreed to purchase, or seek Consumer Credit from the GCTA.

Once the Working Member logs out of the Requesting Member's service login module, and the Requesting Member acknowledges receipt of services, their Willit account is credited. If the Requesting Member does not have enough Willits, the Worker still receives all funds due to them, however, the Requesting Member's account will state a deficit and the Purchase Module will be disabled until their account is in good standing. There are no overdraft fees nor fines, nor are their discounts on BEE -- the People are paid what they are worth.

An individual may register as a service provider with the appropriate Service Labor Union and receive Willits. Service members cannot accept less than their Willit rate, however, they may request payments above their Willit rate.

Producers and Products -- iWAUT members' compensation is based on Asking Price minus True Cost (BEE) which is distributed to an individual's, corporation's, or service provider's Willit Account.

Price and True Cost information are available for everyone to see online, listed upon every product's label, and detailed in service contracts.

iWAUT goods are manufactured after receipt of payment. Products may be produced in advance based on order levels. Full payment thus determines order priority.

Prior to goods or services being confirmed as sold, inventory and production levels are checked, and a date of delivery is estimated based on production levels and open orders -- Supply on Demand.

WILLIT VALUE

The value of Willits does not fluctuate over time due to transparency, standardization, and retirement of Willit accounts at the end of life cycle for every individual (regardless of holdings).

- Willits are a true measure of one's accomplishments

- Wealth cannot be concentrated in a few hands; nor will the Willit Monetary System have the capability of collapse because of debt, inflation, or devaluation.

- Willits are a living, breathing currency, and based on fundamental elements of creation: Life, energy, force, knowledge, and time.

Value Example: The value of a Willit for the United States will have the same value as a Willit from any other country, and will end income disparity between nations.

Income disparity between nations has led to record profits and economic advantages for corporate owners and investors, but wage slavery for developing countries that cannot compete to gain access to international resources, including skilled labor. The migration of skilled workers to nations that are monetarily dominant decreases wages worldwide, and leads to the enslavement of individuals without wealth advantage. Wage disparity leads to more social decline.

Technologically advanced nations will have lower true cost due to efficiency and the automation of production, resulting in fewer work hours for its population and potentially higher standards of living (depending on natural resources). However, the more intelligent a population is the higher the tax grant for one's nation to administrative bodies, and true cost for goods and services.

The Willit monetary system would diminish International trade with exception to natural material resource exchange, as the cost of transporting produced goods could be cost-prohibitive. Each country would deem it mandatory to be self-sufficient. Thus, homeland employment opportunities would increase, and migration to procure employment minimized.

Knowledge and information sharing would continue, as well as travel and tourism. Education and innovation will be essential to obtaining wealth. People would have more leisure time and expendable income to travel. Travel will help foster understanding between people and nations and strengthen international relations based on the pursuit of knowledge, not predatory competition, nor economically forced integration.

The following figure (Figure 8) displays a few examples of international wage rates disparity. Source: http://en.wikipedia.org/wiki/List_of_minimum_wages_by_country 2011

FIGURE 8

Low Income Countries Example						1	2	3
Afghanistan	Argentina	Brazil	Iran	Mexico	United States	Luxembourg	Switzerland	
84.88 mth	546.97 mth	348.39 mth	303 mth	4.8563 hr	51,493	50.610	47.810	
Monthly/Hourly Wage Rates					**Annual Wage Rate**			

GRANT OF WILLITS AND EQUITY COMPENSATION

MULTI-PAYMENT JOB POSITIONS

Some positions may require the payment of both equity and Willit compensation for positions that are vital for society that may be dangerous or undesirable.

Examples: Police Officers, Fire Fighters, Mine and Oil Rig Workers, Teachers and Professors, Independent Investigators, Local Rights Administrators, Medical Doctors, and Mental Health Professionals.

Willit and Equity (WE) designated positions earn automatic equity, and the payment of Willit Compensation may be issued.

PAYMENT OF WILLIT COMPENSATION

Employers **never** pay wages. Once a production agreement is confirmed, all resources including human resources are allocated to Producers and Service Providers at no cost.

The Willit rate is the global minimum one can be paid. Skills and expertise vary greatly; therefore one can be paid more than the minimum, but not less. All compensation received is applied toward maximum compensation levels.

Willit Compensation for work performed is issued by the Willit Administration (GCTA) after work is confirmed by Production Unit Management and processed by the on-site Willit Administrator.

Willits will be of digital format, transferred electronically, will not have a physical essence, and are not printable. Paper checks and credit slips, written against one's account will be acceptable forms of payment only if electronic payment processing problems occur.

EQUITABLE COMPENSATION

- Employee Team Members are tracked and assessed based on their efficiency, abilities, and production and service yields for their department, if required. For example, an individual working as a Human Resource Director would not have a yield requirement, but they are responsible for ensuring all the tasks of their department are completed based on the task management system's time and date specifications.

- Every task is measured by time. Each person acknowledges their energy expense by the completion of tasks confirming their right to compensation or equity.

- Tasks may also have alternate compensation levels (such as hardship levels); that will override the position's compensation levels and thus the individual will be compensated for the completion of the task at the task's Willit rate, as long as the task's Willit rate is no lower than the individual's confirmed permanent position compensation level. The individual will be compensated at the task level only for the duration of time they are performing the task.

- Once a production cycle is completed, a product is assigned a True Cost rate and entered into the virtual market for tracking. Based on the product's Market Status, it is then placed either in the iWaut Market or the Standard Needs Market.

- After a production cycle is completed, rates of efficiency and waste are established and reported to Management and Employee Team Members. The established measures are used as a gauge for production and service efficiency quarterly bonuses – paid by the Willit Administration (GCTA), but excluded from product BEE cost.

- Employees that do not meet personal efficiency, as well as other standards required for quarterly bonuses, are excluded from bonus payments.

- Equitable Compensation is based on the Willit standard compensation rates. However, some jobs are exempt from bonus payments such as: inventors, creatives, and artists.
    - CREATIVE COMPENSATION: ARTIST, AUTHOR, AND FILM MAKERS
      Creatives can set their own pricing for art, books, and films. Funds will be issued to them based on their yearly compensation cap. Income from additional sales that exceed their annual cap will be placed in their escrow account for future distribution – to ensure no individual can dominate nor monopolize resources.

- INVENTOR COMPENSATION
Inventors will be compensated based on their Willit compensation calculation for as long as their original and registered invention or idea is in use.

EXECUTIVE COMPENSATION

Private corporations incur labor costs, as well as the true cost of operation and maintenance. However, all members of society are compensated for work through the GCTA regardless if the corporation is private or public.

Independent Production and Service Provider Agreements

Executive Management Teams (EMTs), receive compensation after the sale of a good or service. Funds in excess of BEE (Base Energy Equity) will be distributed to the EMT's allocated accounts. The Profits may be distributed to the Executive Management Team based on their Executive Team Agreement. However, the distribution of earnings cannot exceed annual compensation caps.

Management teams set pricing rates for production above the BEE, but, their energy investment is not calculated in the BEE. Management is, therefore, compensated based on their success at retaining employees, efficient production, and market development.

The GCTA also issues compensation to non-management personnel, supervisors, and managers at or above their Willit Standard Rate, after the purchased product is received by the purchaser.

ILLNESS AND INJURY

Should an individual become sick, temporarily ill, or unable to work for an extended period, the Standard Needs Earned Equity System would ensure their care. Their equity requirement would be suspended until they can return to work. They will have access to medical services, the expenses covered by the Global Compensation and Transaction Administration, through an Earned Equity - Disability Care Coverage Act.

All expenses paid on an individual's behalf should be recorded in an itemized health care account to determine the amount of equity and Willits required for care. When the citizen is well, and not found to be at fault for self-injury, they will have the opportunity but not the obligation to work extra hours in the Standard Needs Earned Equity or iWAUT Markets to decrease their Care Coverage escrow.

If one's disability is the fault of another individual, the escrow account will be used to determine their financial obligation for care and applicable legal expenses.

VACATION AND LEAVE OF ABSENCE

Each individual will determine the amount and duration of their vacation. Permission to take leave or vacation is not required by iWAUT producers. However, the right or date to return to work must be agreed upon by both parties prior to vacation or a leave of absence. Unions and guilds, by confirmation vote of its members, and agreement by production and administrative units, will have the right to determine work hours, and agreements for sickness and injury, vacation, and leave of absence for the Standard Needs Earned Equity as well as the IWAUT employment markets; and must take into consideration the physical and mental wellbeing of its members, and employment/recruitment rates to ensure efficient production and service provision. See the i-Act System for additional Union and Guild rights and obligations.

FINANCIAL & PRICE STABILITY

The standard factors used to determine Willit Compensation will stabilize costs for goods and services, which will directly affect price strategies. The Base Energy Expense (BEE – Production/Service Cost) will be listed for all products and services.

Global Trade Analysts will attempt to mitigate Bear Market motivation (what the market will bear) during shortages for raw resources and food supplies. But some goods and services may be subject to allocation priority levels.

NATIONAL WILLIT VALUATION

Willits are a universal tender with unified value. In our current system, a nation's currency value compared to other nations is based on floating rates, without sound underlying factors, and can be manipulated. They are without checks and balances, and there is no transparency. Nor, is the current monetary system audited by independent sources who are answerable to the people.

Nations can manipulate their currency and misrepresent gross production and assets used to back their value.

To ensure proper checks and balances, and to assess true production rates and value, each nation's Willits will be designated by the acronym for the source of origination. Thus, each Nation will be issued a Willit Class.

Example - The United States Willit Class would be: Willit.US
Willit classes will be exchangeable for goods and services from the issuing nation.

INTERNATIONAL WILLIT EXCHANGE

To ensure a nation's ability to trade is not impeded, Willits will be exchanged through global Willit and Resource Reserves systems.

Example: (see Figure 9, page 81)

> The United States wishes to purchase oil:
>
> A nation may submit an International Purchase Enactment (IPE), to the people for the purchase of international products, for example OPEC Oil.
>
> The people must approve the IPE, as the people's material resources and labor are in service to fulfill International enactment orders.
>
> - OPEC transfers the oil to the Global Resource Reserve System for transport, which is verified by Global Compensation and Transaction Administrators
> - The United States submits Willits to the Global Resource Reserve System.

OPEC will have the option of purchasing American products, services, or materials; an OPEC nation may also require US-Willit reserves for travel and tourism so that their people may travel to the United States and vice-versa. Or, OPEC may offer the US-Willits to other nations that wish to purchase American goods and services, for which OPEC will receive the option to purchase products, materials and services from those other nations.

Nations may issue Willits up to ten (10) percent of Gross Domestic Production into the Global Resource and Reserve Systems for up to three quarters, based on the 60/30/10 partition agreement. Nations may take on no further resource allocation obligations until the obligation is settled. A nation may also issue Willits or commit resources to maintain a steady ten (10) percent ratio.

Global and Regional Compensation and Transaction Administrations will dispense Willit Compensation and ensure the audit of all transactions, and the efficient and legal distribution of resources.

As a result, only the best products, rare materials, and niche services will be offered for international exchange. Knowledge and training will be of prime importance as well as innovation. Nations, by necessity, will make efficient use of their resources, promote recycling, the best usage of resources (see efficiency calculator Figure 15, Page 55), and conservation. Each nation's cities and states will be vital assets that ensure a nation's longevity; therefore, its people must be well treated to prevent conflict, civil war, and secession.

FIGURE 9

International Exchange

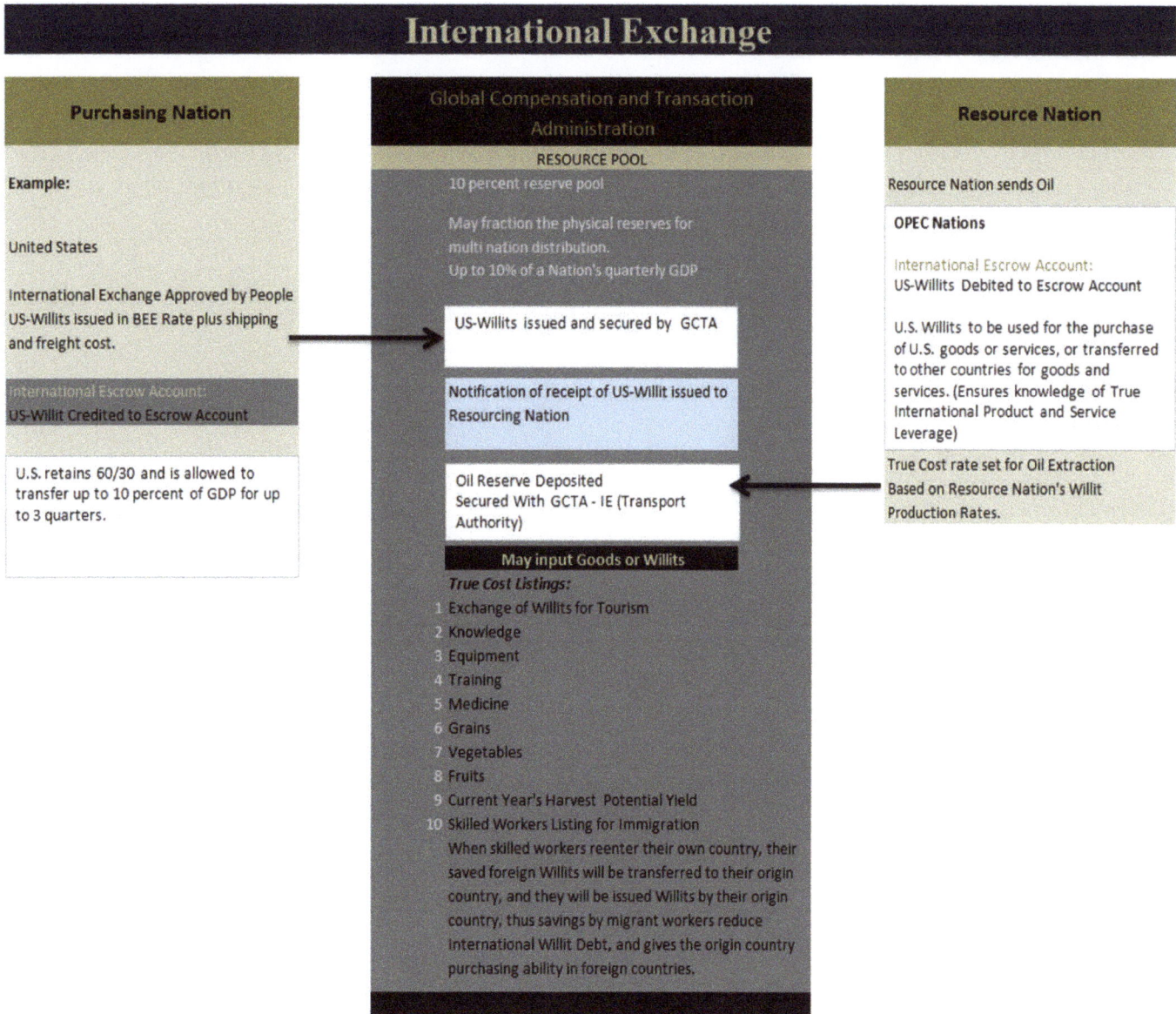

Purchasing Nation

Example:

United States

International Exchange Approved by People
US-Willits issued in BEE Rate plus shipping
and freight cost.

International Escrow Account:
US-Willit Credited to Escrow Account

U.S. retains 60/30 and is allowed to
transfer up to 10 percent of GDP for up
to 3 quarters.

Global Compensation and Transaction Administration

RESOURCE POOL
10 percent reserve pool

May fraction the physical reserves for
multi nation distribution.
Up to 10% of a Nation's quarterly GDP

US-Willits issued and secured by GCTA

Notification of receipt of US-Willit issued to
Resourcing Nation

Oil Reserve Deposited
Secured With GCTA - IE (Transport
Authority)

May input Goods or Willits
True Cost Listings:
1 Exchange of Willits for Tourism
2 Knowledge
3 Equipment
4 Training
5 Medicine
6 Grains
7 Vegetables
8 Fruits
9 Current Year's Harvest Potential Yield
10 Skilled Workers Listing for Immigration
When skilled workers reenter their own country, their
saved foreign Willits will be transferred to their origin
country, and they will be issued Willits by their origin
country, thus savings by migrant workers reduce
International Willit Debt, and gives the origin country
purchasing ability in foreign countries.

Resource Nation

Resource Nation sends Oil

OPEC Nations

International Escrow Account:
US-Willits Debited to Escrow Account

U.S. Willits to be used for the purchase
of U.S. goods or services, or transferred
to other countries for goods and
services. (Ensures knowledge of True
International Product and Service
Leverage)

True Cost rate set for Oil Extraction
Based on Resource Nation's Willit
Production Rates.

MONEY CONVERSION

The conversion of current international currencies into Willits is a simple process, as shown in Figure 10, page 83. Money is converted based on the hours an individual worked to obtain their monetary holdings. Then, those hours are converted into Willits.

Based on our example (Figure 10), the average hourly rate for the individual based on current currency methods yields an hourly compensation rate of 25 dollars. The Willit rate for our sample individual has determined their compensation should have been paid at a Willit rate of Ⓦ32.81 Willits per hour based on the sample age, skill level, and other compensation factors.

Willit monetary conversion rates will ensure every individual is compensated at an equitable level regardless of a nation's previously flawed or arbitrary compensation methods. These rates also ensure that people who wish to acquire a more favorable standard of living are able to do so within their own country, thus migration for economic advantage will decline.

The Willit Monetary System will also help to end the intellectual and labor drain nations suffer, which prevents technological and social advancement.

FIGURE 10

Local Currency Conversion

Used to determine Currency Conversion into Willits

		INPUT FIELDS
		Enter Wage Rate:
STEP 1:	Your Wage Annual Wage:	52,000
STEP 2:	Labor Hours to Earn Wage:	2,080
STEP 3:	Funds to Convert:	3,000
	Average Hourly Rate:	25.00
	Conversion Minute Rate:	60.00
	Hours (to be converted):	120.00
	Minutes Per Hour:	7200.00

STEP 4-8. Complete Fields to determine your Willit Compensation Rate:

Today's Date	4/4/2015
Date of Birth	11/23/1970
Age	44.39
Life Span Expectancy/ Productive Age / or Retirement Age	86

See: Compensation Rate Level (Select Next Tab Below)

Work Level (also consider desirability of the position)

Easy Labor .... Hazard Pay
	7
	50,400

Knowledge/Skill Level of Member

Elementary .... PhD
	13
	655,200

Hierarchy

President .... Student
	4
	2,620,800

Divided by Remaining Years	41.61

FINAL	Willit Compensation Convertion for your cash, savings, fiat currency:	$3,936.72
	True Hourly Rate:	32.81

FIGURE 11

Accurate Past Earnings Compensation Calculations (APEC)

Past Earning Compensation:	$2,366.01
APEC Calculation agreed upon year	2007
Enter Current Year	2018

Note:
A foundation agreement is required to determine the date we will begin calculating wage deficiencies and abuses of the labor force.

Documentation of the wages you were paid are required to make an accurate determination of the energy investment you should have been compensated to determine your reparation amount.

Global Standards

Current Calculation Standards	
Date of Birth	11/23/1990
Retirement Age	86
	40
Hours Per Week	52
Weeks Per Year	
Production Minutes	2400
Work Level	1
At the time of Exchange	1
Knowledge Skill Level	1
Hierarchy	

Year:	Work Level	Knowledge Skill Level	Hierarchy	Weekly Rate	Weeks Worked	Annual
2017	1	1	8	5	52	$253
2016	1	1	8	5	52	$249
2015	1	1	8	5	52	$245
2014	1	1	8	5	52	$242
2013	1	1	8	5	52	$238
2012	1	1	8	5	52	$234
2011	1	1	8	4	52	$231
2010	1	1	8	4	52	$228
2009	1	1	8	4	52	$224
2008	1	1	8	4	52	$221

Total: (APEC) Transferable to Willit Account — $2,366

Work Level

Easy Labor	Medium Labor	Hard Labor	Hazard Pay
1	5	10	20

Knowledge Skill Level

Education and Skill Levels:

None	Graduate	Advanced	Professional	Dr	Master
1	5	10	15	20	25

Hierarchy

Student	Staff Member	Supervisor Manager	Director	Executive	President
8	5	4	3	2	1

REPARATIONS

The Willit Compensation Calculator also includes calculations for Accurate Past Earnings Compensation (APEC) or reparations for unpaid wages, low wages, slavery, and lost wages due to fraud, as shown in Figure 11.

Reparation is paid only to the individual affected or their spouse for the duration of time approved by legislative enactment.

Reparations are not paid to individuals that were not directly wronged, such as an adult child of the victim nor their descendants. Only victims and/or their spouses are compensated.

Once the System Core is operational the people will vote on the date range for which reparations will be issued.

EARNED EQUITY STANDARD NEEDS

The Standard Needs Earned Equity tier of the Willit Monetary systems is vital to ensure that all nations end poverty, and to ensure the people control their nation's destiny.

EARNED EQUITY

Earned Equity is the right to access products and services the people have agreed are Standard Needs for all people -- with exception to those individuals permanently exiled for crimes against humanity and human rights violations.

To place orders for Standard Needs, one's Work Equity Requirement (quota) must be in good standing, or, Willits are required to purchase Standard Needs items at the BEE/R (Base Energy Expense / Rate).

Earned Equity for receipt of Standard Needs is without ranking and is based on each person doing what they do best to ensure the proper functioning of society. Individuals will also receive bonus Willit compensation for efficient production at their compensation rate. Individuals may openly and freely offer their services (non-tangible) and their used products (owned prior to System Core implementation), registered in the x-Change's iWaut Market.

A household or an individual's consumption is reflected in real-time usage: food, utility services, etc. If a household exceeds average consumption for consumable Standard Need goods, their equity requirement is increased, or they may pay for excess consumption with Willits.

An individual may request compensation in Willits instead of Earned Equity, and pay the BEE for standard goods and services at True Cost.

Standard Needs goods and services that will not be calculated as overconsumption, would be: Standard Needs communication services for trade and commerce, physical and mental health and medical services, emergency services, as well as political, judicial, and education services.

Able-bodied citizens should become certified in more than one classification to ensure they have numerous skill sets to earn their equity and Willits.

All citizens (male and female) will be guaranteed the right to work in the Standard Needs Earned Equity System in any field they have obtained certification.

Once a citizen's monthly/annual Earned Equity Requirement is fulfilled, they will be designated as, "standby" in the human resource registry until all willing members of society have fulfilled their Standard Needs Earned Equity obligation.

The Standard Needs Earned Equity System results in one-hundred percent full employment, the reduction of work hours for all people, a robust and dynamic economic system, stability of employment, social and economic security, and individuals having the time to properly care for and nurture their families and themselves. Thus, a stable social and economic system is created.

GLOBAL DEBT RECONCILIATION

You can access the calculator directly at: **Advancian.org/model-3**

Bond Conversion Rate Fi... ×

← → C ⌂ | advancn.org/spreadsheets/Bond_Conversion/Bond%20Conversi...

International Debt Reconciliation - Bonds Stocks Loans and Investmen

		INPUT FIELDS	Low Income Countries Exan	
		Enter Annual Rate:	Afghanistan	Argentina
STEP 1:	Debtor Country's Compensation Avrg (US Dollars) As of 2011	42,980	84.88 mth	546.97 mth
STEP 2:	Enter the amount you paid for the Bond (not face value):	100	100	100
	Debtor Country Hourly Rate: Average Hourly Rate (based on 40 hr work week)	20.66	0.49	3.14
STEP 3:	**Debt Holders' Annual Rate :** Average Hourly Rate (based on 40 hr work week)	51,000 → 24.52	24.52	24.52
	Differential Percentage % (Debtor / Debt Holder)	0.84	0.02	0.13
STEP 3b:	Debt Holder's work hours to purchase bond:	4.08	4.08	4.08
	Debtor Nation's Average Citizen would have had to work the following hrs:	4.84	204.90	31.80
	Work Percentage Difference for Debtor Citizen:	15.73%	98.01%	87.17%
	Percentage of Work Hours counted for Debt Holder:	84.27%	1.99%	12.83%
		100.00%	100.00%	100.00%
STEP 3c:	Hours (to be compensated (x) % Difference) :	3.44	0.08	0.52
	Rate of Debt Compensation (RDC) or Minutes Per Hour	206.22	4.87	31.39

STEP 4. - 8. Complete Field to determine your Willit Compensation Rate:

	Today's Date		4/4/2015	4/4/2015	4/4/2015
	Date of Birth	11/23/19 🗓	11/23/1970	11/23/1970
	Age	44.39	44.39	44.39
	Life Span Expectancy/ Productive Age / or Retirement Age	86	86	86

See: Compensation Rate Level (Select Next Tab Below)

Work Level (also consider desirability of the position)

Easy Labor |———————△———————| Hazard Pay

| 2.681 | 63 | 408 |

Knowledge/Skill Level of Member — Skill Level 1 - 25

Elementary |———△———————————| PhD

| 34,852 | 823 | 5,304 |

Hierarchy

President |———△———————————| Student

| 139,408 | 3,293 | 21,217 |

| Divided by Remaining Years | 41.61 | 41.61 | 41.61 |

| FINAL | **Willit Compensation for Your Bonds, Stocks, Loans and Investments** | **$209.41** | **$4.95** | **$31.87** |

International Debt Reconciliation - Bonds Stocks Loans and Investments

	INPUT FIELDS	Afghanistan	Argentina	Brazil	Iran	Mexico	United States (1)	Luxembourg (2)	Switzerland (3)	Australia (4)	Netherlands (5)	Ireland (6)	Norway (7)	United Kingdom (8)	Denmark (9)	Belgium (10)	Austria (11)
STEP 1: Debtor Country's Compensation Avg (US Dollars) As of 2011	Enter Annual Rate:	$4.88 mth / 42.980	546.97 mth	348.39 mth	303 mth	4.8563 hr	51,498	50,610	47,810	45,385	45,161	45,160	43,607	43,250	42,173	41,923	41,421
STEP 2: Enter the amount you paid for the Bond (not face value):	100	100	100	100	100	100	100	100	100	100	100	100	100	100	100	100	100
Debtor Country Hourly Rate: Average Hourly Rate (based on 40 hr work week)		20.66	0.49	2.00	1.74	4.86	24.76	24.33	22.99	21.82	21.71	21.71	20.96	20.79	20.28	20.16	19.91
STEP 3: Debt Holder's Annual Rate: Average Hourly Rate (based on 40 hr work week)	51,000	24.52	24.52	24.52	24.52	24.52	24.52	24.52	24.52	24.52	24.52	24.52	24.52	24.52	24.52	24.52	24.52
Differential Percentage % (Debtor / Debt Holder)		0.84	0.02	0.08	0.07	0.20	1.01	0.99	0.94	0.89	0.89	0.89	0.86	0.85	0.83	0.82	0.81
STEP 3b: Debt Holder's work hours to purchase bond:		4.08	4.08	4.08	4.08	4.08	4.08	4.08	4.08	4.08	4.08	4.08	4.08	4.08	4.08	4.08	4.08
Debtor Nation's Average Citizen would have had to work the following hrs:		204.90	31.80	49.92	57.40	20.59	4.04	4.11	4.35	4.58	4.61	4.61	4.77	4.81	4.93	4.96	5.02
Work Percentage Difference for Debtor Citizen:		98.01%	87.17%	91.83%	92.89%	80.19%	-0.97%	0.76%	6.25%	11.01%	11.45%	11.45%	14.50%	15.20%	17.31%	17.80%	18.78%
Percentage of Work Hours counted for Debt Holder:		1.99%	12.83%	8.17%	7.11%	19.81%	100.97%	99.24%	93.75%	88.99%	88.55%	88.55%	85.50%	84.80%	82.69%	82.20%	81.22%
		100.00%	100.00%	100.00%	100.00%	100.00%	100.00%	100.00%	100.00%	100.00%	100.00%	100.00%	100.00%	100.00%	100.00%	100.00%	100.00%
STEP 3c: Hours (to be compensated (x)% Difference):		3.44	0.08	0.52	0.33	0.81	4.12	4.05	3.82	3.63	3.61	3.61	3.49	3.46	3.37	3.35	3.31
Rate of Debt Compensation (RDC) or Minutes Per Hour		206.22	4.87	31.39	19.99	48.47	247.07	242.83	229.40	217.76	216.69	216.68	209.23	207.52	202.35	201.15	198.74

STEP 4. - 8. Complete Field to determine your Willit Compensation Rate:

	INPUT FIELDS	Afghanistan	Argentina	Brazil	Iran	Mexico	United States	Luxembourg	Switzerland	Australia	Netherlands	Ireland	Norway	United Kingdom	Denmark	Belgium	Austria
Today's Date	4/4/2015	4/4/2015	4/4/2015	11/23/1970	11/23/1970	11/23/1970	11/23/1970	11/23/1970	11/23/1970	4/4/2015	11/23/1970	11/23/1970	11/23/1970	11/23/1970	11/23/1970	11/23/1970	11/23/1970
Date of Birth	11/23/19[70]	11/23/1970	4/4/2015	4/4/2015	4/4/2015	4/4/2015	4/4/2015	4/4/2015	4/4/2015	11/23/1970	4/4/2015	4/4/2015	4/4/2015	4/4/2015	4/4/2015	4/4/2015	4/4/2015
Age	44.39	44.39	44.39	44.39	44.39	44.39	44.39	44.39	44.39	44.39	44.39	44.39	44.39	44.39	44.39	44.39	44.39
Life Span Expectancy / Productive Age / or Retirement Age	86	86	86	86	86	86	86	86	86	86	86	86	86	86	86	86	86

See Compensation Rate Level (Select Next Tab Below)

	Afghanistan	Argentina	Brazil	Iran	Mexico	United States	Luxembourg	Switzerland	Australia	Netherlands	Ireland	Norway	United Kingdom	Denmark	Belgium	Austria
Work Level (also consider desirability of the position)	2.681	0.408	0.260	0.226	0.630	3.212	3.157	2.982	2.831	2.817	2.817	3.720	2.698	2.631	2.615	2.584
Knowledge Skill Level of Member	34.852	8.23	5.364	3.379	2.938	8.191	41.755	41.039	38.769	36.802	36.621	36.620	35.360	35.071	34.198	33.995 / 33.588
Hierarchy	139.408 / 3.293	21.217	13.514	11.753	32.763	167.030	164.156	155.074	147.209	146.482	146.479	141.442	140.284	136.790	135.979	134.351
Divided by Remaining Years	41.61	41.61	41.61	41.61	41.61	41.61	41.61	41.61	41.61	41.61	41.61	41.61	41.61	41.61	41.61	41.61
FINAL Willit Compensation for Your Bonds, Stocks, Loans and Investments	$209.41 / $4.95	$31.87	$20.30	$17.65	$49.21	$250.88	$246.58	$232.94	$221.12	$220.03	$220.03	$212.46	$210.72	$205.47	$204.26	$201.81

DEBT RECONCILIATION

The reconciliation of all debt, including municipal, sovereign and private bonds, stocks, and commodities will be overseen by the GCTA, to ensure all persons with verifiable claims of debt obligation owed to them are reimbursed, up to their Maximum Compensation Level.

Individuals residing in or holding private property that secures debt obligations will have right of first use, and upon their death, the property will be transferred to the public domain, for lottery distribution and/or recycle. Those wishing to retain private property (with or without an open loan obligation) may do so, however, maintenance of private property must be paid at True Cost for roads, sewage systems and treatment, fixtures, furnishings, water, heating, gas, as well as all Social Benefits/Standard Needs (without subsidies), which would include food, education, training, etc.

Private Property Debt Settlement Example: The loan obligation for the property will be absorbed by the Global Compensation and Transaction Administration, and the payment of Willits is issued to the loan holder. The residing individuals retain their home and are established as Private Owners Without Equity – non-Standard Needs citizens who pay the True Cost for all goods and services. However, no monthly nor annual rental rate nor mortgage is payable, just the cost of upkeep for the property is required. The property must be maintained based on social standards or will be at risk for demolition. Upon the death of the property owner, the property is entered into the public domain.

FIGURE 12

Local Debt Reconciliation

		INPUT FIELDS
		Enter Annual Rate:

Used to determine Currency Conversion into Willits

STEP 1:	Your Wage Annual Wage:	52,000
STEP 2:	Enter your Bond's Value (Purchase $100 worth of Bonds):	100
	Purchase Price (not the face value) is reconciled for payment.	
	Debt Holder's Average Hourly Rate (based on 40 hr work week):	25.00
	Hours (to be compensated (x) % Difference) :	4.00
	Rate of Debt Compensation (RDC) or Minutes Per Hour	240.00

STEP 3-7. Complete Fields to determine your Willit Compensation Rate:

Today's Date	4/4/2015
Date of Birth	11/23/1970
Age	44.39
Life Span Expectancy/ Productive Age / or Retirement Age	86

See: Compensation Rate Level (Select Next Tab Below)

Work Level (also consider desirability of the position)

Work Level

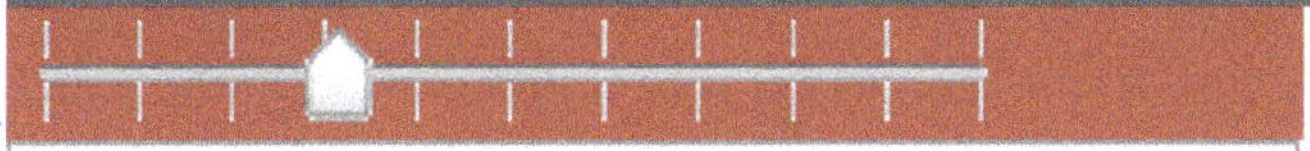

1.680

Knowledge/Skill Level of Member

Knowledge Level

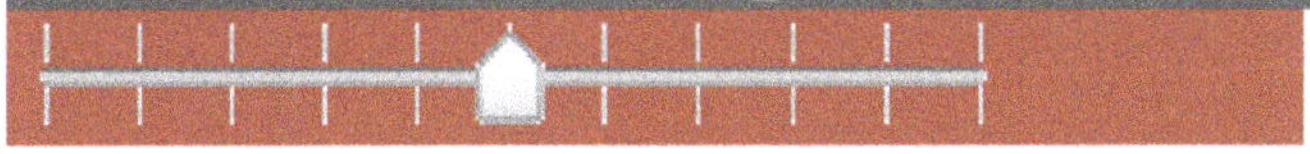

21.840

Hierarchy

Hierarchy

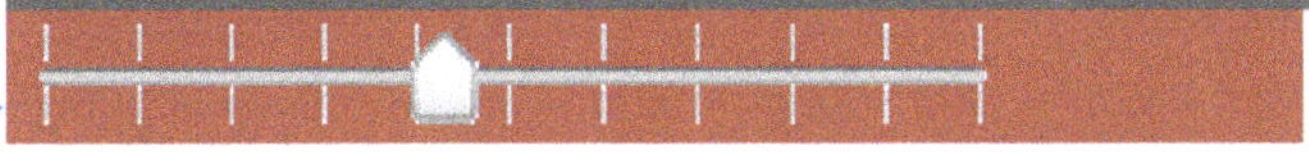

87.360

Divided by Remaining Years	41.61

FINAL	Willit Compensation for Your Bonds, Stocks, Loans and Investments	$131.22

Settlements of each person's or nation's bond/debt is essential to the establishment of a stable monetary system, and will ensure nations are able to restore trust at home and abroad.

The calculation to convert national and municipal bond or sovereign debt the System CORE makes use of, is as follows: (Local debt reconciliation is based on Steps 3c to 8 see Figure 12)

First the debt must be transferred to the individual to whom the debt, loan, stock, or commodity obligation belongs. Within the Willit Economic System, corporations are not people, and therefore cannot claim debts (a claim that another individual owes something to another individual). Thus the debt owed or the shares of the corporation must be transferred to the stakeholders (the individual/s to whom the debt is owed).

STEPS 1 through 3
The average income for the debtor, as well as the debt holder's Average Hourly Rate of Compensation is entered.

- We use a 40-hour workweek to standardize monetary values for the calculation. This yields the Average Hourly Rate.
- Countries that hold another country's debt obligation must transfer the debt holding to all working members. Thus, each citizen that has worked the required minimum hours (per confirmed public enactment) will receive an equal portion of the Debt Obligation (money to be paid to the citizens by the debtor nation) after the debt is confirmed by the International Debt Reconciliation Audit Commission (IDRA).
- Loans received by sovereign nations without the consent of the people, or where the people received no benefits from the loan, would be invalidated, and payable only by those individuals who benefited from the loan. Thus, the debt obligation will be absorbed by the GCTA and the funds deducted from the account holdings of the individual/s involved in the fraud.
- Debt obligations without valid electronic or paper trails will be invalid.

STEP 3b
The hourly labor investment of the bond holder versus the hourly labor of the debtor citizen is used to determine the percentage of work hour difference.

STEP 3c
The comparable percentage of labor hours is used to derive the Rate of Debt Compensation (RDC). This is the minutes/hours the debt holder would have worked, on average, if they were a citizen of the Debtor Country. In other words, you will be compensated at the same rate as the average Debtor citizen (as the citizens pay the debt), because the citizens had no say in how much debt the nation accrued. No one can expect the citizens of a nation to pay

another nation a rate above the average income of the citizens who may or who may not have received any benefit from the investment.

- Usury is the charging of interest. Interest is the demand for additional payment without the expense of energy and is enslavement of another being; is against Divine Law and human rights, is destructive to the individual and mankind as a whole, and an unnatural process conceived in mental illness.

STEPS 4 through 8
After the RDC is calculated, the Debt Holders Willit Compensation is calculated with their Willit Compensation Rate Levels. Willits are then transferred to the debt holders' Willit-IHA (International Holdings Account), for the purchase of goods and services from the debtor nation's international allocation of resources, and no further interest will be accumulated nor paid.

After the Standard Needs (SN) of all citizens are met, every nation that has allocated resources based on the 60/30/10 partition agreement, will commit 10 percent of their yield to the International Exchange to pay off debt owed. Standard Needs include: Housing, food, communication equipment, utilities, infrastructure, security, as well as education, health services, and technological exchange.

Nations may request to purchase an allotment of international debt from its citizens in exchange for its own Willit currency, for the purchase of international products. Nations must disclose what the funds will acquire from the International Resource Pool and how the resources will be used.

Debt conversion into Willits is based on converting the purchase price paid for the bond or the principal amount of the loan to the actual energy investment an individual would have placed into obtaining the bond, if they were compensated at the standard rate of the citizens of the issuing country.

To prevent abuse and loopholes of bond transfer, Debt Conversion is not based solely on the face value of the bond. This is to ensure that an individual cannot purchase, for example, a bond valued at one million dollars, for $1.00, then receive Willits for the face value of the bond, instead of the purchaser's energy output.

Bonds transferred to children, or people that have not held a job prior to the date of transfer or purchase will be considered null and void; as there is no fair income ratio for comparison.

Also, bonds transferred to individuals as gifts, will also be null and void, as the receiving individual did not work for the bonds.

Additionally, the debt holder will be required to provide documentation and provide a sworn statement regarding acquisition of the obligation.

Willit International Holding Account

It should also be noted that a Willit International Holding Account can be created for an individual. However, International Holding Accounts for nations will cluster accounts from individuals to ensure all Willits can be traced back to their original source.

Usually, Willit accounts are limited to individuals, and may not be combined. Willit accounts are exclusively owned by the individual, and upon their death, transferred to their spouse, or minor child/ren (only until adulthood). Thereafter, the Willit account will be disabled and closed. This is to ensure that all people receive only what they earn. And to ensure our system promotes open access to knowledge and resources for all people, so that all can reach their full potential, regardless of perceived class or birthrights.

Debt Settlement Benefits

- International trust can be restored through a stable and equitable monetary and debt settlement system.
- Prevents enslavement of future generations by ensuring they are not obligated for the payment of debt from which they did not directly benefit.

SETTLEMENT OF PERSONAL LOANS ISSUED BY BANKS AND RESERVE SYSTEMS

All loans for homes, cars, education, and corporate assets will be registered and consumed by the Global Compensation and Transaction Administration (GCTA), who will conduct a formal and complete audit of all debt service.

Bank owners and investors may submit claims to convert their debt service investments into Willit compensation.

Once the audit is complete, the people will receive a formal report with claim details.

The people will vote to confirm or deny reconciliation Willit payment to bank owners and Investors.

Why is this important?

Debt is contrived, a form of slavery, and was and is created from nothing but the will/desire of the benefactor, and is without divine/natural Law Authority. The dicode effect (constructive versus destructive), of interest has proven interest to be destructive to financial and economic systems and an unnecessary burden upon households, cities, states, and nations. In layman terms, interest is the request to receive more than what was initially invested without the expense of energy.

All land and material resources belong to nature (God), are meant to be shared, and were never to be sold. Resources are to be shared by all living creatures, thus, the initial act of selling land is a violation of natural/divine Law.

Therefore, sovereigns and banks do not actually own the land they sell, as they never had the right. However, individuals who have invested their energy in developing land and resources must be compensated for their life work/force, or the act of debt reconciliation would result in theft and would also lack legitimacy. No land nor asset can be, nor will be, confiscated to bring the System Core into being.

The reality of True Cost will motivate change.

WEALTH MANAGEMENT

Wealth will be managed in the Willit Escrow System. Wealth will be determined by Willit compensation, patents for relevant products, and copyrights for one's creative works, and will not be associated with property ownership, stocks, commodities, interest, nor business investments.

Neither copyrights nor patents will be transferrable. Once ownership is declared, the party or parties will be compensated for copyright and patent usage by the Willit Administration. Should a private corporation or public production unit make use of the copyright or patent, the copyright or patent owner will be compensated, based on the percentage of the information used and the number of units produced, if applicable.

PAYMENT OF TAXES

Determination of the true value of a resource is not only dependent on the true cost of production, but also on-demand and resource scarcity.

How are we, with use of the System Core, to determine which resources and products are to be allocated to a community when resources are limited? For example, if a city desires to acquire concrete for a building project, how would the community obtain building materials through the Willit monetary process if Earned Equity is in use and Willits are truly reflective of one's energy expense?

You will recall that Earned Equity is reflective of the number of hours one must contribute; yet, one has the option of selecting Earned Equity or Willit compensation for Standard Needs work.

Each nation should make use of the "Sigma Six" percentage standard of 99.9997 for recycling to reduce waste, cost, and inefficiency; however, natural resources for production are not distributed evenly throughout a nation. For example, one state may have coal while another is naturally rich with iron, or materials for mixing concrete, or other natural resources.

Resource distribution determines which neighborhoods and cities decline (ghosting – discussed in the Our New World section page 170) and which are prosperous. Typically, taxation is used to determine resource allocation for communities, along with demand suppression.

Demand suppression (low wages combined with taxation) limits one's ability to acquire resources. Traditionally, the people's acceptance of low wages and taxation has helped to curtail resource-based conflicts. However, crimes: robberies, theft, scams, and fraud connote resistance to man-made monetary constraints.

Taxation is necessary to provide for a community's "social needs" – such as the paving of roads and street cleaning – while ensuring everyone expenses a fair share of energy, yet, the process should be more constructive and produce better results.

The "True Cost" Willit processes and principles, and the Efficient Production Calculator (*discussed on page 113*), are natural conservation methods. We will also make use of **Resource Procurement Tax Grants (RP-Tax Grants),** to prevent tax burdens on the people and to ensure a fair degree of resource procurement potential – without carrying the debilitating burden of debt.

The RP-Tax Grant is a measure to set allocation priority or procurement strength for administrative bodies, without use of negative tactics such as wage theft and threats of incarceration.

The RP Tax Grant will be an intra-nation Willit Class – akin to commodity options for governance administrations.

Resource Procurement Tax Grant Process

Every month, a Resource Procurement Tax Grant (RP-Tax Grant) will be allocated <u>to</u> each working adult (a non-student over the age of 18) at a rate of 30 percent of earned income (national *vote required*) by the GCTA (Global Compensation and Transaction Administration). An individual's income is determined by the Willit Compensation Standards, known as the Willit Rate. Thus the RP-Tax Granted to Administrative bodies is income based, that is not taken from the individual but allocated by the GCTA to an individual to give to an Administrative body for the prevention of income theft. Efficiency bonuses are not considered to be earned income.

The RP-Tax Grant is reflective of Mass Purchasing Power – the will of the people.

The RP-Tax Grant is distributed by each adult <u>to</u> governance administrations, such as one's local neighborhood, county, city, state, or nation, but cannot be used by the individual as income. If the funds are not distributed to governance administrators for resources acquisition, the funds expire within one fiscal year (one year from the date of issuance).

A citizen can use the standard distribution apportionment of 30-25-20-15-10 (see Figure 18 page 136) or select to distribute the funds directly to a resource procurement initiative with no more than two percent (2%) of the RP-Tax Grant distributed to any one initiative. A global vote will be required to limit initiative distribution percentage levels. In the event of dual citizenship the Tax Grant should be without limit to which nation/s one can allocate their grant.

The RP-Tax Grant ensures communities and governance administrators can purchase the resources they require for infrastructure, building projects, and community improvements, and will ensure the People determine how their Grant of Tax Willits to administrators are spent. Thus, it is in the best interest of every administrative body to ensure full employment and education quality – as education is a standard wage factor – and, to ensure responsibly so they cause no undue burden upon citizens, which could lead to the migration of citizens and the RP-Tax Grant under the citizens' control.

Rescinding of a grant due to malfeasance can be initiated through the legislative process. Intimidation or fraud by administrative bodies or personnel could result in their exile (discussed in iEffect page 137).

Resource Procurement Tax Grant Process

Annual Willit Wage	$71,728.37	
OR		
Input Willit Wage	$0.00	
Tax Grant Percentage %	30%	*Vote Required*
Tax Grant Stipend	$21,519	

Standard Distribution Apportionment	**Select Percentage**	Contribution on Average Per-Person
Government Silo	Fraction of Tax Grant	RP-Tax Grant Apportionment
Neighborhood	30%	$6,456
County	25%	$5,380
City	20%	$4,304
State	15%	$3,228
Country	10%	$2,152
	100.00%	$21,519

Est. United States Procurement Power	
if Average Willit Wage is:	*$71,728.37*

Government Silo	Fraction of taxation	Estimated Population	RP-Tax Grant	Annual Willit Purchasing Power
Neighborhood	30.00%	3,000	$6,455.55	$19,366,661
County/District	25.00%	5,203,499	$5,379.63	$27,992,888,863
City	20.00%	2,705,000	$4,303.70	$11,641,514,969
State	15.00%	12,800,000	$3,227.78	$41,315,542,958
Country	10.00%	323,000,000	$2,151.85	$695,047,936,227
Estimated average per-person (RP Tax Grant):	*100.00%*	343,711,499	$21,518.51	$776,017,249,678

FIGURE 13

**The RP-Tax Grant is for material resource procurement, labor is already granted under Standard Needs provision, or Administrative Enactment* *see page 97.*

I-PRESENT: LEGISLATION SYSTEM

iPresent will serve as the central database of Constitutional Rights, community agreements, and social, civic, and private contracts for all parties as well as complaints filed against an enactment. iPresent will also be the recorder of votes for Legislative Enactments and Supreme Court rulings by the people, and the source of reference for all Action Orders legalized by enactment for the payment of Willits or Equity.

BENEFITS

I-Present's legislative system enables individuals and groups to propose Enactments (bills of law) for the production of goods and services for their local, county, state, country, region, and global voting districts.

All people will be able to determine what legislation will be considered, and if the legislation will be placed on the ballot for public vote (based upon achievement of the required support signatures by the public).

iPresent is a completely transparent and interactive system that will enable the people to propose agreements and regulations without cost or need of lobby expense. It will enable the people to be well informed about any proposed legislation that may affect their lives.

LEGISLATION PROCESS

Once an enactment receives the required percentage of sponsor signatures (eight percent of the people within the voting district the enactment will affect), the enactment is submitted for review to determine how the enactment may affect the people, and its impact on resource levels and the environment. Prior to the enactment being activated for public vote it will be subject to review by applicable Legislation Effects Boards and Committees:

LEGISLATIVE A/EFFECTS BOARDS COMMITTEES AND COMMISSIONS:

DIR   District Impact Review Committees

Determines impacts upon external districts to gauge if the enactment should be reclassified for border district sponsorship requirements.

ERA   The Boards of Enactment Review Assignment

Assigns independent reviewers to assess which boards and committees are required to assess the enactment's effects.

EDB   Enactment District Review Board

Ensures proper assignment of affected districts.

RIC   Rights Impact Committee

Determines if an enactment will infringe upon rights, and determines potential effects and human rights violations.

EIC   Environmental Impact Committee

PCR   Production Capacity & Resource Requirements Review Committee

Assesses the impact of an enactment on resources and the labor force.

---

i-Present

db_1c

Public Policy Agreements
Legislative System and Action Orders
FAQ

iPresent
Video Presentations and text documents enactments proposed for agreements, with Negative and Positive effects and counter arguments
Open commenting video/text
Line Item Voting
Optional: Comprehension Questions/Quiz

Global Constitution
Enactment Submission
Laws of Rights & Governance
Production Approval Request
Community Agreements
Global Agreements
Legal Agreements
Marriage Agreement
Contracts: Public and Private
Tools & Applications

Collaboration: Enactment Creation
Group Voting Decision Tools
Enactment Sponsorship 8% of effected populate.
Fact Check -
Voting System
iVote
Local
State

National
Global
Election System
Automated Vote Count System
Official Phone (audio) and video logs of Political Representative
Media, Newspapers, and News Unions - to ensure the truth is deseminated.

One Vote Per Person
Only agreements confirmed by a majority vote of 2/3 with a minimum of 25% of the population voting are recognized as
Political representativies do not possess agreement override authority of the people's vote
Complete Transparency and Open Door Discussions and meetings

Filling System of individual confirmations of community agreements and Social Contracts.

UPLU   Regional Commissions of Urban Planning & Land Use

CDM   Construction Design & Maintenance Review Committee

SDC   Supply & Demand Review Committee

PSRB   Public Security Review Board

WSRC Willit Stability Review Commission

SRRB   Sovereign Rights Review Board

If an Enactment receives the required support signatures, it must be placed on the ballot for public vote. However, the District Impact Review Committees may determine if the enactment requires additional support signatures due to district effects. Boards and Committees will have 180 days to report their research and findings, and may be granted an extension of additional time.

Independent researchers and analyst groups issue enactment committee reports, and any citizen may have their unofficial report or evidence attached to the enactment's list of Report Findings and Evidence.

Review Committee		Enactment Type	Enactment Category
ERA	The Boards of Enactment Review Assignment	2 Legislative Enactment	1 Agriculture
EDB	Enactment District Review Board	3 Standard Needs Enactment	2 Technology
RIC	Rights Impact Committee	4 Resource Allocation Agreement	3 Best Practices
DIRC	District Impact Review Committees	5 Global Agreements	4 Energy
EIC	Environmental Impact Committee	6 Production Agreement	5 Accounting and Finance
PCR	Production Capacity & Resource Requirements Review Committee	7 Service Agreement	6 Administrative Affairs
CDM	Construction Design & Maintenance Review Committee	8 Private Agreement	7 Aging
SDC	Supply & Demand Review Committee	9 Opposition Enactment	8 Appropriations
UPLU	Regional Commissions of Urban Planning & Land Use	10 Amendment of Enactment	9 Data Intelligence and Analysis
SRRB	Sovereign Rights Review Board	11 Appendage To Enactment (request)	10 Commerce
PSRB	Public Security Review Board	12 Marriage Enactment	11 Community Development
WSRC	Willit Stability Review Commission	13 Stop Action Enactment	12 Constitution and Human Rights
		14 District Opt-In	13 Crime
		15 Enactment of Formation	14 Education
		16 Right of Sovereignty	15 Foreign Relations
		17 Supreme Court Judgment - Private Agreements	16 Forestry
		18 Supreme Court Judgment - Public Agreements	17 Health
			18 Housing
			19 Immigration
			20 Judiciary
			21 Labor
			22 Law and Legislations
			23 Natural Resources
			24 Nutrition
			25 Production
			26 Science
			27 Security and Intelligence
			28 Service and Certification
			29 Transportation
			30 District and Community Affairs
			31 Water
			32 Wildlife
			33 Standard Needs
			34 Social Economics

I-PRESENT: PRODUCTION ENACTMENT PROCESS

- Producers submit audio, video, or a formal written request: Business Plans or RRA (Request for Allocation) to the people for resource allocation for a good or service.

- Once the Enactment has gathered the required support signatures (eight percent of the voting population), the Production or Allocation Proposal is sent for board or committee review.

- Enactment Reviewers have 180 days to review and issue a report on an enactment prior to it being placed on the ballot for the public vote.

- The Enactment Board and Committee Review Findings; as well as citizen comments, videos, and interactive real-time forums are made available at one location within iPresent's Enactment Awareness Communication Portal, shown in Figure 14 page 101.

- All voters (within the enactment's applicable voting district) will be notified of an enactment's status, and that the enactment is available for review and commentary by the people.

- Once the 60-day Awareness Requirement is met, the enactment is placed on the next General Ballot for vote.

- The people either vote to enable the enactment, or the enactment is archived. After 12 years the proposal is purged from the system.

- Once enabled, the enactment proceeds to the Board of Resource Allocation.

- The Resource Allocation Board works with enactment producers, unions, guilds, and education and training departments to confirm and detail all the resources, man power, job titles, and position hierarchies required to ensure the enactment is fulfilled.

- If significant variances from the initial proposal are detected, the Resource Allocation Board may request a redetermination by the people.

- Enactment Holds and Redeterminations are to be requested if resource requirements exceed the range approved by the people. For example, if the enactment exceeds more than 40 percent of the resources requested; or, if resource allocation would undermine the ability to produce higher priority level goods, the Resource Allocation Board would place a hold on the enactment and submit a redetermination enactment to the people.

- Global, national, and local labor unions review and confirm positions' hierarchies for compensation and work hardship levels. Should certified union or guild members (certified members actively working in the trade, who are not designated as apprentices), desire alteration to compensation levels, (based on the Willit Monetary System's standardized levels), they would submit a compensation adjustment enactment, and obtain support signatures from their Global Membership body.

The Global Membership Bodies' rates of compensation levels cannot be undermined by corporations, production units, union administrators, nor the people. The rates of compensation determined by all certified members will be the rates of compensation paid by the Global Compensation and Transaction Administration to all union and guild members. Thus, each member of a labor guild will have an active voice and vote in determining the compensation paid to them for their labor, without exception.

Enactment Process Summary

The people enact legislation for the creation of goods or services; use of the System Core will allow for the quick validation of votes and determination of available resources. Global labor unions, trade guilds, and the people pre-determine if the work performed will be either Willit compensation, or Earned Equity. Money is created when work is performed, has true value, and is literally backed by the Will expensed by the people.

FIGURE 14

iPresent Module

CONTRACTS AND LEGAL AGREEMENTS

All contracts and private agreements are to be entered into the Contracts and Legal Agreement databases if they are to be recognized as legally binding.

VOTING & VOTE TRANSPARENCY

To prevent voting fraud and corruption of the legislative process, all votes must be transparent and verifiable by the people. Because the vote of each individual will determine law, it is vital that every man and woman have the right to vote their conscience.

Therefore, Constitutional Rights (permanent laws) will be enacted to protect the individual and will be established to ensure no man, nor woman, is subject to abuse; nor the loss of employment, nor opportunities, because of their voting behavior.

To ensure every man and woman is free to vote their conscience, vote fraud, bribery, and coercion will be exilable offenses (details provided in the iEffect section).

To ensure the people are well informed every citizen will be compensated with Willits at their compensation rate for reviewing legislation. Review confirmations will be established to ensure proper compensation. Review of legislation will not be a requirement prior to voting.

POLITICAL PARTIES

Enactments will have no political party designation, nor will enactments be queried by political party affiliation. This is to ensure that all legislation is considered based on the merit of the proposal.

All Enactments are stand-alone legislation. Once submitted additional legislation cannot be added to an enactment.

Opposition to an enactment will be permitted and is encouraged to balance perspective. Opposition can be submitted by individuals and groups, and will require sworn testimony regarding the evidence submitted.

PROPOSE
Process and Information
Get the details about the process for submitting and Enacting an Enactment

SUBMIT AN ENACTMENT
iPresent
Public Law Legislation
Production Agreements
Private Agreements
Marriage Agreements
Supreme Court Ruling Request

My Enactment IDs

Create Enactment Communication Center

SEARCH
In Construction
Open - Collaboration Enactment

Search: Finalized
Support Signature Required for iVote Ballot

Sponsor or Reject Enactments
Pass an Enactment on for Review and District Voting

View: Sponsors

Opposition Enactment
View Opinions Against an Enactment

View: Watch List

Add To: Watch List
Keep up-to-date with the status of the enactments you support or oppose

AdvanCN.org
ITS YOUR WORLD - BE INVOLVED - WILL IT

▼ Global Community Center
YOU ARE LINKED-IN

▼ Networks Events & Forums
Professional & Social Networks

▼ xChange
For Sell & Will Buy

▼ iPresent Enactments
Legislation by the People

▼ Member Support
Get the help you need

CN TV
LOADED

My Account
Details and Reports

PROPOSE
Process and Information
Get the details about the process for submitting and Enacting an Enactment

SUBMIT AN ENACTMENT
iPresent
Public Law Legislation
Production Agreements
Private Agreements
Marriage Agreements
Supreme Court Ruling Request

My Enactment IDs

Create Enactment Communication Center

SEARCH
In Construction
Open - Collaboration Enactment

Search: Finalized
Support Signature Required for iVote Ballot

Sponsor or Reject Enactments
Pass an Enactment on for Review and District Voting

View: Sponsors

Opposition Enactment
View Opinions Against an Enactment

View: Watch List

Add To: Watch List
Keep up-to-date with the status of the enactments you support or oppose

REVIEW
Enactment Review Boards and Findings
All validated Members and Registered Users can submit reviews for Proposed Enactments. Or, you can become a member of an Official Review Committee. To become an Official Committee Review Person you must submit your credentials to the Board of Review, and confirm you understand the Fiduciary Responsibilities of Enactment Reviewer.
The Board of Review will assign Enactments to you that have gained the required Support Signatures; are within your qualified field of study; and within your travel parameters.

Enactment Reviews
For Passed Legislation and Archived Enactments

Active Enactments Assignments
View Enactment Reviewer Assignments & Positions

Enactment Review Sign up
Earn Equity
Sign up to review and enactment.

Boards of Review & Committees
Contact your Enactment Districts Review Boards

Elected Enactment Board Members and Reviewers
Contact a Board Member or Reviewer

Contact the Interim Board of Review

VOTE
Voting takes place the 1st through the 7th of each month, for enactment that have met the Support Signature and the 30-day Awareness requirement.

REGISTER TO IVOTE
Validate Your Profile

Voting System
iVote - Closed
Note LINK-IN Opens the 1st -7th and for Emergency Vote Enactments

enactment notification system

- Enactment District

  Please select ▼

- Send Type ★

  Cell or SMS Text ▼

- Send To: ★

  [   ]

- Enactment Status

  Type of Notifications ▼

SAVE

JUDGE
You are the Supreme Court.
Sign up to be an arbitrator or juror for community members that wish the judgment of the People

Open Cases
VIEW CASES

File Grievance
Criminal and Civil Grievances
Once submitted an investigator will be assigned to your case. All cases will be investigated, and brought before a judge. The Judge will issue a verdict, or may assign your case for arbitration, or you may request a jury verdict by the People. Submission or the reporting of false evidence is an offense that is punishable by exile.

Evidence
View Evidence for the case you are currently in judgement of.

Submit: Judicial Verdict

ENACTMENT INFOMERCIALS
Finalized Enactment Requiring Support Signatures

OFFICIAL - ENACTMENT REVIEWS
Get the Facts - Supported Enactment Reviews - Unbiased - Full Disclosure

ENACMENT - COMMUNICAITON CENTERS
Videos Docs Forums & Opposition

Get a 360 perspective

Staging Area 1 - Enactments Requiring Support
Staging Area 2 - Official Enactment Reviews
Staging Area 3 - iVote - On the Ballot

ENACTMENT COMPLAINTS

To ensure an enactment achieves its planned goal, all complaints filed against an enactment will be filed with the court. All complaints will go through the complaint process, legal representation will be provided to the plaintiff, and the complaints analyzed and reviewable by all people when the enactment is called for its annual or biannual review. If the enactment does not reach its goals, achieve its mission, causes physical harm, or deprives people of its freedom, the people, based on the complaints against the enactment should repeal and archive the enactment and remove the enactment from active law.

MAKING TIME TO VOTE

How will people have time for legislation?

The people will be compensated at their regular Willit compensation rate for the time they spend reviewing legislation to ensure they are properly informed prior to voting. Page review algorithms will be designed to ensure page review times are met, and a question and answer section will be required to ensure people understand the measures within and the goals of the legislation.

Once the question and answer section is completed, legislation review time will be submitted, and Willits allocated to their account under the heading of Legislation Review with the reference number of the enactment.

Review times will be set for each page of legislation. Parameters will be set to limit the amount of legislation to be reviewed within a voting period, to ensure the people have adequate time to review all legislation.

REMOVAL OF OLD LAWS

Laws are to be removed from active status if they are not confirmed by the people and may not be held on record in an active status, nor reactivated to be used against the people for nefarious purposes by any administrative body.

WILLIT CONTROL PROCESS

Willits will not be seized, nor the transfer of funds intercepted nor impeded, nor will the access of money be restricted without due process and trial.

Business accounts may be temporarily or permanently disabled if one lies about the services they offer. However, no offering shall be prevented that the people approve of – or that which does not cause bodily harm nor death to a consenting adult.

We must have an accurate foundation for our laws if we are to construct a world that is not continuously at war, in pain, or in conflict.

Nature's laws set the heavens, hold the world in place, and establish the boundaries of life. They are the foundation of all existence. Laws do not roll dice nor alter course. They are constant. Their existence is reflected by seasons and stars; the rise of the sun in the east, its settlement in the west, and the tides that rise and fall to their will. Nature dictates that all creatures are birthed - be they man, beast, or seed from within – and that all creatures, regardless of shape, size, or frame, sense their surroundings.

Nature's laws are fixed, and they exact indiscriminate effects regardless of one's ethnicity, race, gender, class, position, or religion. They do not sway with the whims and desires of politics and parties, nor with the agenda of greed, dominance, and imperialism.

Man's laws are arbitrary, changeable, and prone to error. They fluctuate as rapidly as the weather. The laws that govern our social and economic systems are structured based on the prominent belief systems of the dominant social party.

The laws we enact must not inflict greater harm than that which they were conceived to remedy. We have standards for technology and various processes and systems to ensure they function correctly. We must have standards for our laws. Those laws must be based in truth. If our laws are compliant with nature's law, positive effects will result, and our social and economic systems will function correctly. There will be peace, humans will prosper, unity will be commonplace, and our potential will be realized – thus, all laws within the System Core, should be based on a globally recognized Constitution that is enacted and confirmed by the people.

CONSTITUTIONAL-RIGHTS

A constitution is a written declaration of "perceived" rights, a consensus regarding actions, and its authority is backed by force. Without force, the power/will/action of men, constitutions and laws are benign documents – meaningless unless people believe in those rights, and hold people accountable.

Laws, constitutions, and regulations are man's standards of how we are to engage, and, thus far, have been determined, written, and signed into law only by the elite.

A Constitution of Human Rights must be forged that can burn in the hearts and minds of all people.

Laws must be applicable for all people, regardless of class, race, nationality, religion, or position. Any penalty or fine imposed will be applicable for all people who have reached the age of maturity, and to the same degree without prejudice and without regard to class, race, nationality, religion, or position – and without exception.

The people of every nation are endowed by creation with inalienable rights that shall not be transgressed, those rights being the right of life, liberty, knowledge, education, nourishment, and an equitable vote to enact or to abolish any laws of their nation.

SUGGESTED ARTICLES

The following list is an example of what could be included in the Constitution of Human Rights. The actual wording, defined intent, and its effects will reveal the true nature and substance of the people.

- We the people of a divine creator have the right to liberty.
  Our actions shall not be infringed so long as our actions do not physically or mentally damage another, and our actions pose no short nor long-term danger to society and its ability to protect the lives of all people and the ecological systems required for our continued existence.

- We the people have the right to physical security. One's body belongs to self and may not be physically abused, conscripted into service, nor may physical or mental pain be inflicted as a means of punishment or coercion; nor death inflicted upon us by any person or device.

- We the people have the right to defend our bodies and families, as well as our nation.

- We the people have the right to a vote which counts equally in all matters regarding the populous and resources of our nation.

- We the people have the right to free education in our national language and any agreed-upon universal language, from basic studies to the university level.

- We the people have the right to real-time and historical data and information that is not manipulated by governing bodies.

- We the people have the right to clean and safe air and drinking water.

- We the people have the right to earn compensation at an equitable rate of payment, for a task or job, regardless of one's gender, ethnicity, race, nationality, or religion.

- We the people have the right to justice without time constraints.

- We the people have the right to freedom, to be free from incarceration or imprisonment or the threat of incarceration for violations that have not resulted in physical abuse or death.

- We the people have the right to gather and commune with other individuals, so long as such gatherings do not pose ecological damage, unsanitary conditions, or threaten another's ability to travel.

- We the people have the right to the freedom of speech, to speak our minds without fear of job loss, or the loss of home, property, or personal freedom or liberty.

- We the people have the right to religious belief and practice, so long as our practices do not violate the rights of others.

- We the people have the right to add to these rights as determined by the people, so long as those laws are not in conflict.

The people, by majority vote, shall have the irrevocable right to amend any legislation that violates the Constitution of Human Rights, and to remove from office or position of power any person or group who violates the rights of the people.

If the Constitution is applicable to all people, it will ensure any laws that violate our natural and constitutional rights, can be quickly acknowledged and overturned. Thereby, the balance and perfection of law can be achieved.

I-ACT: PRODUCTION AND DISTRIBUTION

iAct receives its mandates from iPresent's confirmed production enactments, and will be the people's central application to ensure production efficiency, full employment, full recycling, and employment security (for all position levels, from staff to executives).

I-Act will work jointly with Labor Unions and Trade Guilds to establish compensation levels for the Willit Monetary System's work-hardship and position hierarchy levels.

iAct's open central data system will link to all aspects of production, refining, and recycling efforts to enable the people to proactively avert shortages, and to determine the best use of human and material resources.

The people will be able to accurately determine the date of receipt for the products and services they have placed orders for; and will be apprised of delays and their causes.

iAct will accurately determine manufacturing waste; and will be the check and balance to aid in resource theft prevention.

iAct will also aid in determining the ecological effects of production, and the effects on documented species, through open and transparent waste and hazardous material placement tracking, and air and water quality monitoring systems. It will track ecological effects of mining and building projects.

iAct will ensure the earned equity percentages for Standard Needs participants are accurately determined, resources are allocated, and the required energy investment is reflective of household size and resource usage. iAct will also ensure requirements are fulfilled and reported accurately to the people, in real-time.

Any producers whose goods do not pre-sell will not have the right of resource distribution (raw and processed material and labor allocation).

Resource distribution will be halted for lack of demand, inefficiency, and waste.

i-Act

db_1e

Production
Production Efficiency
FAQ

Human Will and Resources Allocatio
Labor Request: Standard Needs and iWAUT Exchanges

Producer & Provider Registration
Employment Listing
Action Orders
Independent Producer Registration
Production Unit Registration
Material Use Registration
Skill Trade Profession Registration
Certified Labor
Non Cert. Labor
Service Registration and Availability
Member Appointed Position Registration
iPresentatives
Emergency Services
Officials & Representatives
Analyst

Equity Distribution & Account Log
Human will allocation and distribution
Labor Request & Opt In Tracking
Community Support Equity
Willits Account Deposits and

discipline records

GLOBAL WORKFORCE ADMINISTRATION

The Global Workforce Administration (GWA) is tasked with calculations for workforce requirements to get the job done. Once enactments are approved by the people, the administration works with local labor unions and guilds to input work orders into the automated job placement system.

JOB PROCUREMENT AND STABILITY - EQUITABLE EMPLOYMENT

Individuals that meet certification requirements are automatically placed in job positions by automated Human Resource Systems.

The hiring process is omitted (with exception of creative, executive, and elected positions), to ensure fair placement of all people that meet established work establishment criteria.

Service Order Request - Standard & Willit

Maintenance Request

Required: Reports

State of Membership

Efficiency, Productive, Needs Met

LEAP Will Strength

Labor Request Distribution

Performance valuations tracking

Material Production

Product -

Service -

Requested/Distribution/Variance

Willit Distribution

System CORE: Community

People will be automatically selected from a confirmed pool of applicable candidates based on certification, experience, previous job performance ratings, shift availability, peer reviews, punctuality, competence, and proximity to the work site.

Automated candidate selection is used for all positions of employment including Specialized Work but exclude: Executive Management and/or Teams initiating the original enactment, and creative staff members: artists, designers, writers, singers, entertainers, etc.

- Specialized Work, requires specific personality types. For example, emergency services require individuals who are patient and able to function well during crises; and Customer Service requires individuals who work well with the public. Therefore, Specialized Work will require additional certification that may include behavioral training and behavioral aptitude testing.
- Artists are commissioned independent agents subject to union pay scale minimums, and the GCTA maximum life earning cap.

Employers and Production Unit Supervisors will retain the right of termination, with appropriate Labor Union and Trade Guild oversight.

These measures and system applications will ensure the best people are hired regardless of race, gender, age or nationality; yet, still aim to achieve one-hundred percent full employment of individuals who are willing to work either in the Standard Needs Earned Equity System or the iWAUT Markets.

Human Resource processes and functions are removed from the control of businesses, corporations, and production units with the exception of the right to terminate the employment of an individual. Poor job performance and lowering of corporate moral will be the only reason for which an individual can be terminated.

EMPLOYEE PROCESS
- Employee Team Members are rated based on efficiency, abilities, and production and service yield for their department, if required. For example, human resources would not have a yield requirement, but they are responsible for ensuring all the tasks of their department are completed based on the task management system's time and date specifications.
- Every task is measured by time. Each person acknowledges their energy expense by the completion of tasks, confirming their right to compensation.
- Tasks may also have alternate compensation levels (such as hardship levels), that will override the position's compensation levels, and thus the individual will be compensated for the completion of the task at the task's Willit rate. The individual will be compensated at the task level only for the duration of time they perform the task.
- After a production cycle is completed, efficiency and waste rates are established, measured, and reported to management and Employee Team Members. These rates will be used as a gauge for production and service efficiency to determine quarterly bonuses paid by the Global Willit Compensation Administration (excluded from BEE cost).
- Employees that do not meet personal efficiency, as well as other standards, required for quarterly bonuses are excluded from bonus payments.

CERTIFICATION AND EMPLOYMENT PROCESS
- Trade Guilds review and help to establish training criteria.
- The Board of Education and Certification creates certification programs and testing parameters.
- Once certification programs are commissioned, individuals may register for training.
- Jobs and Certification opportunities are made available to the public, in the iAmwe Community Center's Employment/Opportunity Notification System
- To be selected for employment opportunities, one must apply and input their availability.
- Candidates will be automatically selected to fill available positions, based on their performance ratings.

WORK-PLACE OVERSIGHT COMMISSIONS

The Work-place Oversight Commissions (WPOC) will ensure employee workplace safety, production quality, and productivity quotas for public as well as private facilities. WPOC will work directly with Producers, Education Certification Boards, and the Earned Equity Commission to ensure the proper training, knowledge, and skill level of all citizens.

RESOURCE ALLOCATION BOARDS

The Resource Allocation Boards (RAB) are tasked with answering the questions: What is needed? Where is the resource? How much of it do we have? How much is being used? And, if there is danger of running out of a resource, RAB's mission is to work with Research, Development, Production, and Recycling Centers to find alternatives.

CURRENT SYSTEM COMPARISON

The current system's model for resource allocation for production is not reflective of true demand; nor is it reflective of what products and services are needed to ensure a stable quality of life; and results in over and/or under development, and unnecessary product production.

The use of current monetary measures to determine which goods and services are produced is an inaccurate determinant of true demand and basic needs production requirements, due to the inequality of monetary distribution caused by the concentration of wealth, and the inability of the current system to adequately determine the true cost of production (monetary, social, and ecological impact).

With Willit Economic principles, the interests of the people and entrepreneurs are balanced, and capital incentive for innovation is maintained for the benefit of the people, both the individual and the collective.

MAXIMUM USE CALCULATOR

The efficiency calculator shown in Figure 15 – page 113, will help the people and administrative personnel determine which products are efficient, and which products should be deemed communal to ensure resources are conserved.

The example product used in the calculator is a stove.
Most people consider a stove a vital necessity for their home and quality of life. Yet, based on our calculation, stove production is inefficient and should be deemed a, "Communal Product."

Stoves, plates, forks, knives, and dishware are major production items. Everyone has them in their homes. Many people have their regular dishes, and their fancy dishes. But are they truly necessary in every household?

Would not ambient cafés (local community kitchens) be a better use of the resources? If all food was produced in a restaurant setting, as food is a Standard Need, would this not build and strengthen community bonds? Would it not make our lives more efficient if we did not have to spend two to three hours cooking each and every day? The answer to the last question is yes, and is further evidenced by the increased availability of packaged food.

Our lives would be healthier if we embraced community kitchens that would produce fresh foods, instead of preserved packaged food; which should only be used in times of drought or to prevent famine.

Personal kitchen items will still be produced, in the iWAUT market, to ensure your right to have the products you desire. But, we do implore you to look at the usage rate for these items. Are they a good use of our resources? Or, are they strictly for your personal comfort and convenience? Would it not be more convenient to have all meals in a restaurant setting, if cost was not a factor? Could not community kitchens also have kitchenettes for individuals that desired to prepare their own recipes?

The answers are personal and arbitrary until we account for the energy expense involved in manufacturing the items, versus how often the items are in use.

If you had to pay the true cost for your personal kitchen acquisitions, from refining to product delivery, could you truly afford them? Would ambient cafés and community kitchens decrease our quality of life, or add convenience?

True Cost measures, and time, will tell.

You can access the **Efficiency Calculator** directly at: Advancian.org/model-5

FIGURE 15

Usage_Efficiency_Calculat... ✕

→ C ⌂ 🗋 advancn.org/spreadsheets/Usage%20Efficiency%20Calculation/Usage_Efficiency_Calculation_Final/

sage Efficiency Calculator

Resource Usage Efficiency Calculator (Public - Non-Administration)

Usage Determination Module Calculations - for the determination of a product's usage volume to determine whether an asset should be deemed for personal or community usage to ensue maximum efficiency.

Personal or Public Determination			
Step 1	Our Example: Stove - Households		
	Contamination potential (spread of disease, if communal)	0	Select ▼
	Can contamination factor be contained with cleaning or other policies?	0	Select ▼
	Public or Private Potential Score:	0	
			Potential Communal Product
Step 2	If the Product is communal is or can it:		
	Inconvenience Factor	0	Select ▼
	Can Aid in Socialization	0	Select ▼
	Aid in Security	0	Select ▼
	Public or Private Potential Score:	0	
			Potential Personal Product
Step 3			
	Available Hours of Usage (Based on awake hours: 16) * 30 days	480	Based on 30-day avg.
	Hours used by an individual on an average day	0	Hour/s x 30 days
	(will automatically be multiplied by month factor of 30-days)	0	
	Idle hours	480	
	Idle Percentage	100.00%	
	Percentage of Usage	0.00%	
	Average Daily usage based on 24-hours	0.00%	
	Idle percentage based on 24-hour day	100.00%	
DETERMINATION RESULT:			Asset Best For - Community Usage
	Idle Percentage between 65 % to 100% is determined as inefficient usage.		

Efficiency Determination

When the System CORE is functional actual data will be pulled from labor and production applications:

Step 4	Initial Production - Total Human Energy Expense in hours, for Production and Delivery (Including Extraction of raw materials and refinement, and fabrication) of one unit.	17	HRS
Step 4b	On-going Energy Expense (LABOR HOURS) - What is the additional human energy required for monthly operation of the product: Pipe lines, electricity, etc.	25	HRS
Step 4c	Initial Energy Investment + Ongoing Energy Investment	42	

Step 4d Willit Compensation: set for Average Citizen on 8/31/2012:
DOB: 11/23/1970 Age: 41.8
Work Level = 7 Medium Hardship
Knowledge/Skill Level: 10 = Advanced Studies
Position Hierarchy set to 4 = Manager
Hourly Compensation Rate as of 8/31/2012 = 31.59 Willits   **31.59** Enter Compensation Rate

Step 4e	Willit Expense of initial production - Energy Investment Cost does not include market rate compensation for iWaut	537.03
Step 4f	**Total:** Willit Cost- Ongoing Energy Investment Initial energy plus ongoing energy expense for the operation of product	789.75
Step 5		
Step 5a	Monthly Energy Deficiency Rate percentage On-going energy - Hours Used / On-going Energy Expense	100.00%

Definition   *Energy deficient is:*

The Inefficient use of energy to create and maintain a product, divided by the amount of time the product is in use or operation.

Determination of Efficiency:

FINAL	30-day Efficiencey rate determination	Energy Investment is Not effcient
	Is the 30-day on-going energy expense reasonable, based on the 30-days product is in use?	Asset Best for - Community Usage
	If energy deficiency exceeds 16 percent - the Deficiency Rate is deemed unacceptable.	

WE ARE MATERIALIZED BEINGS, THUS THE ACQUISITION OF MATERIAL SEEMS RIGHT AND JUSTIFIABLE. MANY MISTAKE THE ACQUISITION OF MATERIAL AS A REFLECTION OF SELF, WHICH INFLATES THEIR IMPORTANCE AND EGO – IT IS THE DELUSION OF MATERIAL. NO MATTER HOW MUCH QUALITY MATERIAL ONE TAKES POSSESSION OF, IT DOES NOT MAKE ONE BETTER, NOR MORE INTELLIGENT, NOR MORE BEAUTIFUL. MATERIAL JUST ALLOWS US TO EXIST IN THE MATERIAL PLANE, SO THAT WE MAY LEARN WHAT IS REQUIRED FOR OUR ASCENDANCE – LOVE. LOVE OF SELF, LOVE FOR THE WORLD, AND LOVE FOR OUR CREATOR (CREATION/GOD).

60/30/10 RESOURCE PARTITION PLAN

The 60/30/10 resource partition plan ensures the needs of all people are met prior to desires and whims. And, if international debt has been incurred, resources can be allocated to fulfill the obligation. Resource partition should only take place after the Standard Needs of the people are fulfilled.

- 60 percent of a nation's resources and production are to be allocated to Standard Needs production for Earned Equity.
- 30 percent of a nation's resources and production are to be allocated for fair trade and open markets for the I-WAUT market (capital markets – for Willits).
- 10 percent of a nation's resources are to be allocated to International Resource Pools, to satisfy debt obligations and for trade to quell international tensions that can result in resource wars.

Nations should divert no more than 10 percent of their annual production to international markets. Increases over 10 percent would require a two-thirds majority vote of the people confirming the increase of distribution. A nation cannot be forced, nor should they feel obligated, to provide resources toward the international pool when their nation has yet to first meet their citizens' Standard Needs Agreements due to shortages of resources, knowledge, labor, or technology.

All aid and charity (grants of resources without the requirement of repayment) will be documented by the GCTA, so the people know of the aid extended to them so that they may, when able and when it is required, reciprocate without hesitation.

RESOURCE WARNING SYSTEMS

The responsibility of the Global Trade Analysis Administration (GTAA) is to analyze each Nation's material resource requirements to ensure the well-being of its citizens. And to submit orders to the International Resource Markets to prevent resource related conflicts that could erupt due to water, food, oil, and mineral shortages.

The Global System Core will locate resource shortages, then fluctuate distribution from the 60/30/10 Resource Partition Reserves to needed parties in a manner that is equitable to all nations within the Global Peace Alliance. The Global System Core will also serve as an advance warning system when resources and production levels are in decline, and notify the people when there are legitimate shortages that require conservation.

NATIONAL RESOURCE DISTRIBUTION ADMINISTRATION

International Resource Partition Orders will be submitted by a nation's National Resource Distribution Administration (NRDA), which is responsible for ensuring local communities, cities, and states are adequately supplied to meet the Standard of Living agreement for all citizens.

WORKPLACE OVERSIGHT ADMINISTRATION (WOA)

Service and production units (public, private, and black market), have three Oversight Administrative Units onsite:

1. Willit Allocation Agents (payroll agents and administrators)
2. Production and Service Oversight Agents (operations/accounting/auditor/inventory specialists, production and service efficiency specialists)
3. Independent union and guild representatives (employee rights agents)

Some of the positions listed above are currently positions already within most companies. In the future, the individuals holding these positions will not be beholden to corporations nor business owners, but to the people, and will be sworn in officially and required to uphold their fiduciary responsibilities to ensure the proper functioning of the organizations they oversee.

Union Representatives should have experience working with, or in the industry they will oversee. However, once elected, they cannot work as an employee of the production or service unit. Once elected as a Union Representative by union members, the Willit Administration must compensate all Union and Guild Representatives with either Equity or Willit Compensation (per request of the Union Representative).

Further, recycling, deconstruction, and hazardous material commissions will work with manufacturers and producers to ensure the proper management of waste and materials. An agent from each department will be onsite during production, or as needed.

A PRODUCER/CORPORATION/SERVICE PROVIDER SIMPLY NEEDS TO PROPOSE THEIR PRODUCT OR
SERVICE TO THE PEOPLE AND REQUEST RESOURCE ALLOCATION RIGHTS, AND HAVE THE REQUIRED
ORDERS FOR PRODUCTION.

iWaut producers and service providers are independently operated establishments the people allot resources to through enactment approval to produce items not agreed to as Standard Needs. Producers are subject to the same regulations as Standard Need producers.

Any member of society can operate an independent production unit, upon the people's confirmation of their product or service enactment.

A group of people may also pool their Willits, to acquire resources at BEE cost to obtain what they need to produce a good, or provide a service, without Resource Allocation Approval of the people. A Willit Investment Pool Account can be established to create an independent production or service unit, or black market operation, and a supply on-demand order account established for the entity.

A Willit Investment Pool business will be granted the same opportunities to acquire available resources as any other producer or service provider the people enact.

Startup expense for most businesses will consist of:

- Reach and Development
  Proposals for research and development funding can also be submitted as an enactment, which enables inventors to be compensated during the exploration process.
- Proposal writing
- Awareness building

People will pre-purchase goods to be made in the iWAUT market, so everything produced will be pre-purchased and the business thereby, fully funded.

Entrepreneurs will no longer waste time, money, nor resources attempting to develop products the people do not want and will not buy.

Entrepreneurs are paid by the Global Compensation Transaction Administration based on sales above the BEE, and subject to Willit compensation maximums for lifetime earnings.

PRODUCT RESOURCE ACQUISITION

Acquisition of material resources is based on achievement of order minimums required for a production cycle or lot. The placement of orders by the people through the xChange's Order Processing System ensures a production unit is distributed resources, based on priority and analysis systems ranking.

PRIVATE CORPORATION RESOURCE ACQUISITION

If production approval is not granted by the people, a private corporation of individuals may acquisition materials through the open IWAUT Markets, where 30 percent of resources are allocated, based on the 60/30/10 Resource Partition Plan.

INVENTORS

THE WILLIT SYSTEM ENSURES INNOVATORS ARE COMPENSATED AND ABLE TO BRING THEIR INVENTIONS TO AN OPEN MARKET -- INVESTORS WILL NO LONGER BE REQUIRED.

If an invention is in the I-WAUT market, anything above BEE is transferred to an Inventor Pool Trust (IPT); the funds will be distributed based on the legal agreement entered into by the invention team, which must be enacted within I-Present as a legally binding private contract (within the System Core, a private contract is an agreement between individuals), which will be available for review by the public, but only alterable by a judge or by public trial.

The inventor/s may also set their Willit Compensation Rate within their Production Enactment. Once the product is approved for resource allocation, and the product is produced, the inventor/s will be compensated based on iWAUT sales (previously described as the price, minus True Cost (cumulative BEE)), which is referenced as PIA.

- iWAUT Product Price is equal to: [Demanded Compensation] + [True Cost (BEE x Production and Distribution Workforce Pipeline)]
- Demanded Compensation is the request for Payment for an Idea and one's Acumen, referenced as PIA (thus, the compensation for acumen is Willits – not interest, nor unearned wealth).

If the invention is placed in the Standard Needs Market, the invention is provided to the people at no cost. Therefore, the Willit Administration will compensate the inventor/s for their intellectual property.

Once the System Core is operational, any new inventions will be documented within the system. All Invention Teams will be registered and their time tracked to ensure only those actively working on an invention are compensated, and compensation received if the invention is in use.

PATENT PROTECTION

Patent protections will ensure inventors are compensated for use of their patent by all manufacturers, but will not prevent the use of intellectual findings.

LOGIC

All material and systems are created by God, thus the discovery of a process is not solely the creation of the person seeking patent protection, but acknowledgement of the Laws of the material world, which were set in place from the onset of creation.

No one has the right to prevent the use of knowledge, but one should be compensated for findings that help to develop additional products and advancements. Thus, the compensation for patents is acknowledgement of one's intellect and the energy input for the discovery, by issuance of Willits (real money).

INVENTOR COMPENSATION

INTELLECTUAL PROPERTY RIGHTS ARE PROTECTED WITH COMPENSATION TO ENCOURAGE INNOVATION.

To encourage innovation, to ensure inventors are never without means or resources to bring their ideas to the marketplace, Standard Needs Earned Equity inventors will be compensated at their monthly maximum for as long as their invention, or any fragment of their patent, is used in production.

I-EFFECT PRODUCT LIABILITY

Products, or production or service units that cause injury or death are placed under stop action orders until a thorough investigation is completed and the people confirm Judicial Findings. Any injured parties will be compensated by the individual/s found liable. If an individual is without means of payment their work equity requirement may be increased to cover the injured parties' equity quota.

Individuals found liable for product injury (not due to negligence) will be terminated from their position and employment found for them in another capacity.

Individuals found guilty of injury or death due to negligence will have their Willit and Equity accounts seized, and exile proceedings will be initiated. The guilty parties' Willits, and assets, will be distributed per judgment of the people.

X-CHANGE

The xChange system incorporates several systems and numerous components. And will be the order processing and distribution center of the system; as well as the Real-Time-Demand Inventory and Supply Management System for the Standard Needs market, the iWaut (I Will Accept Universal Tender) market, and the Black Market.

The xChange ensures price stability with use of the Willit compensation system. Willit compensation standards are used to determine base price requirements, also known as the True Cost of provision -- from raw material, to finished product, to delivery.

The Real-Time Demand Systems will ensure resources are used for their best use, so resources do not sit idle in a warehouse or on store shelves.

Once a product or service is entered in the virtual market place, the end-user must pay, at minimum, the BEE Rate and the cost of delivery for non-Standard Needs goods and services.

Figure 16 displays the process of exchange.

1. Corporate compensation paid to an individual
2. Deposit of compensation into the account of an individual
3. Purchase of an item
4. Transfer of funds for a product
5. Inventory System Management
6. Shipping of the good to the individual

See enlargement beginning on page 123

---

xChange

db_1f

Distribution and Allocation
Earned Equity and Willit
FAQ

Product Service Request

Standard Needs xChange:
Earned Equity
Order placed for Standard Needs and Products and Services and **WAUT xChange:**
Willit Purchased Goods/Services
Global Reserve Depository and International Shipments

Order System
Product Orders
Standard Need
Food Transfer to Restaurant

Production/Service Request
Material- Raw & Component Request
Production Request
Service Request

Goods and Services Deposit/Inventory Sys
Recycled Material Centers

Raw Materials and Components
Agricultural Products
Housing & Building Construction Materials
Usery Item - Perishable and Non
Communication Device etc.
Heavy Equipment/ Machinery
Services

Transportation
Shipping/Freight

WAUT xChange
Willit Transfers
Distribution Priority level
Product Useful Lifetime Calculations determine priority and access for redistribution of goods to end users.

100%Transparity
Real Time - Open transaction, consumption, and contact logs
Inventory Systems
Needs/Service Assessment
Needs/Service Locator
Needs/Service Distribution

x-Change System

FIGURE 16

GCTA
Global Compensation and Transaction Administration

NCTA
National Compensation and Transaction Administration

LCTA Local

Corporations or Production and Service Units - Willit Account

Transaction Description	Payments Received	Expense Paid	Balance
Opening Balance	849,000		749,405
Compensation Order 22487736		-90,000	759,000
Wages payable 01/01-15/2020			
200 Compensation Payments			
Transaction: 02012020-2899824683	405		759,405
Smart Phone SMTP8			
Order 224888621		-10,000	749,405
Fiberglass (500 lbs.)			

(1) **(2)** **(4)**

Individual - Willit Account

Transaction Description	Payment Received	Expense Paid	Balance
Opening Balance	1,000		0
Compensation Order: 22487736.186	500		
Compensation from Employer: Corporation X			
Transaction: 02012020-2899824683		-405	
Title: 052248766821487 - Samsung Smart Phone SMTP8			

Production & Inventory System

Inventory	Sold to	Sold	On hand
Samsung Smart Phone SMTP8			210
Title: 052248766821487 - Samsung Smart Phone SMTP9	02012020-2899824683	-1	209

(5) **(6)**

Shipment Confirmation
a) Item removed from Corp's Inventory System
b) The product is shipped
c) Consumer Registers Products
d) Transfer Title Transferred (Recyclable Good)
e) Item entered into household inventory and is able to be recalled automatically should an issue occur

Household Inventory System

Item	Qty	Value	Recy
Title: 052248766821487 - Smart Phone SMTP8	1	405	25

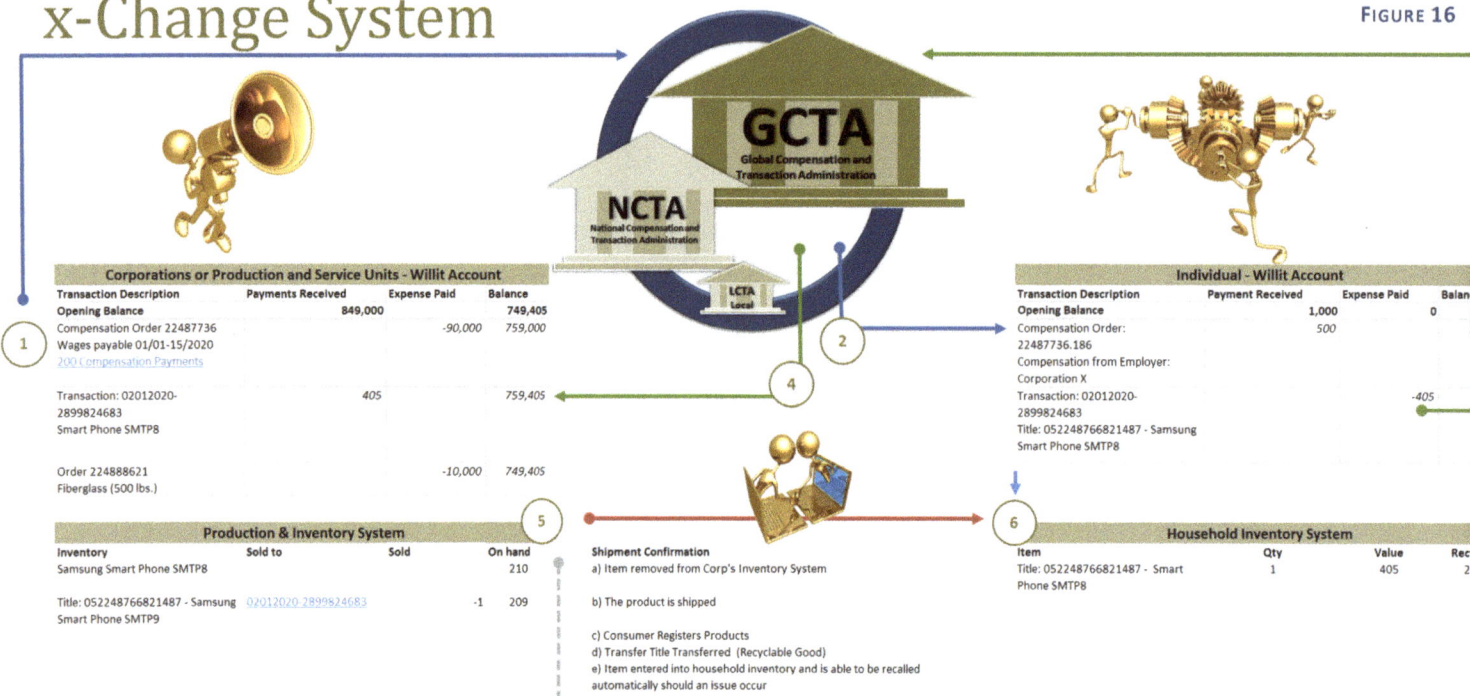

National Display Based Order Management System:

No fees for any product or service sells - Standard Needs System Process

Smart Phone - 6.4 in Screen and 128GB - Blue
by Corporation X
4.0 out of 5 stars   815 ratings   967 answered questions

Price:	**$369.00**
BEE:	**$280.00**
Shipping:	**$36.00**

In Stock.
Color: **Ocean Blue**
Size: **128GB**
Options: 128GB | 512GB

3-Year Life of roduct Guarantee.
Renewed products work and look like new. These pre-owned products have been inspected and tested by Amazon-qualified suppliers. Box and accessories (no headphones included) may be generic. Wireless devices come with the 90-day Amazon Renewed Guarantee. Learn more
The largest battery in a Note, ever. When you have a long-lasting battery, you really can go all day and all night.
The Note9 has twice as much storage as the Note8, which means more music, more videos, more pictures, and less worry when it comes to space on your phone.
The Note9 gives you a quick network connection for incredibly fast streaming and downloading, so you can do more, uninterrupted.
Still amazing on screen, but now the S-Pen has more power off screen. Remotely control different applications and use the S pen to capture shots from far away, scroll, and play music.

Compare with similar items

Report incorrect product information.

Approximate Order Date: __/__/____

$405.00

Delivery Date
Tomorrow by 9:00pm CST

Life of Product: 3-Years
Annual Maintenance: $75.00
Annual Energy Usage: 2,000 w
Annual Energy Cost: $12.00
Recycle Value: $25.00
Life Time Cost: $641.00

Annual Cost: $216.67
Daily Cost: $0.58

Resources Usage Efficiency Rating:
Market: iWaut - USA **(Orange)**

Buy Now

Apply for Credit

Add to Order List

Add to Wish List

Accessories
Simular Products and Ratings

Market Place Segmentation

Standard Needs
iWAIT
Black Market
   Option to Disable

Administrative
   Simular, yet administrator privillages are required for purchases

Buy Now (Green)
Buy Now (Yellow)
Buy Now (Black)

Green Market
• Natural Products
• Recycling Rating More than 50%
• Human and Animal Friendly or Safe (May still need to check for your allergen reactiors)

Orange Market
• Highly Refinded
• Poses Environmental or Health Hazards

Black Market
• Hazardous to life or well being
• Must sign proof of understanding
• Must watch hazard and warning video notices.
• Must be over 21
• Your right for product harm lawsuites may be effected

Delivery Methods

Shipping

Pick-up
   Local Store

Delivery
   Regular Mail
   Shipping Parnters

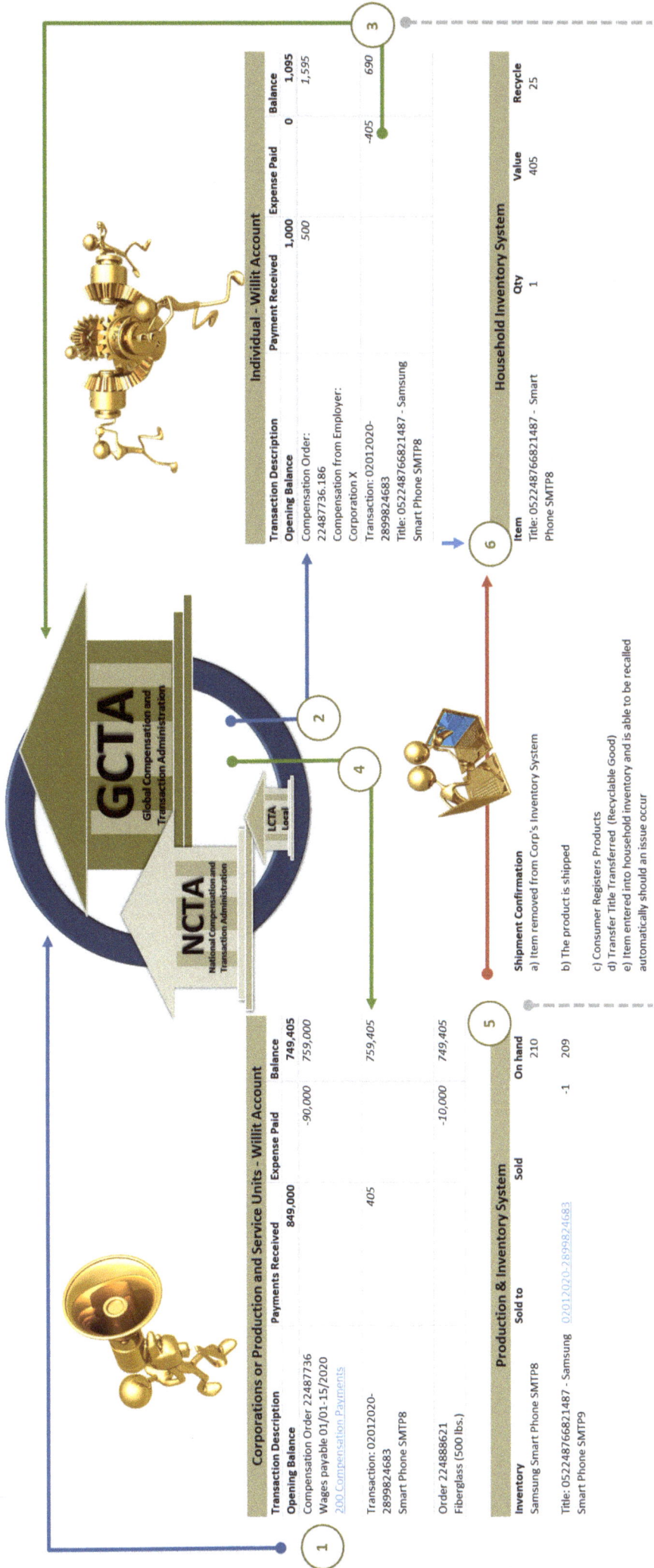

FIGURE 17

Individual - Willit Account

Transaction Description	Payment Received	Expense Paid	Balance
Opening Balance			0
Compensation Order: 22487736.186	1,000		1,095
Compensation from Employer: Corporation X	500		1,595
Transaction: 02012020-2899824683 Title: 0522487666821487 - Samsung Smart Phone SMTP8		-405	690

Household Inventory System

Item	Qty	Value	Recycle
Title: 0522487666821487 - Smart Phone SMTP8	1	405	25

Corporations or Production and Service Units - Willit Account

Transaction Description	Payments Received	Expense Paid	Balance
Opening Balance	849,000		749,405
Compensation Order 22487736 Wages payable 01/01-15/2020 200 Compensation Payments		-90,000	759,000
Transaction: 02012020-2899824683 Smart Phone SMTP8	405		759,405
Order 224888621 Fiberglass (500 lbs.)		-10,000	749,405

Production & Inventory System

Inventory	Sold to	Sold	On hand
Samsung Smart Phone SMTP8			210
Title: 0522487666821487 - Samsung Smart Phone SMTP9	02012020-2899824683	-1	209

Shipment Confirmation

a) Item removed from Corp's Inventory System

b) The product is shipped

c) Consumer Registers Products

d) Transfer Title Transferred (Recyclable Good)

e) Item entered into household inventory and is able to be recalled automatically should an issue occur

GCTA Global Compensation and Transaction Administration

NCTA National Compensation and Transaction Administration

LCTA Local

National Display Based Order Management System:

No fees for any product or service sells - Standard Needs System Process

Smart Phone - 6.4 in Screen and 128GB - Blue

by Corporation X
4.0 out of 5 stars   815 ratings   967 answered questions

Price:	$369.00
BEE:	$280.00
Shipping:	$36.00

In Stock.
Color: **Ocean Blue**
Size: **128GB**
Options: 128GB | 512GB

3-Year Life of Product Guarantee.
Renewed products work and look like new. These pre-owned products have been inspected and tested by Amazon-qualified suppliers. Box and accessories (no headphones included) may be generic. Wireless devices come with the 90-day Amazon Renewed Guarantee. Learn more
The largest battery in a Note, ever. When you have a long-lasting battery, you really can go all day and all night.
The Note9 has twice as much storage as the Note8, which means more music, more videos, more pictures, and less worry when it comes to space on your phone.
The Note9 gives you a quick network connection for incredibly fast streaming and downloading, so you can do more, uninterrupted.
Still amazing on screen, and now the S-Pen has more power off screen. Remotely control different applications and use the S pen to capture shots from far away, scroll, and play music.

Compare with similar items

Report incorrect product information.

Approximate Order Date: _ _ / _ _ / _ _

$405.00

Delivery Date
Tomorrow by 9:00pm CST

Life of Product: 3-Years
Annual Maintenance: $75.00
Annual Energy Usage: 2,000 wh
Annual Energy Cost: $12.00
Recycle Value: $25.00
Life Time Cost: $641.00

Annual Cost: $216.67
Daily Cost: $0.58

Resources Usage Efficiency Rating: 12.5
Market: iWaut - USA (Orange)

Buy Now

Apply for Credit

Add to Order List

Add to Wish List

Accessories
Simular Products and Ratings

Market Place Segmentation

Standard Needs
iWAIT
Black Market
Option to Disable

Administrative
Simular , yet administrator
privillages are required for
purchases

Buy Now

Green Market
- Natural Products
- Recycling Rating More than 50%
- Human and Animal Friendly or Safe
  (May still need to check for your
  allergen reactions)

Buy Now

Orange Market
- Highly Refinded
- Poses Environmental or Health Hazards

Buy Now

Black Market
- Hazardous to life or well being
- Must sign proof of understanding
- Must watch hazard and warning video
  notices.
- Must be over 21
- Your right for product harm lawsuites
  may be effected

Delivery Methods

Shipping

Pick-up
Local Store

Delivery
Regular Mail
Shipping Parnters

FREE OPEN AND FAIR MARKETS (FOFM)

The x-Change will be the central system for locating and purchasing products and services from registered companies, production units, and independent producers and service providers. Fees and commissions for sales will not be charged for listing and selling products in the xChange.

Free Open and Fair markets are standard needs services required by society and a service provided by the System Core Administration.

Consumer goods and services, and products and services used in production or construction will be segmented with different access control restrictions.

The xChange will have a graphic interface with categorization and filter options that are easily searchable based on a consumer's search criteria – and similar to the display systems of Google, Amazon, and eBay.

Consumers will have the option to rate the items they have purchased and the customer service provided by the company, production unit, service provider, or independent producer.

xChange systems will also exist for the purchase of grains and farmed foods – thus commodities will not be traded in the market place, but commissioned based on production levels, for standard needs such as breads and cereals.

xChange system employees will receive Willits for their services. The xChange will not charge fees nor will commissions be paid for placing a good or service in the centralized exchange systems.

Benefits of a centralized exchange systems:

1. Automated reordering of materials for production
2. Accurate accounting of all goods, services, and finances
3. Automated reporting
4. Fraud prevention
5. Abuse prevention of the labor force
6. No corporate taxation

STANDARD NEEDS MARKET

Standard Needs goods purchased by individuals who select not to earn equity may not be inflated nor decreased in price; it must be provided at no less, nor greater than, the True Cost.

Local and Global Compensation and Transaction Administrations ensure all people pay no less than the True Cost for goods and labor-based services.

Standard Needs goods are produced based on automated real-time demand trends and available for immediate use in the Standard Needs market place.

Once a product is purchased, the item is entered in the individual's household inventory system for centralized product recalls, product sharing, recycling confirmation, and fair allotment check and balance systems.

Fair Allotment Check and Balance (FACB) is used to ensure all people wishing to order a product have the opportunity to place an order and receive the item, and establishes distribution priority. This does not prevent the placement of multiple orders; however, it does place subsequent orders, or quantities of a good or service at a lower fulfillment ranking – if the item is not a Standard Needs item and in high demand.

Items excluded from fair allotment checks and balances would be common household items: band-aids, toothpaste, bathroom tissue, bathing soap, and sanitary supplies -- typically, "everyday staples of life" and emergency supplies.

End-users of a product have the right and responsibility to report all product defects in the **Product Information and Review** Central Data System.

Products that are defective are analyzed, deconstructed, recycled, and the materials remanded to processing plants.

Product hazard alerts will be available immediately to consumers in real-time within the iAmwe community center, and notices submitted to anyone with the product in their household or business inventory management system.

I-WAUT

Willits are used in the iWAUT market for the exchange of goods and services not offered as Standard Needs.

Goods and services provided in the IWAUT Market must be provided at no less than the True Cost. A production unit's Executive and/or Management Team can charge any amount they desire, over True Cost to obtain their Earning Cap. The True Cost and price will be on the labels of and listed with all products. Service providers must provide customers with a statement of True Cost for services and their PIA, prior to the enactment of a private contract or agreement.

The price set for an independent product is thus also reliant on market demand.

BARTER AND TRADE

The trading of resources between individuals is not hindered, nor infringed.

Willits cannot be exchanged for previously owned resources unless the resource has an assigned true value to determine production value. Therefore, if one wishes to trade a product for Willits, the true cost of producing the item, and its recycle value, will need to be established.

Individuals will be able to take products to local licensed appraisers, who will then enter the good into the X-Change, and store the item until it is purchased. Once the item is purchased Willits are transferred to the seller's account.

To prevent the theft of pre-System Core goods, households will be required to add an item they may wish to sell to their household inventory account. Any item not added prior to the date established for Old World household inventory input, will require a receipt or bill of sale, or may not be applicable for Willit Trade with other consumers, nor allowed entry into the Barter application system.

BLACK MARKET

Adult only products and services will be allowable to ensure compliance with the Law of choice. The black market may not prompt or compel product or service consumption, but may respond to product or service inquiry and offer their products or services with full disclosure of all known hazards.

Examples of Black Market goods: animal flesh, tobacco, recreational drugs, alcohol, adult services; as well as guns and military weaponry.

The selling and enslavement (trafficking) of women, children, and men, will be illegal; and punishable with Exile Level – 1 for the purchaser; the sequential exile process from level 4 to 2, will be applied to the seller if sworn testimony is provided.

The request for, or payment of, compensation to a parent or guardian for the marriage of a minor or adult will also be defined as trafficking.

LAW OF CHOICE

God gives man the right of choice of action and effect. The System Core will also be compliant with the Law of free will.

The System Core will incorporate the Black Market as a subsystem to facilitate financial transactions and full disclosure.

Each individual must determine for themselves if they will help to produce and distribute weapons, guns, militarized equipment, and meat products. If individuals decide to produce these products Willit Compensation will not be denied. However, full disclosure laws will designate the production unit as a Black Market Producer, and will fully disclose the products one helps to manufacture, or that one purchases.

The markets will be regulated to ensure product and service safety, and will require full disclosure of potential side-effects regarding an individual's consumption or usage. In other words, the individual (consumer) must acknowledge they are fully aware of the potential negative effects they may experience, and the product's or service's effects on their health. With written, audio, or video consent by the consumer, a black market producer or service provider will not be held liable for any adverse effects the consume acknowledges – nor will a producer of service provider be arrested or jailed for offering or supplying their product or service to a consenting adult consumer. Nor, will the right of employee, benefits, or promotion be denied to a black market consumer based solely on black market consumption activity.

The effects experienced by the individuals will be tracked, and the cumulative effects of a product disclosed, to ensure the people will be fully informed about the effects of detrimental products.

The purchase of all items will be fully disclosed including black market items to ensure an individual can determine for him or herself if they wish to engage individuals that support the Black Market. Truth is essential to building trust, restoring bonds, and healing ourselves.

MEAT CONSUMPTION

The word *"anima"*, is defined as soul, spirit, life – it is the acknowledgement of the existence of the life force, will, and power within other beings. If one demands the right of life for self and freedom from abuse, one should and must extend the right of life and freedom to all beings.

The killing, eating, or enslavement of animals is strongly discouraged and no less egregious or perverse an act as the killing or enslavement of a human being.

Because meat and animal product consumption is equivalent to the actions of killing and enslavement, it will be designated as Black Market activities. Individuals who desire to consume meat or animal products will be required to assist with maintenance and butchery. Households will also be required to slaughter, for themselves, the animals they wish to consume at butchery farms or centers.

It is hoped that when mankind becomes more conscious and loving, the majority will vote to make the killing of animals an illegal (ill) act. To ensure the development of the System Core and the eventual conscious evolution of mankind, the provision to free all beings is left to the spirit and good will within each of us, in the belief that the counterfeit spirit – the destructive, perverse part of our being – will be removed.

PRODUCT AND SERVICE CENTERS

Communities will have a merchandise and/or service marketplace where consumers can interact with products or learn about services prior to the purchase of the product or service. Once a good is purchased, the product is manufactured, with exception to items designated as on-hand products. An example of on-hand products are emergency medical supplies and staple-goods.

DISTRIBUTION SYSTEMS

i-Act's Order and Distribution System will enable all people to submit orders for the products and services they require (Basic and Standard Needs) through an on-demand-supply system; thereby ensuring we conserve resources for their best use, while limiting the production of unnecessary goods that strain a nation's resources and production capacity.

RECYCLING

To ensure we achieve our mission of at least 95 percent recycling of products, when an individual returns a used product, Willits are returned to their account based on material extraction rates of compensation. Willit credits for recycling are not counted as compensation towards an individual's maximum compensation.

RESOURCE SECURITY - RESOURCE USAGE COMMISSION

The Resource Usage and Security Commission (RUSC) reports to the people the state of resources and how resources are allocated and used. RUSC may obtain an override vote by the people to produce products with higher priority ratings, or place a Stop Action Order to prevent resource distribution or usage.

Each nation's Resource Usage Commission (RUC), has the right to override priority of enacted legislation, if an enactment would place the nation in harm or shortage of vital material resources for governance or defense.

All reports must concur with System Resource tracking barometers and inventories that are completely transparent and open for public review, and based on each individual's reporting of their yield or production and service rates.

This measure ensures best use is considered prior to any major distribution of vital resources that will affect a nation.

ALLOCATION PRIORITY

The centralization of production will ensure people have full knowledge of every available resource, and details regarding how their resources are being used.

The solution to ensure fair distribution of resources and products is the right of usery; and collaborative discourse by all people regarding allocation, with the goal of "Maximum Use" set as the principle objective to ensure access and to improve efficiency.

The assignment of "Usery" rights, of all materials by all people, will ensure the bonds of attachment to material goods are forever severed. When the bonds of attachment are severed, we end the ideology of entitlement, inheritance, and the control of material for selfish motives. Embracing the right of Usery ensures all resources are used to fulfill the needs of the people without causing harm or violating rights.

PROACTIVELY MITIGATING THE IMPACT OF
CONSUMPTION, PRODUCTION, AND IMPROPRIETY

I-EFFECT: JUDICIAL SYSTEM

iEffect is the judicial proceedings roster, judicial findings and reviews datacenter, and action order enforcement application.

iEffect will enable the people to quickly address public, private, and criminal grievances and corruption to ensure the people are in receipt of justice.

All complaints entered into the Grievance Center, by *Rights Enforcement Officers* are open to the public, completely transparent, and will be independently investigated and brought to a judge for an initial finding.

Judges determine the initial findings of guilt or innocence. If all parties are satisfied with the finding, the case is finalized. If all parties are not satisfied, the case can be remanded for arbitration, then a jury trial, Supreme Court review and findings, and finally to the people. Judgement by the people is the final judgement.

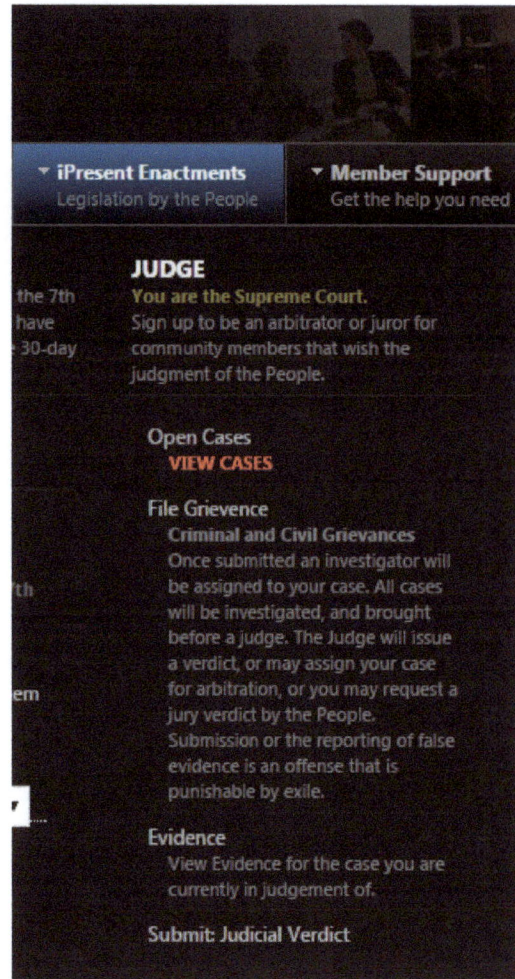

REPRESENTATION

To ensure justice is received by all citizens, every citizen will have the right of representation, whether the citizen is the plaintiff or the defendant; whether the case is civil or criminal.

Payment for judicial services will be paid at the base Willit rate by the Global Compensation and Transaction Administration (GCTA) for the filling of the case, investigations, depositions, witnesses and expert testimony, and court reporter fees, with exception only to fines levied by the court upon the litigators.

Any judgement issued to the prevailing litigant will be paid by the losing party. To ensure financial compensation due to the plaintiff is free of any charges or fees, and to ensure full compensation for injuries, counsel of record and the opposing attorney will have no right to recover fees from the winning party.

The attorneys and/or counsel on record for the prevailing party will receive a bonus of twenty percent (of the standard compensation they receive), from the GCTA for every case they receive a successful judgement for.

A civil complaint may be initiated by any citizen for non-frivolous concerns. The complaint will be reviewed and an attorney or counsel assigned.

Citizens will have the right to select an attorney. The attorney will review the case, determine the likelihood of receiving an award, and may file the case with the appropriate court. Once the case is filed an attorney may submit all expenses for payment to their Nation's Compensation and Transaction Administration (NCTA) accountant.

If a party is unable to pay the compensation due to the successful litigant, the GCTA will pay the compensation due to the litigant based on the order issued by the court. The compensation, attorney's fee and court cost will be assigned to the losing party's NCTA account and deducted based on a payment schedule that is fair to the litigant.

JUSTICE AND CIVIL RIGHTS PROTECTION AGENCY (JCRPA)

To ensure the right to seek and ensure justice every citizen will receive representation or have the right to file a case pro se.

Currently the right to seek justice is infringed upon by the necessity of court system processes which require an indigent plaintiff to pay for all expenses except court cost.

Thus, low income individuals who have been wronged have no means to ensure justice. Attorneys reject legitimate cases due to the cost of legislation:

- compensation of the attorney's time
- investigations
- expert and witness fees
- court reporting cost

---

i-Effect

db_1d

Legislative - Judicial Agreements
True Justice
FAQ

iVote Rights & Justice

Supreme Court - is the Right of the People

No cost to request justice
Justice is a Standard Need.

No person is detained for any offense that does not involve physical injury. People that enter a nation must apply for community relocation services.

Death sentences, nor physical harm, may be imposed upon any person.

iEffect - Jury Voting System
iAct Stop Action Application
Agreement Dissolution
Arbitration
Complaint Resolutions

Criminal Actions Judgment
Civil Disputes
Exile Determination
Member Extractions
Product / Service Liability
Right Infringement

Data and Tracking System

Social Misconduct Complaints
Grievance and Criminal Action
Investigation and Evidence System
Product Recall
Citation Data System

Enforcement Systems
Warrants for Arrest
Sentencing Tracking System

This breeds hatred animosity and exploitation and further abuse of the poor and/or financial hardship on indigent individuals as well as potential financial hardship upon attorneys.

Attorneys, lawyers, and or counsel will be compensated for their time by the Justice and Civil Rights Protection Agency (the judicial oversight body of the GCTA), at the agreed upon Legal Services Union Rate Agreement.

An attorney or a law firm, will review a case, determine if the complaint has merit, and file the case with the JCRPA to ensure accurate time accounting for payment of service.

The attorney or law firm will contract with service providers who will also be compensated by the JCRPA (GCTA) for:

1. Court Cost
2. Depositions
3. Transcripts
4. Audio and video services

5. Investigation Services
6. Mediation Services
7. Experts and witnesses
8. etc.

The payment of all judicial costs for civil and criminal plaintiffs and defendants will be ensured for all people regardless of sex, race, ethnicity, income level, or sexual preference.

Assurance of justice and representation will ensure all people are in receipt of justice. And will ensure the people do not have to settle their court cases under private agreements of non-disclosure, which would allow an individual or corporation to hide their wrong-doing.

JURY COMPENSATION

Jurors will be compensated for jury duty based on their personal Willit rate. This ensures Jury Services is non-punitive for the individuals who serve to right wrongs.

VERDICT BONUS COMPENSATION

Attorneys will receive (up to) a 20 percent bonus, if the judge or jury finds in their favor regardless if they are counsel for the plaintiff or the defendant – this is to ensure every person has excellent representation and a true advocate during court proceedings.

Ten percent of the attorney's bonus will be based on the client's perception of how their case was handled, if they were well informed, and if they perceive they were adequately represented.

JCRPA – will compensate all lawyers and legal service professionals for their time and will be an arm of the Global Compensation and Transaction Administration – and will be primarily responsible for auditing payment requests and ensuring all legal professional ethics regarding citizens are adhered to. They will also aid individual citizens in finding legal representatives who are in good standing in their local community.

RIGHTS VIOLATION ACCOUNTABILITY – PUBLIC DISCLOSURE PROJECT

Private personal litigation will not be covered under the JCRPA. Any legislation that will not be available for public disclosure during or after litigation will be required to be personally financed by the individual or organization.

BLACK-MARKET – LEGAL REPRESENTATION

Representation will be provided to black-market businesses for contract disputes so long as the contract is within the public domain.

FINANCIAL RECOVERY

The JCRPA will also ensure fraud prevention:

- Accurate accounting of billable time
- Complaint Legitimacy – frivolous claims penalties
- Reimbursement of cost by losing parties
- Case Auditing which may entitle JCRPA to access all records and public domain judicial verdicts and mediation results
- Non-public contract disclosure review

CASES REMANDED TO THE PEOPLE

The people will determine the guilt or innocence of an individual or group, and will determine if an individual will have:

- Resource usage rights suspended;
- The amount of restitution payable by a guilty party;
- If the guilty party will receive cause and effect education and training;
- The level and the time duration of an individual's exile:
  - Level 4 - Temporary Exile (1 to 3 years)

- Level 3 - Temporary Exile (4 to 7 years)
- Level 2 - Temporary Exile (8 to 10 years)
- Level 1 - Permanent Exile

Evidence from the jury trial will be available for the people to review, including video testimony; evidence will be logged, scanned and/or filmed for public review, as shown in Figure 18 page 136:

- All parties will be given an opportunity to submit video testimony and their evidence.
- All testimony must be sworn.
- Any party found guilty of submitting false testimony, regardless of their position or status, will be subject to a term of exile.
- All jurors will have the right to submit their judgement without group persuasion.

THE PEOPLE WILL BE THE SUPREME COURT, WITH THE POWER TO DETER AND CORRECT CORRUPTION AT ANY LEVEL.

Judgement by the people will ensure all people are in receipt of justice and that no one escapes due process because of corrupt judges, officials, monetary influence and bribery; or unjust laws.

The people at any time may overturn a judicial judgement; and a judge, investigator, the police, or Rights Enforcement Officers removed for negligence of their duty to ensure justice.

All equivalent crimes will receive the same sentence of punishment, regardless of gender, race, or nationality.

INTERNATIONAL GRIEVANCE REGISTRY

All grievances regarding impropriety or corruption are to be filed in the International Grievance Registry, investigated, and the investigation records maintained until the death of the individual in question. The grievance registry will be open for public review and comments. And individuals may file unofficial grievance reports (complaints) to ensure the public is aware of impropriety that may not be illegal, but potentially harmful.

Full disclosure of an individual's actions ensures the public is informed and on guard, and helps to prevent crime.

FIGURE 18

CASE NUMBER: IL 445864666 | Parties :: United States vs. John Doe | Complaint type: Willit Fraud | Court: Civil Court | Case Status: Awaiting Jury Decision | ▶ Logout

JURY DISCUSSION LOG

Juror Login: Wrina Iamwe   CP

1/23/2013 08:30am
Statement clarification request.
P-Council of Plaintiff:
Am i correct in understanding
that your testimony is that you
were given authority to ...

REVIEW CASE Q&R
Questions and Responses

SUBMIT QUESTION
Proceeding Question to Judge
Submit Question to Plaintiff
Submit Question to Defendant

ENTER TEXT

COURT MONITORS

JUDGE
PLAINTIFF
P-COUNCIL
DEFENDENT
D-COUNCIL

Citizen Profile LINK-N

TRANSCRIPTS

CN: 445864666 – 1/15/2013 08:30am

By the Court:
Please state you name for the record.

Witness:
My name is Jennifer Murran.

By the Court:
    Q. Do you swear to tell the whole truth under
penalty of perjury – Perjury holds a sentencing
judgment of Exile Level II for a duration of no less than
one year?

A.   I do

MS MURRAN:
    Q. Ms Murran what is your relation to the
defendant?

A.   Mr. Doe was my employer

    Q. How long have you worked for Doe and what
was your position?

A.   10 years – i was a compensation admin.

    P - COUNCIL:
    Q.   What was the work environment like?

A.   Stressful.

    Q.   What caused this work environment to be
stressful?

A.   Mr. Doe insisted that i request compensation for
employees that i was not familiar with, nor had i ever
seen these individuals. Their Wallit Accounts were active
and the documentation seemed authentic. I didn't
question it for sometime because we have many offsite

ACTIVE CAMERA FEED

PLAINTIFF
DEFENDENT
JUDGE
WITNESS STAND

Active Monitors: 1 2 3 4 5 6 7 8

VIEW LIVE PROCEEDINGS   Full Screen | Normal View
ON DEMAND PROCEEDING FEED REVIEW
AUDIO RECORD
TRANSCRIPTS

PROCEEDINGS MULTI CHANNEL DISPLAY: 1 4 17 8

On Record: Charges | Complaint | Response | Evidence | Witnesses | Jurors | Verdict & Judgement | Sentencing & Settlements

Witness for Plaintiff
CP Jennifer Murran   LINKED Testimony: ✔ Video [5] ✔ Text [5] Audio [0]
CP Peter Huffman   LINKED Testimony: Video | Text | Audio
CP John Jacobs   LINKED Testimony: Video | Text | Audio
CP Patricia Jones   LINKED Testimony: Video | Text | Audio

SUBMIT: Decision

Decision: Due By date 1/30/2017 (30-day decision requirement)

DETAILS OF CHAGES:

Charge 1   Misdemeanor Larceny $500.00

Decision Option:

    1. Defendant is innocent of crime

    2. Defendant is guilty of crime

Line Item Order Request if defendant is found Guilty (Sentence and or restitution Requested):

1   If defendant is found guilty - We request Defendant receive Cause and Affect Training for a term of one year.

    Line item Request: Approved | Denied

2   We, further request that True Cost Restitution be compiled, and that the True Cost be transferred from the defendant's Willit Account to the plaintiff's (GCTA), and the Legal Defense Offset Accounts.

    Line Item Request: Approved | Denied

Confirm your non biased judgment and that there is no conflict of interest. Then, submit your Decision.

| Upload Video Affidavit | Record Video Affidavit | SUBMIT: Video Affidavit |

Decision Confirmation:

☐   I confirm that I entered into these preceding without bias nor malice, and that my decision is based on the evidence presented

☐   I affirm that, my decision is without bias nor conflict

| Compile and File Decision |

EXILE

Exile is the termination of common rights, the seizure of all assets and property, (with exception to earned Willits), and the removal from society to a secluded inescapable landmass that has no benefit of community, technology, nor human interaction, other than with those of like effect and gender.

Medical and mental health provisions may be provided by volunteers at the exile medical facility, and medical cost covered by the individual's Willits, Family, or Community at cost. A family or community may also vote not to provide care to exiles Level 2 (8 to 10 years) to Level 4 (1 to 3 years).

When sentenced to exile, the individual will forage for their food, construct their own shelter, tailor their own clothing, mend their own injuries, and have time to contemplate the necessity and benefits of civil society.

Goal of Exile

The objective of exile is to ensure individuals understand the need of community, and, to provide a true deterrent to prevent crime. Currently, communities are burdened with the care of individuals who are anti-social. To provide care for anti-social individuals condones destructive actions. Exile ensures an individual's enlightenment will come by the natural Law of cause and effect, and prevents our social systems from condoning killing.

OFFENSES APPLICABLE FOR EXILE

Offenses that have not resulted in death or major injury to another individual may be sentenced to Exile Level 4 to Level 2. For example: the violation of human rights, theft of property or Willits, or the purchase of stolen property; physical assault with injury – with exception to conflicts initiated by, arising from, or caused by the injured party (provoking or coaxing an assault); threats of physical violence, fraud, bribery, voter coercion, false testimony, false claims of injury, lies of omission, and any person who co-conspires to commit the offenses previously mentioned.

Exile - Level 1 Offense (Permanent Exile):

Murder, misleading information or testimony that has resulted in the wrongful death or exile of another individual; rape, and child molestation.

EXILE PROVISIONS

Exiles may take with them (at their own expense): books, clothing, blankets, food rations during non-harvest months, and camping equipment they can carry. Survival Training skills/manuals will be provided upon request.

Recommended provisions for Exile - Level 1: Just ice.

PERMANENT EXILE

Permanent exile results in the termination of all common and global rights (except for the right to one's own life), and removal of the individual from society to a secluded inescapable landmass that has no benefit of community, technology, nor human interaction – except with individuals of like offense and the same gender (to ensure children are not born into the punishment of their parents).

The goal of permanent exile is to ensure the safety and security of civil society, and to rid civil society of predatory human beings.

RE-ADMISSION

Once an exile's time is complete (Level 4 to Level 2 only), they must submit an application for re-admission to the community of their choice.
The re-admission application must be approved by no less than eight percent of citizens who cannot be related by blood or marriage.

Previously exiled individuals may not confirm re-admission.

An Exile's right to vote may be reinstated after five years.

RECURRING OFFENSES

An exile level should not be repeated, but should be assigned in sequence regardless of the crime, unless the crime is one punishable by permanent exile – Level 1.

Example: The first offense will yield – Level 4 Exile; Offence 2 – Level 3 Exile; Offense 3 – Level 2 Exile; Offense 4 – Level 2 Exile. If an individual commits a 5th offense, he or she would automatically be assigned Level 2 Exile – 10 years. And any offense thereafter would also yield an exile sentence of 10 years.

Prisons are considered by most citizens to be a benefit that helps to keep them safe. Yet, those who violate laws do not suffer ill effects. They are clothed, housed, fed, and provided with medical care.

The growth of the prison population is confirmation that prison is not a deterrent that prevents crime.

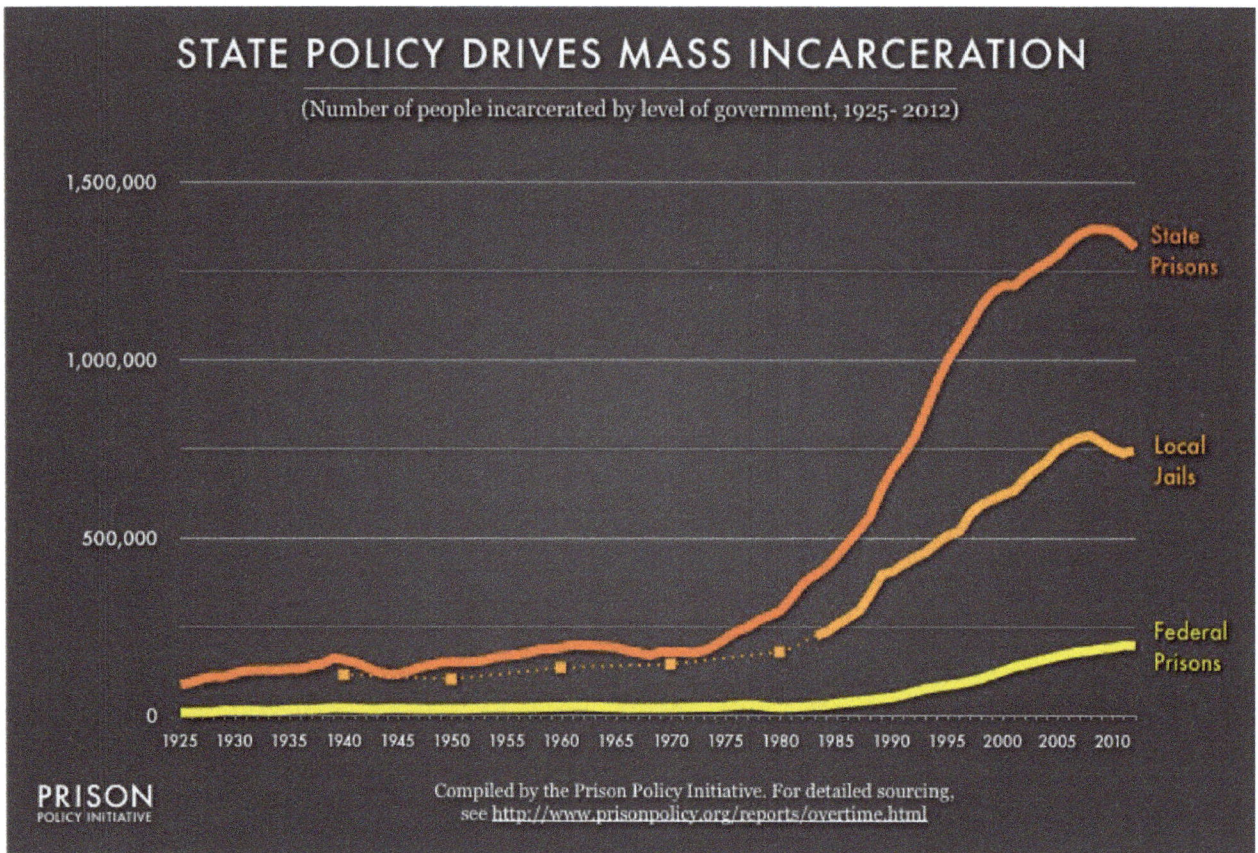

STATE POLICY DRIVES MASS INCARCERATION

(Number of people incarcerated by level of government, 1925- 2012)

Prison and jail are not places most people wish to be because of the lack of freedom, rape, and physical harm initiated by other inmates. The offenses that occur in prisons and jails are a blight not only on the inmates who commit crimes; the offenses are also a blight that confirms prison authorities' inability to control and manage the inmates placed in their care.

The care for inmates is a burden upon society and allows convicted individuals to further victimize citizens. Resources used for the care of inmates could be used to feed and clothe deserving members of society.

Exile is an alternative that lessens the burdens on civil society, and a real deterrent to crime because of the lack of social benefits.

Enforcement Officers may only approach an individual for the violation of law where a citation can be issued. Citizens may only be arrested for the violation of law that results in the physical abuse of another individual; if they pose an immediate danger to themselves or others; if identification (identification card, verbal, or electronic confirmation) is not presented to an enforcement officer (police) for a citation; or if a warrant for arrest is issued by a judge.

If an individual is arrested, a Rights Administer (local civil rights agent) must be present before the individual is removed from the arrest location.

All citations and arrests are registered, linked to an individual's personal account and open for public review.

Citations

Law enforcement will issue citations for the violation of laws. Citations will result in cause and effect course requirements, and may be used as evidence for other crimes.

Use of Force

We do not condone killing; however, God allows self-defense.

If an individual is determined to be dangerous, our preference would be the tranquilization of individuals. Then, a public trial to determine guilt or innocence, and if found guilty, exile. However, some individuals are extremely dangerous and without care of who they hurt. Thus, law enforcement agents must determine the extent of force they deem appropriate.

Drug Related Enforcement

Drug related law enforcement will no longer be under the supervision of police.

The manufacturing of recreational drugs will be delegated to recreational drug manufactures, and regulated. Recreational drug manufactures will comply with full disclosure laws. And a recreational drug user will be required to sign a liability waiver.

The distribution of drugs will be consigned to licensed home delivery companies, or to licensed Adult Recreational Establishments (ARE). AREs must retain a licensed physician on staff in case of emergencies and to monitor a patron's usage.

Individuals registered as purchasing recreational drugs will be temporarily disabled from Earned Equity and the Willit Human Resource login deactivated. Driving privileges will be revoked until they have tested negative for recreational drug usage. A recreational drug user must visit a primary care physician to reestablish the right to return to work and driving privileges.

Upon entry to an ARE, patrons must scan their identification (Identification cards are embedded with access rights) and valet their vehicle (surrender the key or access code).

It is conceivable that an Adult Recreational Establishment (ARE) will have a medical center in close proximity (which may not be under the same management nor operation unit of the ARE). An individual could visit a medical center, post-entertainment, for a medical checkup and to have driving and work privileges reestablished.

All Adult Recreational Establishments will be designated as Black Market (BM), and will be subject to Black Market laws:

- BM establishments' websites are restricted to adult citizens only
- BM establishments are not allowed to advertise publicly
  nor may they solicit to procure business, nor may the business have any displayed signage
- No BM establishment may have a place of business within a mile radius of an education facility
- The selling to, employment of, or abuse of a minor will result in exile.
- Drug addiction, any self-inflicted injury, will not incur disability benefits (for the avoidance of earned equity requirement).
- Other regulations as determined by local districts

The right of compensation for employment through Black Market businesses will not be infringed by Willit Administrators, nor by the Global Compensation and Transaction Administration (GCTA). Both must transfer earned Willits in the same manner as any other product, service, or industry.

Goal: The prevention of drug abuse by accurate determination of the effects and volume of drug usage; and the education of individuals and society about the effects of drugs on the body.

LOGIC

Killing people to end drug consumption is no less negative than the act of drug consumption. We cannot stop nor prevent people from doing what they desire. Drug enforcement attempts to date have resulted in many deaths, and is a major strain upon resources and police efforts.

If one wishes to end a negative or destructive act, education is the key, not killing.

We must make life worth living by making the world a better place to be, so people will not desire to be removed from it through hallucinogenics and risky behavior.

Tracking the use of drugs through physicians will enable the individuals to view real evidence of the effects of their drug use upon their body, and possibly motivate self-change. The evidence will also be used in drug prevention education programs.

Individuals will have the option of selecting not to engage with individuals who consume drugs (based on full disclosure laws). However, the right of employment will not be infringed, with exception to temporary prevention of employment login of the individual until they are deemed medically fit for work.

Arguably, not everyone who uses recreational drugs becomes an addict, but for those who do become addicted, their addiction will be solved with positive actions. Only when the patient is ready, will they end their addiction.

INVESTIGATORS

Police Officers issue citations and make arrests. All crimes and crime scenes will be investigated by Independent Investigation Units to ensure proper oversight and checks and balances. Investigation Units and Rights Administrators are sworn to protect the truth and the evidence of the crime scene to ensure justice prevails; and are housed separately from Police Officer Units; and, Administrative oversight is under separate management and directives.

Video and Media Evidence

A Rights Administrator or an Independent Criminal Investigation Unit may request immediate sharing of video, audio, or media, captured by surveillance equipment.

Citizens may not interfere with an arrest, but they may film an arrest from a safe distance that does not interfere, nor endanger police officers, nor themselves. Any Citizen with video or media evidence may apply to upload unaltered video and sound to have the evidence attached to a case.

The police and any official from any administrative office may not at any time, nor for any reason, confiscate any person's, company's or business' video, sound, nor media equipment. Independent Investigators, however, must be granted access to copy the data.

GUARDS

Jail guards are to ensure that arrested citizens are safe during their confinement until they stand trial, and guilt or innocence determined.

No guards are provided in exile facilities. Those who wish to provide services to Exile Level 4 to Exile Level 2 facilities, must protect themselves. Willits will not be granted to protect nor to secure the existence of exiles, nor those who wish to aid them.

I-LEARN

The iLearn system application will ensure education opportunities, and the open dissemination of information (public and private).

The iLearn application will enable an open system for the people to become knowledgeable and proficient in any area they wish to acquire certification or knowledge to meet their personal as well as professional goals, and to create universal achievement standards for mathematics, science, and technological proficiency.

iLearn will also be used for collaborative research and development for public and private industries to ensure the sharing of research findings; prevent the corruption of data; and to ensure accurate information regarding research findings are open and transparent to make certain the people have accurate information regarding true causes of effects of production, products, medical procedures, and system effects; and to acknowledge the contributions and achievements of the appropriate individual/s.

The Boards of Education along with Labor Unions and Trade Guilds will work to ensure fundamental and advanced education requirements are met by all citizens. And will work directly with producers and manufactures to ensure the people are trained to meet job-specific certification requirements.

The Global Education Board will ensure the people are trained in the maintenance and programming of the System CORE to assure its continued advancement with societal needs. Programming and coding will be taught as a basic educational requirement.

EDUCATION PROCESS

Education for grades up to the 12th level (high school) will take place in regular classroom settings, and will be led by an

i-Learn
db_1g
Academics and R&D
Information & Knowledge
FAQ

Board of Education and Certifications
Education is a Rights
Education and Certification are Standard Needs. Pre K - Professional: BA, MS, PhD's

CERTIFICATION AND LICENSING
Skills
Trades
Service Providers

Certification
Academic Profiles, Records, and Test Score - Public Review

Knowledge Access
Online Learning
Lecture Series
iBook
Knowledge Assessments
Interpreters

Research & Development

Research Team Registration
Health Care
Mental and Physical Health
Natural Cures
Disease
Global Medical Records
Technology
Science

Universal Laws - Publication
Recall Tracking Applications
Food and Product Effect Tracking System
Production Effect Application Integration

Fact Check - Freedom of Information

Unlimited Open Access
Transcripts and Recordings for

History
BC, AD, NE History Archives
Remembrance Archive

in-person instructor. Computers and web-based learning systems will also be used for At-Your-Pace Learning.

Grade levels will be applicable, but, an "at your pace" learning style will be implemented to ensure students are fully competent in a subject before introducing curriculum that is more advanced.

CURRICULUM

Many people, teachers, administrators, business professionals, and scientists will be involved in establishing curriculum standards for basic education, and for the skill set requirements for each job profession for each industry segment.

EDUCATION SYSTEM

TEACHERS AND PROFESSORS

Teachers and college-level professors will record their lessons, which they will be compensated for, and lessons will be made available to the public.

After video recording of coursework, teachers and college-level professors will be available for interactive question and answer sessions, in a physical classroom or in a virtual setting.
A virtual classroom mockup is shown in Figure 19, page 147.

Teaching professionals will not depend on a college to secure employment (tenure). A teacher's tenure will depend on the knowledge they offer, and the attendance levels for the question and answer sessions they offer, which will be available globally for virtual classrooms.

Knowledge is based in truth, either it is factual or false; the outcome of the processes taught are constructive or destructive. Thus, if one acquires true knowledge, the ranking of the institution one receives knowledge from is irrelevant.

With use of the System Core, alumni, fraternity, and societal relations will be immaterial, and professors and teachers will be able to focus on the most important aspects of teaching to ensure academic success – understanding (the ability to reflect, relate, and associate likeness and difference).

TRANSFERABILITY

All courses will be registered with the Global Accreditation Department. Degrees will be awarded based on the course work completed regardless of where the course was taken so long as the course is accredited.

All universities and institutions of higher learning will recognize all course work taken by an individual. All transferred credits are assessed and applied towards a program degree.

PROCTORS AND TESTING

Online and onsite testing proctors will monitor students during testing sessions.

Testing will be computer, lab, or residency based, and administered by testing officials regardless of the school or college an individual attends.

Certification or licensure by the Board of Education Certification and Licensing (BECL) will be required to confirm a degree, regardless of the institution one attends.

Thus, an individual's final testing scores will be the driving factor of their ranking and job opportunities, and not the institution they attended, as the curriculum, regardless of the institution, is the primary importance.

Thus, self-taught individuals may be certified and licensed in fields without having attended college, provided they pass test requirements. This provision is provided to encourage and detect abstract thinkers, and geniuses.

FIGURE 19

Virtual Course | Assignments | Activities | Test |

Course Schedule | Account | Mail (5) | Site News | ▲ Logout

White Board | My Notes | Translate | Private | Transcript

Active Student

Joel Rampstone

Class Discussion

Instructor: W. Iamwe
3/31/2015 08:30am

Good morning every one.
Please confirm you are able to
see and hear me.

Michael Myer:
Good Moring professor. You're
clear, audio is fine.

Anna Pekija:
GM. Ur AV - Perfect

Jon Hamm:
""

Christopher Hendricks:
Audio is Good, Video is Fine

Vincent Jones
AV Good

ENTER TEXT

Live Course : ACTIVE CAMERA FEED

Professor: Wrina Iamwe : Date: 03/31/2015

Full Screen | Normal View

VIEWING LIVE COURSE
SYLLABUS
ON DEMAND VIDEOS
AUDIO RECORDINGS

Course: Exploring Understanding and Decoding Prophecy...

Course Aid

Course Aid

Bill Halsted

Joel Rampstone

Elizabeth Kartheiser

Vincent Jones

Natalie Merry

Michael Myer

Anna Pekija

Jon Hamm

Nicholae Sellers

Christopher Hendricks

Course Aid

Enrolled: 30 **Online:** 26 **Video:** 22 **Audio:** 4 **Queue:** 10

Online Learning Applications

Online learning will consist of the following applications:

- Online Lesson Plans
- E-learning Online Courses
- SCORM Technologies
- Tests and quizzes
- Social and collaborative learning
- Video learning

- Online training (various trades):
  - Customer service training
  - Sales training
  - Customer training
  - Safety training
  - IT training
  - Product training
  - Healthcare training

Basic Education

Basic education materials and applications will be available for at home and at your pace learning.

- Hundreds of educational books, interactive games, songs, stories, and activities
- Customizable worksheets
  Powerful worksheet generators will create custom worksheets based on student performance to help them build skills in subject areas they require assistance.
- Progress tracking
- Learning programs track progress through dozens of skill-based lessons and submit weekly test scores to the GCTA. Students are rewarded for learning and information retention.

STUDENT COMPENSATION CALCULATOR

Willit compensation for students is calculated in similar fashion to Willit compensation for production and service provision.

Willits earned by students can be traded for the goods and services they desire in the iWAUT Market upon parental approval. Student compensation is an incentive to ensure students understand their future earnings will directly correlate with their education and competence levels, and teaches students the value of hard work.

Basic, intermediate, and advanced levels for a grade level are used to determine rates of compensation, as well as weekly test scores.

The first step in processing Willits for students is the entry of School Hours and Study hours.

I

II

Student's Weekly Education Time Sheet

HOW THE SYSTEM WORKS:
You will login every day in your class rooms to start the education timer for your coursework, and exit the system prior to leaving each class. Home school students will log into the same education tracking system. Teachers can upload unedited video of the day's lesson for absent students, for clarification of subject discussions, and parental viewing, with permissions set to only allow parents of students in a particular class to view the day's events.

All study time will be tracked from the online tutorial assistance system. If you study outside of the system, you can add those hours with your mobile phone, or log your study hours when you login with your computer. The more you study and attend classes the more you Earn.

Student's Login: Mark Hinner   Week starting 4/6/2015
Teacher's Login: Wana Iamwe   Week ending 4/12/2015

1) Sample Data Provided, Please Enter Your regular School or Study Schedule

	Sunday	Monday	Tuesday	Wednesday	Thursday	Friday	Saturday
School Hours	4/6/2015	4/7/2015	4/8/2015	4/9/2015	4/10/2015	4/11/2015	4/12/2015
Time In	9:00 A	8:00 A	8:00 A	8:00 A	8:00 A	8:00 A	
Time Out	2:30 P	2:30 P	2:30 P	2:30 P	2:30 P	2:30 P	
Study Time							
Time In	1:00	1:00 A	1:00 A	1:00 A	1:00 A	1:00 A	
Time Out	6:00	1:00 A	6:00	1:00 A	1:00 A	1:00 A	
Total	4.50	6.50	6.50	6.50	6.50	6.50	0.00

Paid Student Age Range   Bachelors   Masters   PhD.   CMS

Age 5-9	Age 10-12	Age 13-15	Age 16-18	Age 19-21	Age 22-23	Age 24-26	
Elementary	Pre Junior High	Junior High	Advanced Studies	College 1	College 2	College 3	Production
Level 1-3	Level 4-6	Level 7-9	Level 10-12	Level 13-15	Level 16-20	Level 21-25	Level 30-35

Education and Skill Levels

Basic		Intermediate	Advanced	
Levels 1	Level 2	Level 3	Level 4	Level 5

Student	
8	You Have Potential Baby!

Your Weekly Willit Value for your Efforts

Weekly Averaged Test Scores for all Subject Masters (0% to 100%)
This is the Amount you will be compensated for each week
Willits Lost Amount

Annual Wage: If less than 75 hours per week, with 100% on all test scores

Willit Compensation Calculator (II)

How does it calculate your true value! Complete the form below. Then, select "UPDATE" to view your true compensation rate

STEP		
3	Today's Date	4/4/2015
	Date of Birth	1/1/1999
	Age	16.27
4	Life Span Expectancy/ Productive Age / or Retirement Age	85
	Potential Will Power Energy (Willits) in minutes	44,676,000
	Days - used to date	5,937
	Minutes - used to date	356,220
	Estimated Remaining years (or	68.73
	Estimated Remaining minutes	44,319,780

Estimate of Willit Energy

39.00	School and Study Hours From Student Time Sheet	2340
0	Minutes	0
39.00	Total Production Minutes	2,340

5	Education Level	
10		23,400

6	Knowledge/Skill Level of Member	
5		117,000

7	Hierarchy	
8		936,000
	Divided by Remaining Years	68.73
		$212.78

Weekly Test Scores
Select the percentages you usually achieve for your test scores, then adjust the rate

8	83%	
		$176.60
		$-36.17

Select Update at the bottom of the form to view
9   your Willit

    $11,064.35

advancn.org/spreadsheets/willit_calculation/WillitCompensationCalculator%20Final/WillitCompensationCalculator%20Final.htm

Your True Value | Maximum Compensation | APEC Past Earning Calculator | Inventors Production Units | Student Time Sheet | Student Compensation Calculator | Working Youth

Student's Weekly Education Time Sheet

HOW THE SYSTEM WORKS:

You will login every day in your class rooms to start the education timer for your coursework, and exit the system prior to leaving each class. Home school students will log into the same education tracking system. Teachers can upload unedited video of the day's lesson for absent students, for clarification of subject discussions, and parental viewing; with permissions set to only allow parents of students in a particular class to view the day's events.

All Study Time will be tracked from the online tutorial assistance system. If you study outside of the system, you can add those hours with your mobile phone, or log your study hours when you login with your computer. The more you study and attend classes the more you Earn.

Student's Login: Mark Hirmer

Teachers Login: Wrina Iamwe

Week starting: 4/6/2015

Week ending: 4/12/2015

STEP 1:

1) Sample Data Provided, Please Enter Your regular School an Study Schedule

	Sunday		Monday		Tuesday		Wednesday		Thursday		Friday		Saturday	
	4/6/2015		4/7/2015		4/8/2015		4/9/2015		4/10/2015		4/11/2015		4/12/2015	
School Hours														
Time In	9:0 ▼	Total	8:00 A ▼	Total	8:00 A ▼	Total	8:00 A ▼	Total	8:00 A ▼	Total	8:00 A ▼	Total	▼	Total
Time Out	3:3 ▼	6.50	2:30 P ▼	6.50	2:30 P ▼	6.50	2:30 P ▼	6.50	2:30 P ▼	6.50	2:30 P ▼	6.50	▼	0.00
Study Time														
Time In	1:0 ▼	Total	1:00 A ▼	Total	1:00 A ▼	Total	1:00 A ▼	Total	1:00 A ▼	Total	1:00 A ▼	Total	1:00 A ▼	Total
Time Out	1:0 ▼	0.00	1:00 A ▼	0.00	1:00 A ▼	0.00	1:00 A ▼	0.00	1:00 A ▼	0.00	1:00 A ▼	0.00	1:00 A ▼	0.00
Total	6.50		6.50		6.50		6.50		6.50		6.50		0.00	

Total School and Study Hours: 39.00

FIGURE 20

WillitCompensationCalcu ×

advancn.org/spreadsheets/willit_calculation/WillitCompensationCalculator%20Final/WillitCompensationCalculator%20Final.htm

How does it calculate your value? Complete the form below to determine the true value of your labor.
Then select 'UPDATE' to view your true compensation rate

STEP

3

Today's Date	4/4/2015		
Date of Birth	1/1/1999	Days in Year	Minutes in days
Age	16.27	365	1440

4 Life Span Expectancy/Productive Age / or Retirement Age **85** (oldest living relative at time of death)

Potential Will Power Energy (Willits) in minutes 44,676,000
Days - used to date 5,937
Minutes - used to date 356,220

Estimated Remaining Years 68.73
(or
Estimated Remaining minutes 44,319,780

Estimate of Willit Energy
39.00 School and Study Hours From Student Time Sheet 2340
0 Minutes
39.00 Total Production Minutes 2,340

5 Education Level 10 23,400

6 Knowledge/Skill Level of Member 5 Skill Level 1-20 117,000

7 Hierarchy 8 Skill Level 1-20 936,000

Divided by Remaining Years 68.73
$212.78

8 Weekly Test Scores
(select the percentage you usually achieve for your test scores, then adjust the rate)
83% $176.60
$-36.17

9 Select Update at the bottom of the form to view your Willit

After age 26, compensation is no longer paid to students. However, you may obtain schooling for free at any age. Rights of Passage can only be obtained once you enter the work force as a full time equity member. Should you have children prior to completion of your education goal, both parents must enter the workforce as an equity member and can pursue their education goals at their leisure, yet absent the student based compensation. It is in your best interest to refrain from child rearing until you have achieved your academic goals. Yet you, nor your child, are penalized with substandard living should you choose otherwise.

Paid Student Age Range

			Bachelors	Masters	PhD.	CMS
	Age 16-18	Age 19-21	Age 21-23	Age 24-26		
	Advanced Studie	College	College 2	College 3	Production
	Level 10-12	Level 13-15	Level 16-20	Level 21-25	Level 30-35

Paid Student Age Range

Age: 6-9	Age: 10-12	Age: 13-15
Elementary	Pre Junior High	Junior High
Level 1-3	Level 4-6	Level 7-9

Education and Skill Levels:

Basic	Intermediate	Advanced
Levels 1	Levels 2	Levels 3	Levels 4	Levels 5

Student You Have Potential Baby!
8

Your Weekly Willit Value for your Efforts

Weekly Averaged Test Scores for all Subject Matters: (0% to 100%)
This is the Amount you will be compensated for each week
Willit Loss Amount:

Annual Wage: If less than 75 hours per week, with 100% on all test scores

$11,064.35

We will determine the compensation for a student named Angela (see Figure 20, page 151):

Reference Step 3/5:
We will give Angela an age of 16, and a Grade Level of 10

Reference Step 6:
Angela is studying an Advanced Level 5 Curriculum (honor roll).

Reference Step 7:
Angela is a student so the Hierarchy will remain constant.

Reference Step 8:
Angela scores 83 percent on her weekly test.
Angela will receive Ⓦ176.60 Willits per week for her studies, yet she is losing Ⓦ36.17 Willits because she is not yet 100% competent based on her test scores.

Students also receive monthly bonuses for healthy living and acceptable social behavior.

THE GOAL

Students who achieve academic success are rewarded. Students that have performed below average will have a visual tool to measure their success and potential. Students are also motivated to acquire the things they desire through academic success. Students will learn from a very early age they must work for the things they desire in life.

Unlike our current economic system, the Willit compensation an individual receives is earned based on an individual's merit.

PARENT-TEACHER COMPENSATION

A parent who desires to stay home with their child will be compensated for teaching their child. Their pay will be based on how well their children perform on their weekly or bi-weekly examination at a fractional rate based on class size.

Compensation will be available to the parent for children aged four to fourteen so long as there is no physical abuse of the child and the child has achieved 80 percent competency on their test, based on the nation's home study teaching plan.

IAMWE

APPLICATION COMPONENTS

Iamwe is used to access the resources required to live a fulfilled and informed life.

Access to forms, records, and reports with drill-in analytics and auditing features will be available.

Access to information regarding proposed legislative enactments, as well as the ability to report abuse and fraud, and to schedule vacations and time-off requests, will be centrally located for easy access.

To ensure international and community trust is developed, the System Core's data will be open for review, with exception to ongoing criminal investigations and military activity.

The Transparency System will detail all public and private account holdings - Willit compensation, Earned Equity, Standard Needs, resource production allocation and contracts, and public and private agreements. Without complete transparency, one can be deceived.

Iamwe system applications and reports will consist of (but not limited to):

- Centralized Electronic Mail System – Official Correspondence for your records.
- Willit Account Maintenance and Audits
- Community and International news
- Dwelling Allocation Request
- Health and Mental Health Services – Appointment Scheduling
- Medical Records
- Household Inventory
- Immigration request
- Local and International Online Community Sites
- Maintenance request:
  Products, infrastructure, buildings, and dwellings
- Private Communication Records
- Real-time health, product, and legislative effects reporting

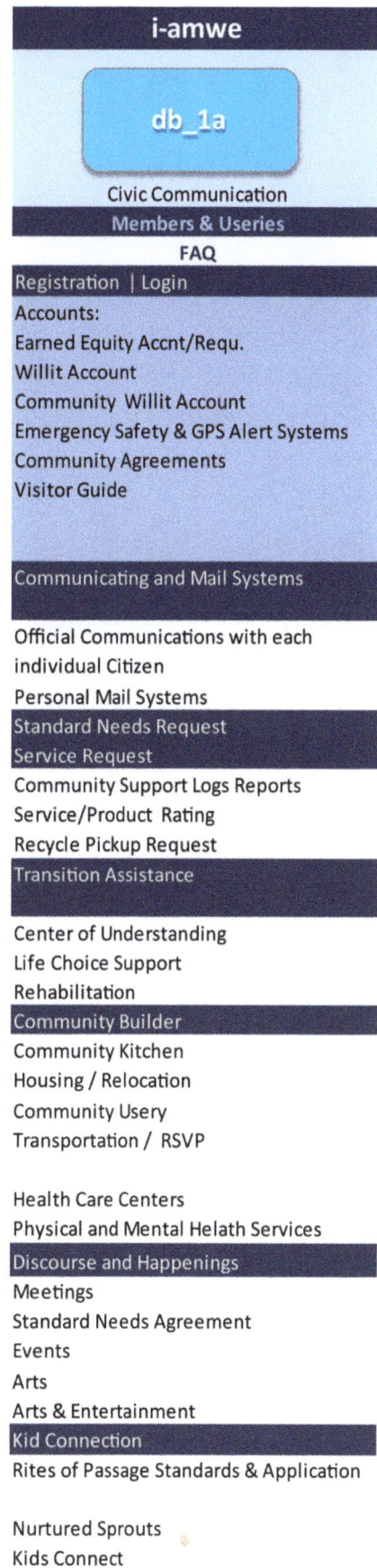

i-amwe

db_1a

Civic Communication
Members & Useries
FAQ

Registration | Login
Accounts:
Earned Equity Accnt/Requ.
Willit Account
Community Willit Account
Emergency Safety & GPS Alert Systems
Community Agreements
Visitor Guide

Communicating and Mail Systems

Official Communications with each individual Citizen
Personal Mail Systems
Standard Needs Request
Service Request
Community Support Logs Reports
Service/Product Rating
Recycle Pickup Request
Transition Assistance

Center of Understanding
Life Choice Support
Rehabilitation
Community Builder
Community Kitchen
Housing / Relocation
Community Usery
Transportation / RSVP

Health Care Centers
Physical and Mental Helath Services
Discourse and Happenings
Meetings
Standard Needs Agreement
Events
Arts
Arts & Entertainment
Kid Connection
Rites of Passage Standards & Application

Nurtured Sprouts
Kids Connect

- Reservation Systems: Vacation Housing, Restaurants, Community Kitchens, Car sharing (Availability and Usage Request), Mass Broadcast Studios and Channels...

COMPLETE TRANSPARENCY IS THE KEY TO THE PEOPLE'S POWER

FREEDOM OF INFORMATION

Request for Information will <u>not</u> be required to be filed for any information within the System Core.

The people may view all allocation rights, inventory distribution, orders/confirmations/audit history, employee automation criteria, job placement statistics, etc., in real-time. User friendly drill down information analytics will be built into the system to ensure all members of society can see the details behind the numbers within all reports.

The meetings of all administrations, boards, and commissions will be electronic, transcribed, and made available for public review; with exception to ongoing criminal investigations and national security information.

News
Global
Local
Enactment and Vote
Announcements & Updates

Media League
Fact Cast
TECH Knowledge
Idea Exchange
Announcements
Travel Connection
Lodging
Transportation

Cultural Exchange
Archives

Remembrance

History: BC, AD, NE

GLOBAL MEDICAL TRACKING SYSTEMS

Global medical tracking systems will ensure medical information for every individual is available to any doctor a citizen desires to contract as their physician, to ensure continuity and the quality of care over time.

HEALTH SYSTEMS

Health systems will be used to track and analyze effects of physical and mental disease due to production, products, and social stresses; track food contamination and infectious diseases; and will be monitored by the *Healthy Citizens Commission* (HCC)

Health and Wellness Systems will integrate with Emergency Services. If an individual has not interacted with the system for more than 48 hours a wellness check will be initiated.

SYSTEM CORE

The System Core will be a multi-tier introspective system as shown in Figure 21. The System Core's applications and components will be mirrored for each district, and each district's data pulled through a branched system, of four layers, to compile, calculate, and report on various aspects of a nation's economic and social systems. Language applications will convert the core systems for multi-national usage. Updates to core system templates will be seamlessly reflected in mirrored districts.

Thus, an individual could access seamless reports based on: various districts, cities, and states, and compile global data to ensure the equality of trade.

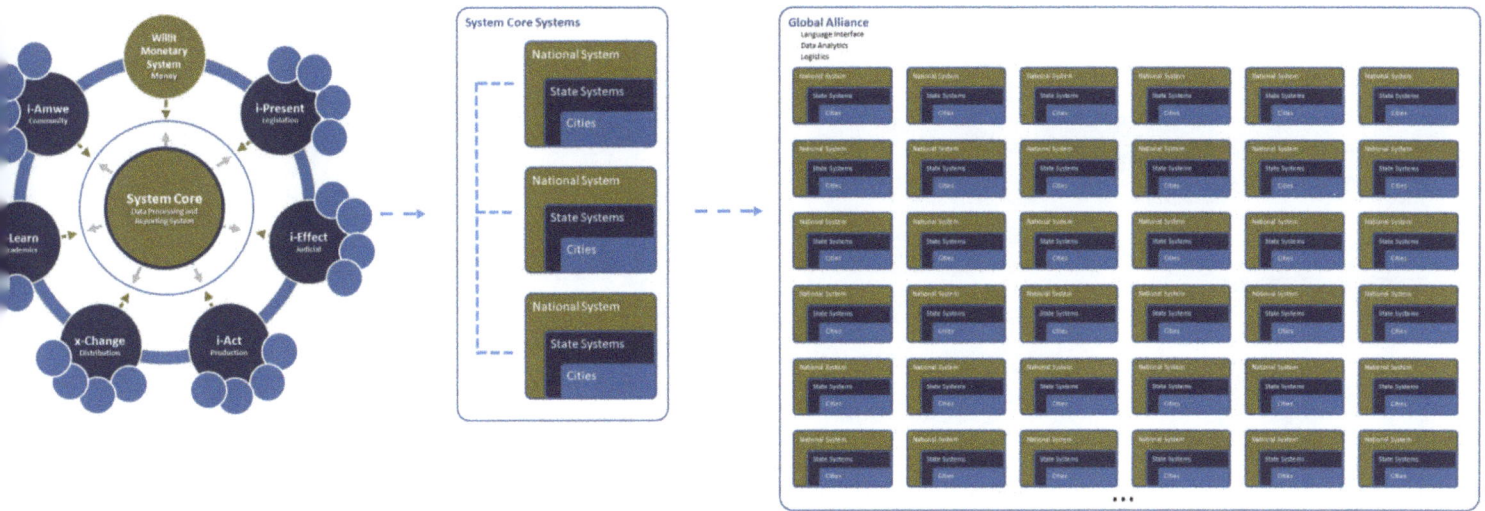

FIGURE 21

i-amwe	i-Willit	i-Present	i-Effect	i-Act	xChange	i-Learn
db_1a	db_1b	db_1c	db_1d	db_1e	db_1f	db_1g
Civic Communication	Monetary System	Public Policy Agreements	Legislative - Judicial Agreements	Production	Distribution and Allocation	Academics and R&D
Members & Useries	Money with Real Value	Legislative System and Action Orders	True Justice	Production Efficiency	Earned Equity and Willit	Information & Knowledge
FAQ	FAQ	FAQ	FAQ	FAQ	FAQ	FAQ

i-amwe	i-Willit	i-Present	i-Effect	i-Act	xChange	i-Learn
Registration	Login	GCTA	iPresent	JVote Rights & Justice	Human Will and Resources Allocation	Product Service Request	Board of Education and Certifications
Accounts:	Global Compensation and Transaction Administration	Video Presentations and text documents enactments proposed for agreements, with Negative and Positive effects and counter arguments	Supreme Court - is the Right of the People	Labor Request: Standard Needs and IWAUT Exchanges	Standard Needs xChange:	Education is a Rights
Earned Equity Accnt/Requ.					Earned Equity	Education and Certification are Standard
Willit Account	Intelligent Automation Systems for Bulk Compensation Approval and Audits	Open commenting video/text	No cost to request justice		Order placed for Standard Needs and Products and Services and WAUT	Needs. Pre K - Professional: BA, MS, PhD's
Community Willit Account		Line Item Voting	Justice is a Standard Need.		xChange:	
Emergency Safety & GPS Alert Systems		Optional: Comprehension Questions/Quiz			Willit Purchased Goods/Services	CERTIFICATION AND LICENSING
Community Agreements			No person is detained for any offense that does not involve physical injury. People that enter a		Global Reserve Depository and	Skills
Visitor Guide					International Shipments	Trades
			nation must apply for community relocation services.			Service Providers
Communicating and Mail Systems	Action Order Reviews and Confirmation	Global Constitution		Producer & Provider Registration	Order System	Certification
		Enactment Submission		Employment Listing	Product Orders	Academic Profiles, Records, and
Official Communications with each individual Citizen	Compensation Login Systems	Laws of Rights & Governance	Death sentences, nor physical harm, may be imposed upon any person.	Action Orders	Standard Need	Test Score - Public Review
	Worker GPS Tracking System	Production Approval Request		Independent Producer Registration	Food Transfer to Restaurant	Knowledge Access
Personal Mail Systems	Work Confirmation Systems: Yield and inventory, Service Completion and Order Confirmations	Community Agreements		Production Unit Registration	Production/Service Request	Online Learning
Standard Needs Request		Global Agreements		Material Use Registration	Material- Raw & Component Request	Lecture Series
Service Request			iEffect - Jury Voting System	Skill Trade Profession Registration	Production Request	iBook
Community Support Logs Reports	Management Confirmation	Legal Agreements	IAct Stop Action Application	Certified Labor	Service Request	Knowledge Assessments
Service/Product Rating	Payroll Submission Systems	Marriage Agreement	Agreement Dissolution	Non Cert. Labor	Goods and Services Deposit/Inventory Sys	Interpreters
Recycle Pickup Request	Willit Account	Contracts: Public and Private	Arbitration	Service Registration and Availability	Recycled Material Centers	Research & Development
Transition Assistance	Willit Issue Order		Complaint Resolutions	Member Appointed Position Registration		
		Collaboration: Enactment Creation		iPresentatives	Raw Materials and Components	Research Team Registration
Center of Understanding	Equity Issue Order	Group Voting Decision Tools	Criminal Actions Judgment	Emergency Services	Agricultural Products	Mental and Physical Health
Life Choice Support	Willit Escrow Account	Enactment Sponsorship 8% of effected populate.	Civil Disputes	Officials & Representatives	Housing & Building Construction Materials	Natural Cures
Rehabilitation	Personal Willit Account	Fact Check -	Exile Determination	Analyst	Usery Item - Perishable and Non	Disease
Community Builder	National Willit Account	Voting System	Member Extractions		Communication Device etc.	Global Medical Records
Community Kitchen	Earned Equity Calculations and Account Confirmations	iVote	Product / Service Liability		Heavy Equipment/ Machinery	Technology
Housing / Relocation	Global Trade Analysis	Local	Right Infringement	Equity Distribution & Account Log	Services	Science
Community Usery		State	Data and Tracking System	Human will allocation and distribution	Transportation	
Transportation / RSVP	International Will Exchange				Shipping/Freight	
		National	Social Misconduct Complaints	Labor Request & Opt in Tracking		Universal Laws - Publication
Health Care Centers	Employee Bonus Compilation Data Systems	Global	Grievance and Criminal Action Investigation and Evidence System	Community Support Equity	WAUT xChange	Recall Tracking Applications
Physical and Mental Helath Services	Health Citizen Confirmation System	Election System	Product Recall	Willits Account Deposits and	Willit Transfers	Food and Product Effect Tracking System
Discourse and Happenings	Employee Evaluations	Automated Vote Count System	Citation Data System	Employee rievance, and discipline records	Distribution Priority level	Production Effect Application Integration
Meetings	Social Systems	Official Phone Tracing and video logs of Political Represententive	Enforcement Systems	Service Order Request - Standard & Willit	Product Useful Lifetime Calculations determine priority and access for redistribution of goods to end users.	Fact Check - Freedom of Information
Standard Needs Agreement		Media, Newspapers, and News Unions - to ensure the truth is disseminated.	Warrants for Arrest	Maintenance Request		
Events			Sentencing Tracking System	Required: Reports	100%Transparity	Unlimited Open Access
Arts				State of Membership	Real Time - Open transaction, consumption, and contact logs	Transcripts and Recordings for
Arts & Entertainment		One Vote Per Person		Efficiency, Productive, Needs Met	Inventory Systems	History
Kid Connection		Only agreements confirmed by a majority vote of 2/3 with a minimum of 25% of the population voting are recognized as		LEAP Will Strength	Needs/Service Assessment	BC, AD, NE History Archives
Rites of Passage Standards & Application		Political representativies do not possess agreement override authority of the people's vote		Labor Request Distribution Performance valuations tracking	Needs/Service Locator	Remembrance Archive
Nurtured Sprouts		Complete Transparency and Open Door Discussions and meetings		Material Production	Needs/Service Distribution	
Kids Connect				Product -		
News		Filing System of individual confirmations of community agreements and Social Contracts. And, affirmation of Social Contracts, by youths for the Rites of Passage		Service - Requested/Distribution/Variance		
Global				Willit Distribution		
Local						
Enactment and Vote				System CORE: Community secession/potential, and Integrations		
Announcements & Updates						
Media League						
Fact Cast						
TECH Knowledge						
Idea Exchange						
Announcements						
Travel Connection						
Lodging						
Transportation						
Cultural Exchange						
Archives						
Remembrance						
History: BC, AD, NE						

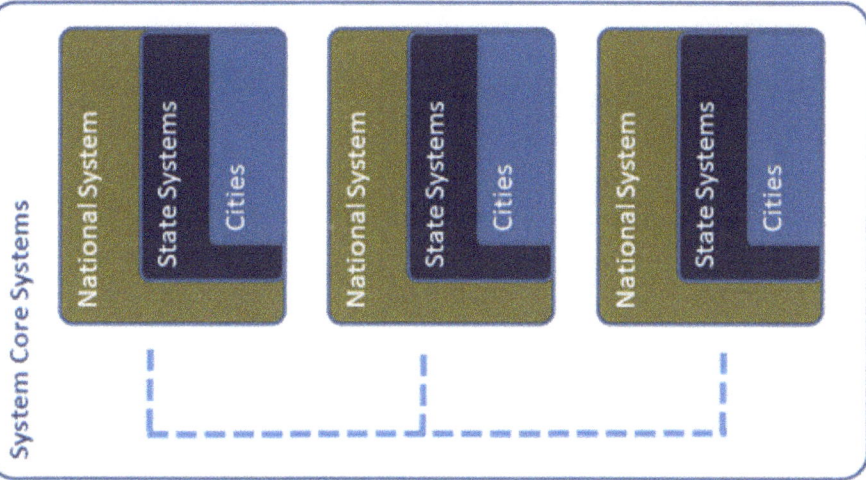

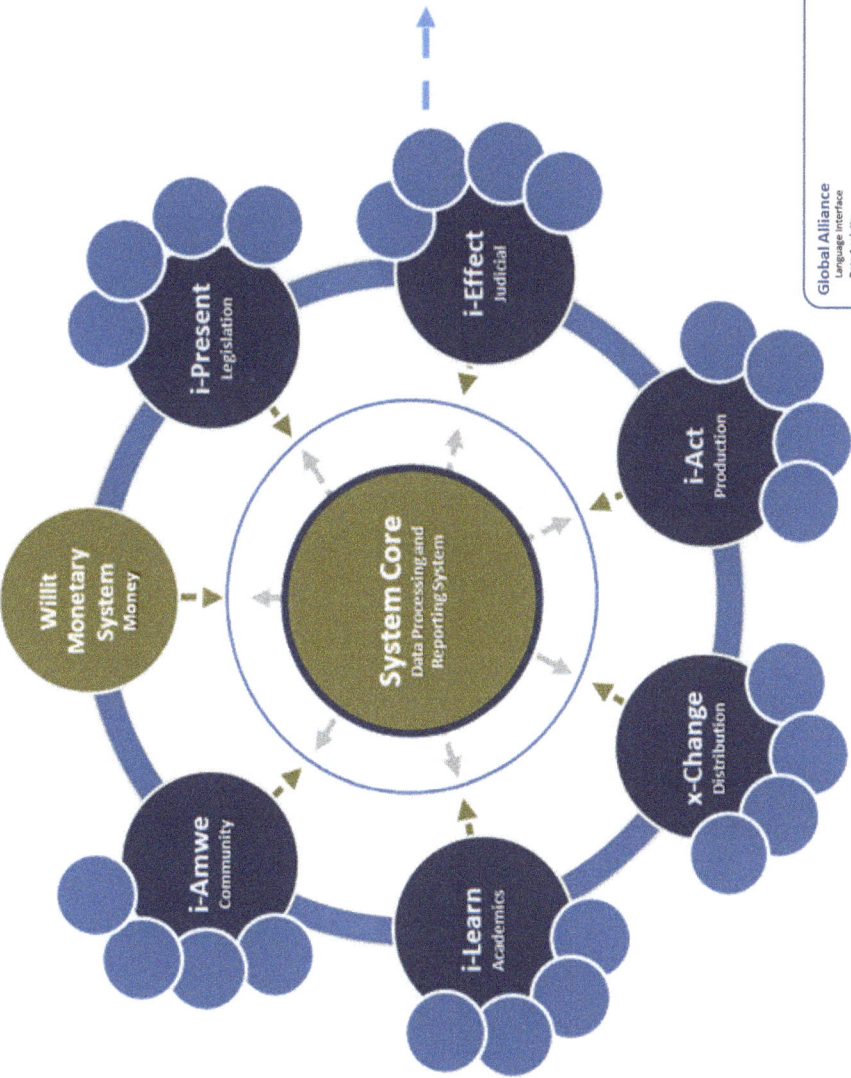

REPORTING SYSTEMS

The reporting systems will give individuals access to detailed reporting functionality for their district, city, state, and country, as well as global information for specific regions. The reports will be dynamic, with 3D imaging, maps, and multimedia integration, and will include, but will not be limited to:

- Production and agriculture yields
- Product and service orders
- Production efficiency
    - Corporate and production unit product efficiency rates and service scores.
- Compensation and equity rates and levels
- Willit usage, savings, escrow
- Reserves and shortages
    - Foods, grains, minerals, oil and gas reserves
- Consumption rates
- Imports and exports
- Energy usage: individual households and business units
- Medical Reports: individual, research Studies, Epidemics
- Audits: Willit allocation, inventories, production yields, orders, legislative and Judicial votes
- Production and legislative effects
- Criminal activity reports
- Judicial outcomes and reviews
- Administrative reports
- Systems errors

Warning systems

- Resource shortages
- Cause and effects
- Product recalls – recalls will be issued only to the individuals that have ordered or purchased a recalled product.
- Community incidents and locations

The System Core will also use effect perspective algorithms with set tolerance levels that will warn users of potential harms.

ACCURACY OF REPORTING FOR ALL NATIONS

Once report driven data is entered into the system, it must be confirmed by order confirmations, documentation, auditors, etc. Once confirmed, the data will not be alterable; adjustment entries will be required by an auditor with the input of the proper electronic or scanned documentation to support and validate the adjustment.

AUTONOMY

The System Core will enable communities (districts), cities, states, and nations to enable or disable applications and components specific for their use.

Example: Legislation and Enactment Applications and Components
To ensure autonomy of agreed upon laws, each community district's System Core would be sensitive to its independent laws, as well as the hierarchical laws of cities, states and nations. Yet, the structure of law approval, infraction ledgers, etc., would be standardized and centralized, and enabled with law crossover ability. Example: If one district initiated a law that would geographically affect the resource rights of other districts, the law would be up-scaled to a different hierarchal level to ensure the voting rights of all affected communities.

Each nation's mirrored system will be autonomous. Security features will be built into the system to prevent other countries from manipulating data that does not belong to them. Data sabotage would be deemed a violation of the Global Peace Alliance Agreement; trade with the offending nation would be halted until the culprits are brought to justice and placed on public trial.

ORDER BASED SYSTEM

The System Core will function based on Legislative Enactments.
Enactments must delineate the actions to be performed.
Action orders ensure each task performed is assigned to an approved enactment, ensures accountability, and will be required prior to issuing compensation to an individual. Action orders will also detail the manager or agent issuing the order, the action to be performed, and the party that will commit said act.

If an individual does not receive an action order, compensation cannot and will not be issued, and they should not perform the action.

For example: within the capital IWAUT Market – for an item to be produced, an order from a customer must be received. Likewise, if an administrative action is to be performed, an order must be issued for the performance of the action to ensure proper documentation of all tasks.

Action Orders can specify a date and time and can be open-ended until a new party takes over the action order.

Action orders will have template options so that orders can be quickly copied and assigned.

Executives, managers, and supervisors will have the ability to issue action orders in alignment with enactments approved by the people.

FRONTEND AND BACKEND USER INTERFACES

The frontend and backend user interfaces will be graphic and user-friendly with detailed instructional links and videos.

There will be various segments of the System Core's Applications and Components that will be viewable but not enabled for input by the public.

All programming code will be available and detailed for the people to view.

LANGUAGE PROGRAMS

The System Core will have a base language program set of the agreed upon universal language, and translation modules will be integrated into the system for every major language.

CENTRALIZED ACCESS SYSTEM (CAS)

The CAS is centralized and departmentalized. It controls the permissions for accessing various systems, for each citizen. For example, access to mass transportation systems – which would determine if you have Standard Needs access or must pay True Cost, and helps with determining usage rates for scheduling and the proper allocation of transportation resources.

TECHNOLOGICAL AND INFRASTRUCTURE REQUIREMENTS

See Appendix A.

OUR WORLD VISION

The following envisionments are summaries of how the System Core's applications and components could affect our lives.

OLD WORLD IDEOLOGY VERSUS NEW WORLD IDEOLOGY

Today, in 2020, our governments own all the lands, resources, and houses the people make use of and reside in, regardless if one's mortgage is paid off or not. If land can be seized and assets confiscated, then land and assets can be used, but they can never be owned.

Banks are the buffer to protect governments from civil unrest, and facilitate a covert scheme of energy theft from the people through the demand of production for the payment of paper money that can be used to pay other people and taxes. Taxes are the payment of money to the same governments that initially approved the printing and issuing of money. Federal Reserves and Central Banking Systems usually are not part of a government, but, they do rule governments.

- Governments print and issue money, or authorize the printing and distribution of money.
- Governments request the repayment of the same money they issued in the form of taxes.

If governments have the power and authority to issue money, why do they need it returned to them in the form of taxes?

The process of money creation and taxation is nonsensical, and an old scheme of kings, lords, and serfs (slaves) that has been renamed, yet conceptually more complex. It is clever marketing with mental chains that promote hard work for the reward of resources provided freely by nature. The schemes of these systems offer a false sense of security, opportunity, and freedom. If a government is truly sovereign and a legitimate authority, it has no need of taxation.   Yet, to ensure international trade (the acceptance of another sovereign nation's currency), bonds and interest were conceived to convince others of the value of external currency (thus bonds which pay interest to ensure extra benefits were created, and helped to decrease resource acquisition conflicts).

Our system of governance is an old system that is skewed for the benefit of the elite.
A system of provision is necessary to ensure needs are met, but the system of entitlement is not.

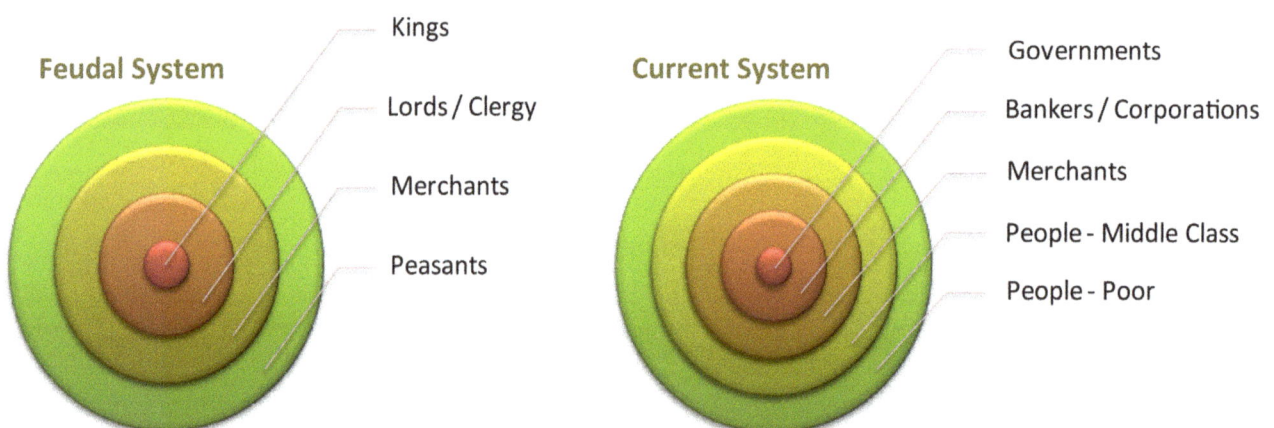

Feudal System

Kings

Lords / Clergy

Merchants

Peasants

Current System

Governments

Bankers / Corporations

Merchants

People - Middle Class

People - Poor

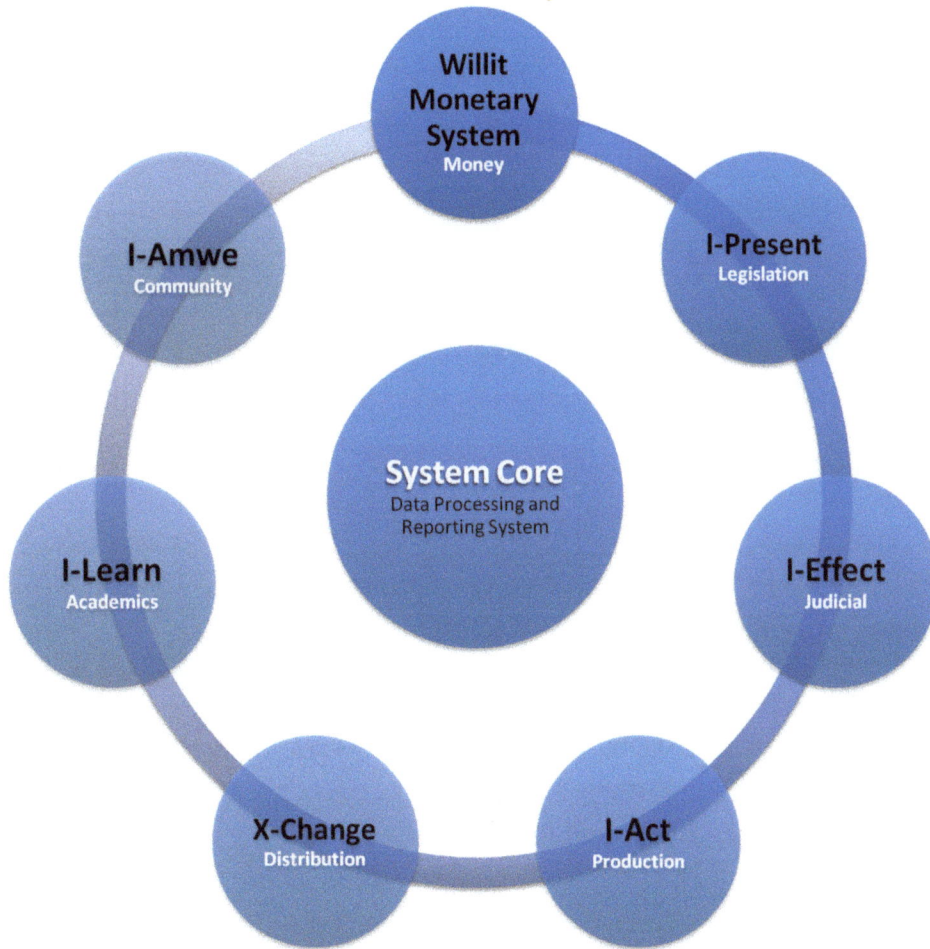

Willit ideology ensures balance between our social and economic systems; governance by all members of society through the equality of vote for all people of legal age and the right to propose, amend, or annul laws; the education of all people, and the ability for any individual to be a merchant or service provider.

PROPERTY OWNERSHIP

Many believe property ownership is what determines wealth. Yet, money is required to purchase and maintain land and to extract resources to make products. Wealth can only be obtained with access to the means of production, which is controlled and granted by governments who create money, and have the forces to commandeer land and command compliance.

Prior to man's existence there was land. Man cannot claim ownership of that which he did not create, nor that which will exist after his demise, no matter how much energy one places into it or how much blood one spills to hold on to it.

The ownership of land is an old-world concept conceived from greed, and the madness and fear of self-protectionism, in a parasitic and predatory world.

The confiscation of land is not being condoned herein. True Cost principles employed by the System Core will inevitably prove private ownership of land and houses to be impractical in a truly equitable world.

HOMES

Instead of banks issuing mortgages for procurement of land and houses, housing will be a Standard Need obtained through earning equity.

FARMLAND

Farmland will be managed by individuals, families, and corporations – who will be paid Earned Equity and Willits for land management.

Example: Farmers may select to retain their lands, however, they will pay the True Cost for all goods and services rendered to them, as well as the true cost for gas, labor, transportation, and the social allowance of infrastructure usage. Farmers can sell 60 percent of their products to the Standard Needs Administration at True Cost (which offsets their initial investment after the product is brought to market), offer 30% exclusively to the iWAUT Market (I Will Accept Universal Tender), and 10% to International Reserve markets, and receive Willits for their transactions.

However, farmers that select to yield property ownership rights will be paid the full Willit value for their lands, will incur no upfront cost in bringing products to market, and can be designated as Land Managers. They will have the option of residing in their homes for the duration of their life should the people determine the best use for the land is that of agriculture. Should the people decide to reject farmland usage, the farmers will be provided with housing as part of their Standard Needs Earned Equity – in which they may opt to provide agricultural services for their Earned Equity and/or Willits.

The time of private property rights will end due to population growth. Yet, the right to, and fair assignment of usage, will help to stabilize families and create an unbreakable bond between the people for the care of all resources.

Retirement of the ideology of private property will end the inclination for resource wars. With a system of collaboration, equity, and justice, all people will have access to the resources required to sustain themselves and society without the necessity of poverty and war.

There are many people who believe it to be impossible to meet the needs of all people. Their belief is based on observation of the enormous requirements needed to complete the task. However, their belief is not founded based on facts because their flawed systems are not adequate to compute all needs; nor to account for all resources, nor resource usage efficiency; nor to assign and determine fulfillment of the required tasks.

AdvanCN envisions property usage rights will be assigned by lottery, and not social status, nor executive privilege, and prime real-estate used for vacation lodging and made available to all members of society for the exchange of Willits. The True Cost of maintenance for large estates and prime property will be cost-prohibitive for almost everyone.

With the incorporation of the System Core's ethos and the peoples' social agreements, a property or land-owner will have the option to retain their property for the duration of their life. A land-owner may select to pay the True Cost for resource usage, by opting not to become a Standard Needs citizen who Earns Equity.

REGIONAL COMMISSIONS FOR URBAN PLANNING & LAND USE (UPLU)

Local UPLU commissions will review community needs and prioritize building and infrastructure projects and maintenance; determine best land use; and report their findings to the people for enactment approval. Within the UPLU, will be the Department of Property Management, who will be the oversight agency for property inventory, management, and acquisition.

SOLUTION OR APPLICABLE SYSTEM CORE APPLICATION/S

The Standard Needs Earned Equity system and markets will be used to ensure every person has an apartment or home, a central location to schedule maintenance and repairs, and to find available housing units or to access temporary housing for travel, vacation, or business needs.

The UPLU administrative body will ensure that home usery is limited to one housing unit per individual or family unit.

Current landlords who rent housing or apartment units will be compensated for the property, and the dwelling unit placed in the Standard Needs Market. The landlord will receive compensation for upkeep, maintenance, and management of the property, without the burden of ownership.

STANDARD NEEDS HOUSING

Standard Needs Housing allocation will be by application and lottery. Every individual will be granted Standard Needs Housing. Housing will consist of units for individuals, families, seniors, supportive housing, co-op housing, and student housing.

The people will determine square footage requirements and design, based on available resources and construction standards and building codes.

NON-STANDARD HOUSING (PUBLIC DOMAIN)

Non-equity Standard Needs properties that have been placed in the public domain, that exceed agreed-upon Standard Needs criteria for square footage and fixtures, could be leased through the I-WAUT market for the True Cost of maintenance.

If a property cannot be maintained at True Cost levels once the System Core is implemented, the people within the district the property is located may vote to confirm the UPLU's recommendations or co-op the property.

PRIVATE HOUSING

Private houses and lands are those homes or properties that are owned by individuals who have determined they will retain ownership rights, for which they will be required to pay the True Cost for the maintenance of the home. As well as the true cost for all utilities, sewer, trash removal, and road maintenance; as well as the True Cost for all social benefits.

Upon the death of the home-owner and their spouse – the land and property will revert to the public domain. A community may select to place the property in the Standards Needs market, or the I-WAUT Market, or condemn the property for recycling.

HOUSING MAINTENANCE

Maintenance of all housing units will be part of the Standard Needs system, and required material resources paid for by a Community's RP-Tax Grant. All housing units and homes must be up-to-date with housing regulations enacted by one's district, city, and state.

Repairs may be paid for by the residing members and quickly reimbursed by the UPLU, for all expenses that were not the fault of the occupant.

PROCUREMENT PROCESS

Banks will no longer issue mortgages for the procurement of land and houses; housing will be a Standard Need obtained through earning equity or Willits.

In-lieu-of ownership people will have usery rights – the right of use. Properties will be managed by property management organizations, companies, or agencies registered with the UPLU.

The Global Compensation and Transaction Administration, may not, nor any System Core Administration, deprive the people of the land they have placed their energy into by seizure.

However, the people of a nation may acquisition land and resources by enactment, so long as the land holder is adequately compensated, the land acquired by the people is used to benefit the entire community including the owner/s the land was acquired from, and the use of the land will pose no ecological nor physical danger.

Once property is entered into the Standard Needs Earned Equity System, it may not be bought nor sold for private ownership.

HOUSING ACQUISITION PROCESS

Once the System Core is approved for activation:

- Every person residing in a dwelling or rental unit will retain possession of their home.
- Ownership of housing units will be transferred to usery rights, and the debt obligation settled by a National Compensation and Transaction Administration, and if applicable with the International Debt Obligation Settlement Administration.
- Prior owners will be compensated.
- Housing units will be listed with the UPLU, maintained, refurbished, or demolished for building materials and the land cultivated for raising crops, if possible.

BENEFITS

- Resource Conservation - Housing will be built based on need, not speculation.
- Stronger Communities
  - Safer Communities
  - Lower Crime Rates
  - Communities will have the option to request people who do not comply with standards to relocate
- Housing always maintained - No dilapidated buildings
- Improved lifestyle and quality of life
- End of housing debt and taxation

ONE FAMILY ONE HOME

Goal: To ensure affordable and safe housing for all People.

AdvanCN supports not only affordable and safe housing but the means to ensure that every person has a home, without the burden of debt, and to end the antiquated landlord system.

Our mission is to ensure every individual and family has a home that is safe, well maintained, and provided to them based on Earned Equity.

LOGIC

Housing is a fundamental right and basic need for every human being. And, should not be a for profit endeavor.

Minimum Square footage for housing should be determined by the people, based on the land mass available, with 50 percent left unused, 25 percent for agriculture and 25 percent for housing and infrastructure.

Building Designation

CLASS	UNIT TYPE	STATUS		Min. Sq. Ft.
Class A	Homes			
Executives	Level 1-A	Family	Three to Four - Bedrooms	2000
	Level 1-B	Couple and Child	Two - Bedrooms	1800
	Level 1-C	Single	One - Bedroom	1200
Managers	Level 2-A	Family	Three to Four - Bedrooms	1800
	Level 2-B	Couple and Child	Two - Bedrooms	1600
	Level 2-C	Single	One - Bedroom	1000
Staff	Level 3-A	Family	Three to Four - Bedrooms	1600
	Level 3-B	Couple and Child	Two - Bedrooms	1400
	Level 3-C	Single	One - Bedroom	800
Senior Housing	Level 4-B	Couple	Two - Bedrooms	1400
	Level 4-C	Senior	One - Bedroom	1000
Student Housing	Level 5-C	Student	One - Bedroom	450
Class B	Business and Corporate Buildings			
	Level - B1	Manufacturing		
	Level - B2	Commercial		
	Level - B3	Business		
	Level - B4	Secure Off-site Office		
Class C	Temporary Lodging			
	Level - D1	Business Temporary Lodging		
		Class A		
		Class B		
	Level - D2	Vacation Temporary Lodging		
		Class A		
		Class B		
	Level - D3	Transitional Temporary Lodging		

TAXATION AND MONEY

Taxation is not a means to ensure government operations. Governments can print as much money as they desire and can skew belief and confidence in the monetary system through control of the media and distribution. Taxation ensures governmental control over people, cities, and states. Monetary distribution determines access to resources; determines membership of the elite; is used to ensure a modicum of resource conservation; and to prevent the chaos that could erupt from immediate mass demand upon the economic system.

With use of the Willit Monetary System's global monetary creation standards and Standard Needs Earned Equity, taxation will be obsolete, and immediate mass demand quelled through True Cost ideology and cooperative sharing programs.

© Reuters

GHOSTING

Implementation of the System Core may result in a phenomenon termed ghosting. Ghosting is the abandonment of cities that become economically obsolete (ghost town).

Instead of abandoning these sites, if feasible, the sites could be converted into sky farms and solar towers; or, the building materials recycled.

The following public domain illustration and images are examples of sky farms. Currently, sky farms are not a viable alternatives to farms, and will only be a viable alternative for producing leafy produce when they are completely mechanized.

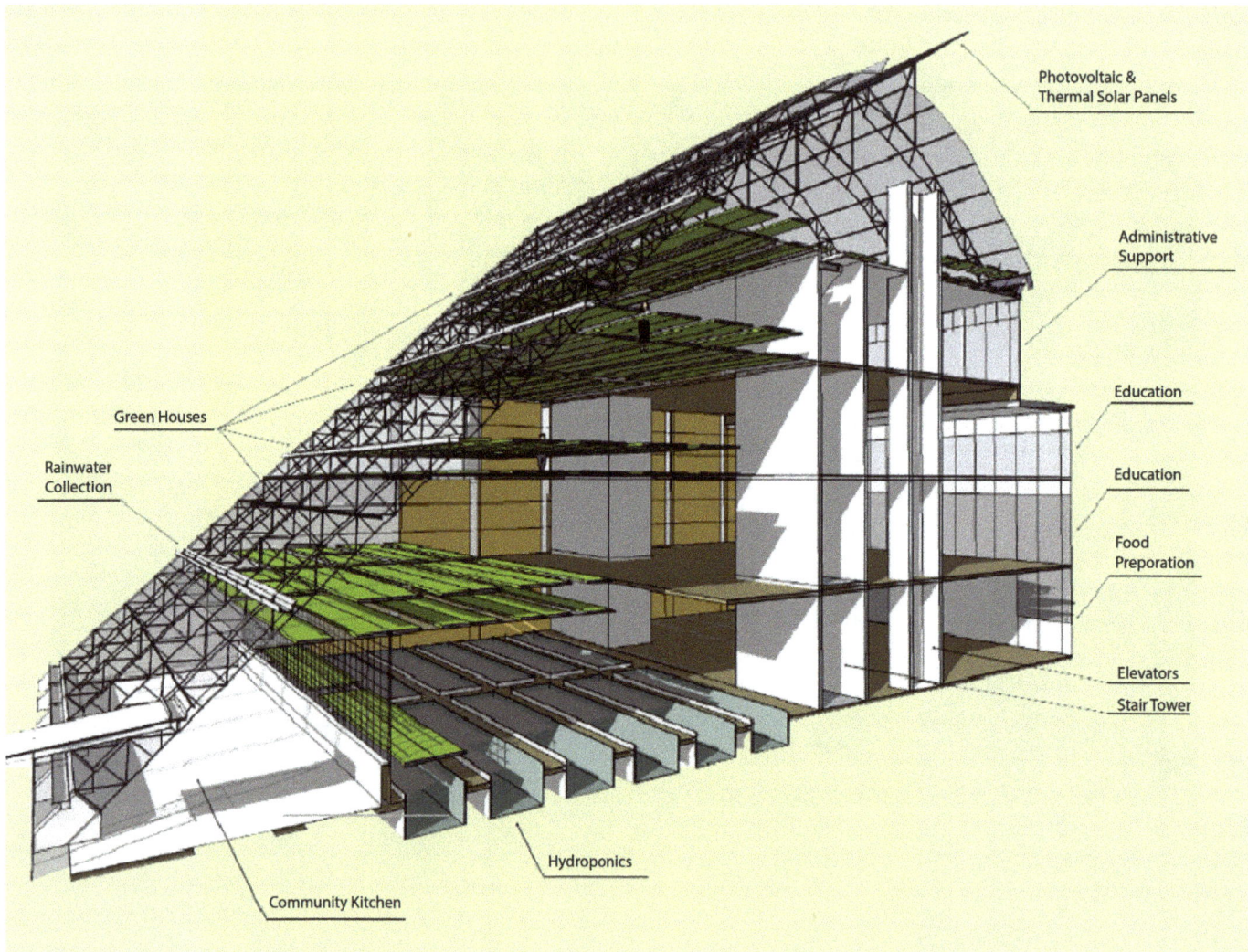

WELFARE STATES

Welfare states will be nonexistent. Every able-bodied person will work their fair share and will have time to rest and care for their families. The elderly have helped to create the world we inherited and will be cared for by the people. Individuals who cannot care for themselves due to mental or physical incapacitation will be cared for and nurtured because every person born to the world has required aid, and should reciprocate when there is need.

Able-bodied individuals who refuse to work, should not receive aid; as there will no longer be any excuse, just the requirement and opportunity to earn equity.

RETIREMENT

Every individual will be cared for through the Standard Needs and Earned Equity system once they reach retirement age. They will have a clean and comfortable home, medical services, nourishment required to sustain them, and the Standard Needs of Life.

One can also retire early by meeting their maximum income cap and have the purchasing power for the items they desire in the iWAUT Markets.

Funding one's retirement has been an issue of concern for many people and has supported a system of debt and interest required by an antiquated system of continuous growth, debt, and interest. No one should expect to retire in their early 50's when they are still able-bodied and of use to society. And society should not be burdened with funding a retirement system that continually takes from the people so those who work for governing bodies can retire after twenty years.

INHERITANCE

A parent has the right to secure their lineage and to pass on their possessions to their children. The world has the responsibility to ensure equitable distribution of resources, a level playing field, and to guard themselves against the destructive mindset of entitlement, reward without work, unearned access to resources, and ego inflation.

The Social Agreements adopted by the people for the transition to the Willit Monetary System will end the right of inheritance; thus ending the transfer of land and money upon an individual's death. Yet, in doing so, all mankind ensures a system of equality for their family, in which they and their children will have equal opportunity and access to education, resources, and the ability to prosper based on the knowledge, skills, and energy they offer to the world, without exploiting their brothers and sisters.

Sole Proprietors of a successful business will have the right to determine their predecessor/s.

Money (Willits), land, and homestead property will not be inheritable assets. Every individual will work for the money they acquire. Inheritance will be limited to the physical goods left to them through the inheritance inventory system.

An individual may grant possession of the assets within their estate inventory system to an individual or individuals, by assigning the asset to a beneficiary.

Account

EXPENSES & REVENUES   MANAGEMENT LOG   MILEAGE   INVENTORY   MY INHERITANCE   MY ACCOUNTS   ✉

Assets Inventory

Name of Asset	Description	Value	Status	Asset Split	Asset Beneficiary	Inheritance Amount	Asset Image	
Wicker Furniture	Indoor wicker furniture	1500	On-Site	1	792	1500		VIEW

DISPLAY # 10

Estate
Trust Repository

CORPORATIONS AND OUR NEW WORLD

Corporations will <u>not</u> be the determinants of wealth; nor will they have overwhelming influence upon the political, nor legislative process; nor will they be subject to the whims of law and financial constraints. They will only concern themselves with the efficient production of products and service provision. They will produce that which is required, needed, and desired, by the people without exploitive profiteering.

And, they (corporations) will be without worry of investment dollars and without cash flow concerns.

LOGIC

Corporations are not beings unto themselves, their actions are not immune from effects. Their sole purpose is to make use of the earth's resources to produce products people require and need to sustain their lives. As such, corporations are answerable to the people of the world, who will determine and approve the need and validity of the products produced, and jointly determine if the sacrifices required for production are worth the negative impacts that may result.

Corporations are not creators nor geniuses unto themselves, as they require product feedback to innovate and to perfect their products. Thus, corporations should not have the ability to destroy lives and determine destinies; they are not gods, they are need fulfillment processors.

Therefore, within Willit System ideology, corporations will not determine legislative agenda, and their power limited to the production and provision of goods and services.

RESEARCH AND DEVELOPMENT

Research and development will be an industry unto itself. The findings and creations of inventors will be submitted to the people for production rights. Once production rights are approved, corporations and production units will manufacture the products.

The industry of invention and legislated production rights will result in:

- Open markets
- Robust entrepreneurial systems and innovations
- The proper acknowledgment and compensation of the individuals who innovate

NONPROFIT ORGANIZATIONS

Nonprofit organizations will remain viable entities and will help bring about awareness of conditions the people need to address. Nonprofits will be fully funded by Standard Needs and Earned Equity through iPresent's legislative system for Service Enactments. Service Enactments state the mission and goals of the nonprofit organization, targeted completion date for the project, and the expected outcomes to be achieved.

COPYRIGHTS & PUBLIC DOMAIN

Copyrights will remain in effect for literature and creative works until the death of all contributors. The benefit of Willit compensation for copyrights will not be extended to relatives, nor any member of society for the purpose of inheritance. Once the copyright expires, the work is entered into the public domain.

FRAUD PREVENTION

Corruption Malfeasance and Theft Prevention

There is no absolute method to prevent theft by administrators of the Willit system, nor theft by individuals that wish to commit fraud. However, auditing teams and completely transparent transactions and allocation systems that all people can view and audit will be a major deterrent. The punishment of exile for theft and lying will also be a major deterrent.

TRANSPARENCY

Transparency, open access, and full disclosure are essential to ensure the System Core is not corrupted by destructive individuals; and will help to restore trust between married couples, families, communities, and nations.

STATE AND NATIONAL INDEPENDENCE

It is essential for cities, states, and nations to remain intact to ensure resources can be shared and needs met, so long as a nation does not physically or mentally abuse its citizens or prevent the advancement or growth of its citizens.

All states within one landmass or continent should be seen as one region and the people as one body, each with the right to resources, and the assurance they will be fed, clothed, housed, educated, and properly cared for, provided their equity is earned.

SOCIAL COMMUNICATIONS MEDIA AND TRANSPARENCY

Information will be derived from various sources, and the freedom of information and the right of communication will not be impeded for any reason.

The internet will be a free source of communication for all people and nations. Every person will be granted access to explore various networks and sites.

The internet will not be disabled for any reason. Nor any site disabled with exception to sites that:

1. infringe the right of life
2. promote or allow for the enslavement of another being
3. promote the death or physical abuse of any being
4. promote inequitable treatment of another being

EDUCATION MATERIALS GRANT

Every person will be granted an allotment for the purchase of books and materials that aid in social and/or personal development to ensure a well-rounded education.

COMMUNITY KITCHENS (SIMILAR TO RESTAURANTS)

Community kitchens will help to prevent food waste and reduce packaging material requirements for processed foods. The true state of our food supply levels will be apparent immediately based on the availability of meal offerings. Obesity will be managed by healthy food options and portions guidelines.

People would eat together and stronger community bonds would develop.

FINANCIAL MARKETS

What will happen to financial markets for items such as stocks, commodities, bonds, equities, securities, and derivatives?

Trading of the financial markets will be obsolete. All financial rewards will be received based on the Willit Compensation Standards.

Investments will be secured by a nation's Standard Needs or Willit Credit System.

Commodities will only be purchased by organizations and corporations that actually use the goods in production. The commodity will be acquired at the BEE rate.

Bonds will no longer require lending agreements and interest will no longer be charged with the use of the Willit Credit System.

Equity dividends will be obsolete as investment income will no longer be utilized, and thus no longer applicable.

Securities will no longer be traded as no debt will be incurred by any entity.

A derivative is a contract between two or more parties whose value is based on an underlying financial instrument, such as bonds, commodities, currencies, interest rates, market indexes, and stocks. Thus derivatives will also be obsolete.

RIGHTS AND RESPONSIBILITIES

ADMINISTRATIVE ACCOUNTABILITY

Administrative bodies are to act as a divine entity that ensures justice for all people regardless of the individual's gender, race, ethnicity, or religious beliefs or sexual preference. They are to be accurate and they are to give account of any error and to ensure the error is corrected.

Administrative bodies have the responsibility to ensure accurate information is disseminated without bias, and that all systems are well maintained.

They are also to remain impartial and without favoritism to any individual, corporation, or organization.

They are to be without corruption.

CORPORATE AND ORGANIZATION ACCOUNTABILITY

Corporations and organizations have the responsibility to ensure the products they make or the services they offer are offered in a timely manner and are accurately described to ensure the consumer is in receipt of what they have purchased or utilize; and to inform the people of any potential harms from production, consumption, or usage of the product or service.

All products will accurately detail materials and ingredients whether natural or manufactured. A listing of materials and ingredients will be available online for every product and accessible through barcode scanning.

All product-related injuries will be centrally located on the front page of the product's or service's online xChange page and corporate website. An impartial team unrelated to the corporation or organization will investigate all incidents to ensure accurate reporting and the findings reported to the people and located on the xChange page of the corporation or organization.

INDIVIDUAL ACCOUNTABILITY

The individual has the right and responsibility to ensure their systems are fair and without prejudice. The individual has the responsibility to ensure they are informed about every aspect of their social and economic systems.

The individual has the right to gather with other like-minded individuals and remove any individual from a position of authority if they are found to be corrupt in the handling of the duties they have been assigned.

The individual does **not** have the right to physical assault, harm, nor to kill another being.

Rites of passage confirmation is the entitlement to all social benefits based on the social contract.

Every individual will be educated about the rights and responsibilities of adulthood.

High school students will be educated in raising a family, the cost associated with raising children, all laws, and how they can engage the legislative and judicial systems.

They will also be educated in the social contract and how to resolve conflicts without physical abuse of another person.

Prior to the Rights of Passage an individual may explore other communities within or outside of their nation to determine the best location for their residency.

Parents will be compensated and awarded Willit compensation after the child receives the Rites of Passage and upon confirmation by the child that the parent was a good steward.

OIL – THE BLOOD OF THE EARTH

The resource wars for the control of oil field reserves has begun, and will continue until mankind creates viable energy alternatives.

Our industries and lives are stubbornly entrenched and obsessed with oil. Oil is thought of as a cheap means of energy that enables our societies to function, but at the cost of many lives for its procurement and profit.

1790

Industrial Revolution, Start date

Industrial Revolution

Turning point

The Industrial Revolution was the transition to new manufacturing processes in the period from about 1760 to sometime between 1820 and 1840. Wikipedia

Humans survived without mass production of refined oil before the industrial revolution. Work was hard, labor abuses were suffered; but, even without oil millions were clothed and fed. Now, there are many more people to share the burden of care and provision.

With aid of the System Core, the changes that are required to switch from oil dependency to alternative energy can be accomplished. Oil conservation will be required.

The implementation of True Cost principles, Community Kitchens, manufacturing upon purchase (with a three percentage inventory allotment of produced products), and production consent by the people, will change the focus of our global economy from growth and profit, to conservation and needs provision. These changes will help to heal our ecological systems and our domestic and international relationships.

SHOULD ONE KILL AND ENSLAVE OTHERS FOR PROFIT, LEISURE, AND COMFORTS?

Oil is the blood of the earth, and should only be used when necessary. Yet, many people still commute alone in their cars to jobs that are not vital to our economy (with exception to the fact, their work provides them with the money required to purchase the necessities of life), in cars that set idle 80 percent of the time.

Until mankind creates the technological advancements required to prevent resource wars, and to better manage our social and economic systems, oil conservation will be required.

Efforts the System Core will aid:

- Technological advancements in clean and renewable energy will be of primary importance.
- Non-fossil fuel dependent mass commuter rail systems that link communities and cities.
- Communal use of resources to avoid non-essential use of resources
- Self-sufficient communities and cities to lessen transportation requirements.
    - Telecommuting and Multi-Business Work Centers

Communities must be designed so the use of electric/solar vehicles, commuter rail systems, and vehicle sharing programs are feasible.

WAR

If war is ended by treaty, then there is never a reason for war. What is required is the acknowledgement of rights and just treatment.

The administrative bodies of the System Core will not engage in acts of war, nor sabotage. Should war occur, the System Core's administrative bodies will ensure the restoration of all nations' economic systems and data, in the hope that when sane minds prevail, the System Core can aid reconstruction and recovery efforts.

INITIAL FOUNDATION ENACTMENT REQUIREMENT

Our rights are only effective if man agrees to abide by them. The effect of any law created by man must ensure life and freedom; and if a law violates these inalienable rights, the people must amend it.

With this ethos in mind, the following eight foundational laws for the System Core are offered for consideration:

ENACTMENT 1 – APPROVAL OF LEGISLATION

No law shall be enacted, enforced, nor funded, without a confirmation vote of the people.
All laws will be reviewed no less than every five years to determine their validity and to review their documented effects.

The people are to determine if the law is fair to all people and constructive of peace, security, life, and freedom. If the law is destructive of peace, security, or life, it is to be deactivated from active Law Code. Sub-enactments constructed based on the initial law, may also be deactivated and archived.

No law will be enacted that prevents the people from amending or suspending an enactment or law.

Goal of Enactment 1: The Perfection of Law

ENACTMENT 2 – ASSURANCE OF JUSTICE

No law shall be enacted that prevents due process; nor shall any law be enacted that prevents the investigation or filing of charges for corruption, theft, or lies against any individual charges are to be brought against, regardless of their position, class, or social status.

Every individual will have right to a trial by a jury of the people, whose judgement is final, so long as the people's judgement does not condone, nor the punishment result in, killing or theft.

Goal of Enactment 2: The Assurance of Justice

ENACTMENT 3 – RIGHT OF LIFE

The right of life and freedom from physical abuse is to be protected.

No government, nor their administrative bodies, contractors, corporations, or mechanical constructs, may subject any person to physical abuse; nor can any writ (by verbal, physical, electronic, or any other means of communication) be issued; nor any law enacted that will authorize, condone, fund, nor manage, nor bring about the killing of, or physical abuse of, any human. Self-defense against immediate and imminent danger is the only exception to this provision.

The punishment for violations of this act will be exile, Level 1 (if approved by the people).

Issues concerning abortion or a woman's reproductive rights and health will be the private concern of women and their physicians – no, administrative body, nor group, may propose legislation that will hinder or limit a woman's rights or freedom of choice regarding the concerns of her own body.

The killing, eating, or enslavement of animals is strongly discouraged and no less egregious than the killing or enslavement of human beings. If one demands the right of life for self and freedom from abuse, one should and must extend it to all beings.

Goal of Enactment 3: End of physical and mental abuse by governments

ENACTMENT 4 – RIGHT OF SELF DEFENSE

No law shall be passed, nor sentence of exile issued, for individuals that protect themselves from direct and immediate danger. Coaxing or actions that incite violence, which result in physical harm or death are exilable offenses.
Goal of Enactment – Right to protect self from physical harm, if one is innocent.

ENACTMENT 5 – RIGHT OF PRIVACY

The Right of privacy is to be extended to all, and is limited to the confines of one's home or dwelling – for actions that one commits in that space so long as such actions do not impede the right of life, liberty, safety, and freedom of other individuals.
Goal of Enactment: To ensure the right of privacy of the individual – just as one has the privacy of one's thoughts.

ENACTMENT 6 – OPEN COMMUNICATION AND TRANSPARENCY

No law shall be passed that infringes the People's right to peaceable assembly.

No law shall be enacted that limits or prevents the distribution or sharing of information, or knowledge, in real-time, book form, or any other means of information exchange between individuals or groups.

And, no law shall be passed that prevents individuals from collecting and sharing information. Likewise, to ensure full disclosure by all parties, the administrative bodies for governance will have the right of information collection and dissemination.

To ensure the truth may be known at all times: No law shall be enacted that will discontinue or impede the right of communication between people or groups of any nation, for any reason. Local and global communication systems must be maintained in a state of excellent repair to ensure the ability of communication, trade, and information exchange, to ensure information is shared with all people, at all times, and in all locations – except those in exile, and the communication of national defense plans.

Hacking of the System Core will be an exilable offense.

Goal of Enactment: Full disclosure and transparency
Informed Individuals can only make wise decisions if the information they receive is accurate.
Knowledge is the key to self and system perfection.

ENACTMENT 7 – FREEDOM FROM UNLAWFUL INCARCERATION

No being shall be incarcerated (jailed or imprisoned) unless they have committed a crime that has resulted in the physical injury or death of an individual.

Exception: temporary holding of individuals for exilable crimes, or those individuals for whom a warrant of arrest has been issued for failure to appear to answer for violating a law.

Goal: End threats of incarceration for the violation of laws that pose no physical harm.

ENACTMENT 8 – ADVANCEMENT OF MANKIND

To ensure the advancement of mankind, laws can not hinder the development of mankind; it is the intent of creation, the founders, and the ancients that mankind achieve perfection (right actions that result in constructive effects for the individual and the whole); as such, any law that would prohibit achievement of this end will not be binding.

Thus, each man must be free to act in accord with his or her conscience, so long as their actions are not destructive to other people. Thus, the freedom of ideology, previously known as the freedom of religion, and the freedom of choice shall not be hindered, so long as the person can prove in a court of law that their belief and action is constructive for self and society, or, socially benign.

Goal: the freedom of religion and belief.

SYSTEM CORE IMPLEMENTATION PROCESS

The implementation process will be **without** the seizure of assets and without forced coercion; nor will the System Core be implemented without global cooperation.

Date	Phase	Planning
2020	Phase I	Planning
2021	Phase II	Development
2023	Phase III	System Review
2025	Phase IV	Testing
2027	Phase V	Testing
2029	Phase VI	Full Implementation
9	Total Years	

PHASE I – PLANNING (2020)

- Formation of System Core Planning Council
  Selection of technical analysts, user logic and flow designers, and industry expert teams from around the world.
  - Planning of the System Core applications and systems integration will be open to the public - meetings are to be broadcast and video made available online for complete transparency
- Analysis of and the planning for Global Communication Systems and Data Center infrastructure upgrades and/or development to ensure every community has access
- Appointment of media with full access and disclosure rights
- Public Collaboration
  The people - Gather online for the collaborative creation of:
  - The Law of Rights and Governance (Global Constitution and Bill of Rights)
  - Compile Agreements: Nonaggression, Aid, Global Resource Contributions for the 60/30/10 Resource Partition Plan, and the Debt Reconciliation Plan
  - Standard Needs: Discussions regarding which Goods and Services will be deemed Standard Needs items and which items will be marked for the IWAUT or Black Market
- Determine acquisition and compensation for assets and infrastructure for system integration
- Every person is to maintain all compensation statements for Proof of Funds that will be transferred into the Willit System.

PHASE II – DEVELOPMENT (2021)

- All nations collaboratively write the code for the System Core with technology and integration requirements
- Enter preliminary data for testing
- Nation-states Privacy Security Systems checks – Conducted by Each Nation's System Core Council

PHASE III – SYSTEM REVIEW (2023)

- Introduction to the people
- Registration of the people to test the System Core
- The people review the System Core application plans and submit comments, questions, and recommendations
    - Comments and feedback for improvements
- Update and reintroduction
    - World Peace Expo 2022

PHASE IV – SYSTEMS INTEGRATION (2025)

- Activation of iPresent voting applications
- Confirmation of voting districts and communities
- Confirmation vote by the people for the Foundational Agreements and the Laws of Rights and Governance
- Confirmation of the Agreement of Nonaggression by the people of each nation.
- Community Agreements confirmed by community members
- Vote of Standard Needs production and services by the people
- Confirmation of Global Debt Settlement Plan
- Negotiation of compensation for investors and capital assets for the exchange of Willits
- Gifted assets to the people to be entered into the System Core
- Vote of asset compensation claims – approved by the people
- Data entry of:
    - Resources, Raw Materials, and inventory
    - Products and available services
    - College degrees and academics – certification and licenses
      Medical Records, etc.
- Confirmation vote for the allocation of resources to Production Units, Management Teams, and Independent Producers
- Citizens enter household inventory for upgrades, recalls, priority allocation, and previously purchased goods

- Human Resource Administrations (local, national, global...) confirm skill-sets for each member of society and outlines training requirements for enactment approval for allocation of work and resource orders.
- Confirmation of Willit Administrators and Auditors
- Confirmation of Independent Media Service Members
- Citizens provide Proof of Funds to Transfer into the Willit System
- Reflective Funds Account creation –
  Monetary holdings of individuals will be reflected in their Willit account prior to bank account liquidation.
- Acquisition of public and private corporations:
  Per the Debt Settlement Plan (upon approval by the people) a public company's board of directors, employees, and shareholders will be given the option to exchange their voting stock to Willits; with the maximum exchange per individual limited to their lifetime earnings cap.
- Double accounting entries (Businesses' Current Accounting System and the System Core) to ensure the System Core is up-to-date with current inventory levels and orders

PHASE V - TESTING (2026 - 2027)

During the testing phase, the System Core will be completely operational and available for free everyday use (unofficially).

Full implementation of:

- Willit Monetary System
- Human Resources Components
- Production and Distribution System
- Market System
- Legislative System

The first test of the System Core is to establish the System's ability to process all the people's orders, generate work orders, have the people confirm their work orders, and to compile efficiency rates and production yield reports without glitches, system overloads, or shutdowns.

- The people enter their Standard Needs orders
- Producers are to review system order levels, confirm, and submit resource requests
- The people receive Work Order requests and confirm their commitment
- The System is to confirm orders and estimate delivery dates

PHASE VI IMPLEMENTATION (2027-2029)

- Data Integrity Confirmation by Auditors and the people: Inventories and Willit Reflective Funds Accounts
- Official Vote by the People for Full System Integration Date and Time
  - Old systems are officially voted obsolete; set to offline status, and decommissioned.

When 75% to 85% of the people within a nation confirm approval of the applications' functionality and the System Core's ability to meet the needs of the people, full implementation should commence.

When 86% to 94% of the people confirm the ability and functionality of the System Core - Complete System Integration and automation processes should be activated.

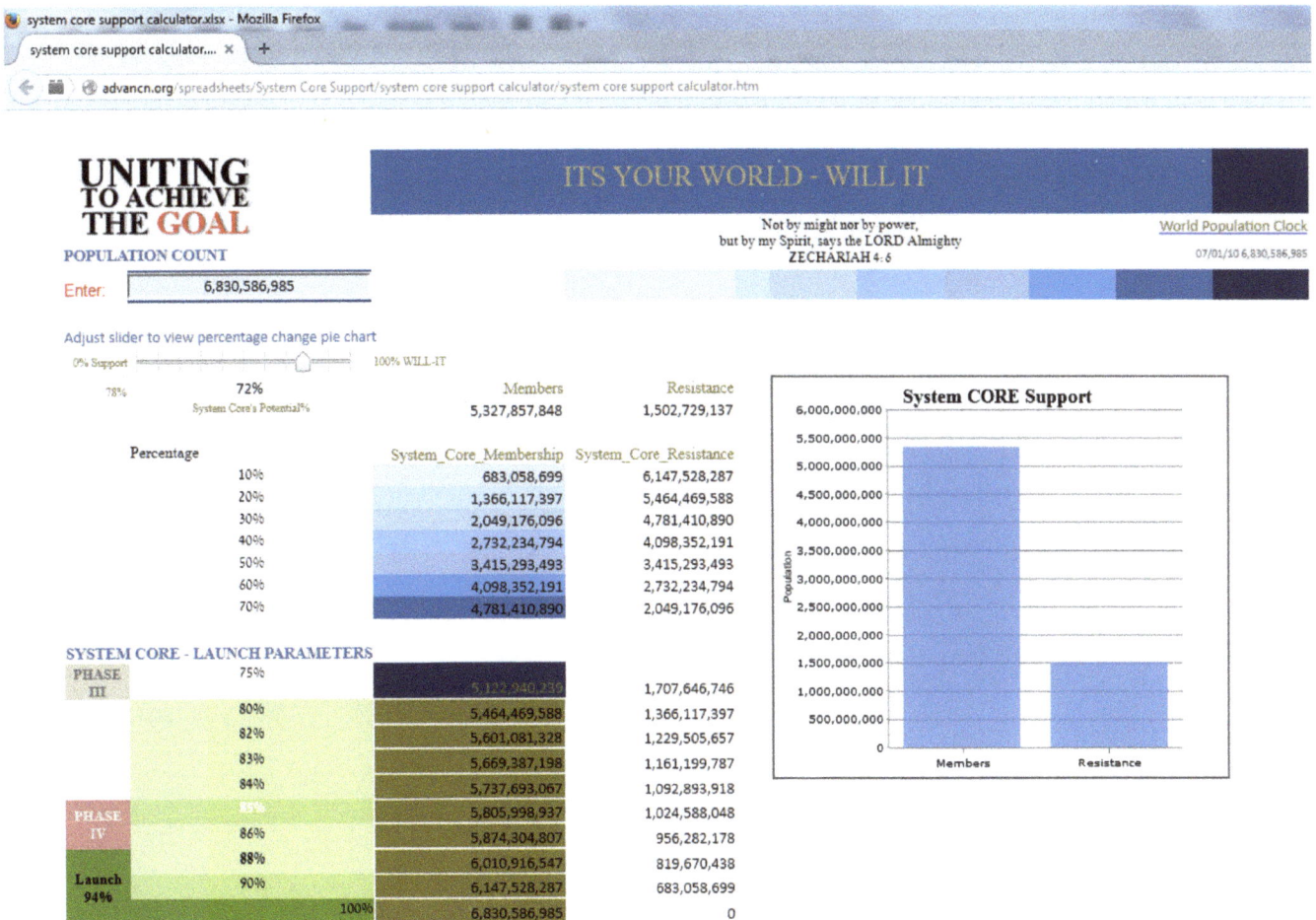

PHASE VII –UPGRADES MODIFICATIONS AND IMPROVEMENTS

- Upgrades to Processing and Manufacturing plants to ensure they meet system standards, and air and water quality regulations enacted by the people.
- Strategic recall of obsolete products for disassembly and redistribution
  Examples:
  - Internal combustion cars will be recalled for the exchange of Solar Electrical Vehicles
  - Obsolete computer and technical equipment
  - Dwelling reconstruction
  - The decontamination of lands
  - The break-down and recycling of abandoned and/or unused materials and landfills (as required)
- Global Communications System and Data Center infrastructure Upgrades and Development

THERE WILL BE CHALLENGES - WE WILL OVERCOME THEM TOGETHER

BUDGET | BUILDING THE SYSTEM CORE

The world we reside in today resulted from past errors. Errors which we must now correct to ensure we have a future. Our current economic system requires the raising of funds to show power, and will be required to resurrect the knowledge tree that will help prevent future errors.

It would be ideal if the System Core could come about by wishing. But wishes and prayer will not make it so. Actions that right past wrongs are required. There is no other way. Evil prevails when good men ignore the truth and do nothing.

The estimated cost for planning, development, and the testing phase is approximately 82 million dollars per year for four years.

Cost estimates for the planning and development of the System Core are estimated at $628,000,000 for Phase I - Planning, through Phase V - Testing. With an estimated 144,000 foundation members contributing $622 per year for seven years, the cost is roughly $51.86 per month, or $1.73 per day per foundation member.

Estimated development cost does not take into consideration World-Wide implementation.

Implementation of the System Core will be part of the Global Standard Needs Agreement, once the people approve integration and infrastructure acquisition.

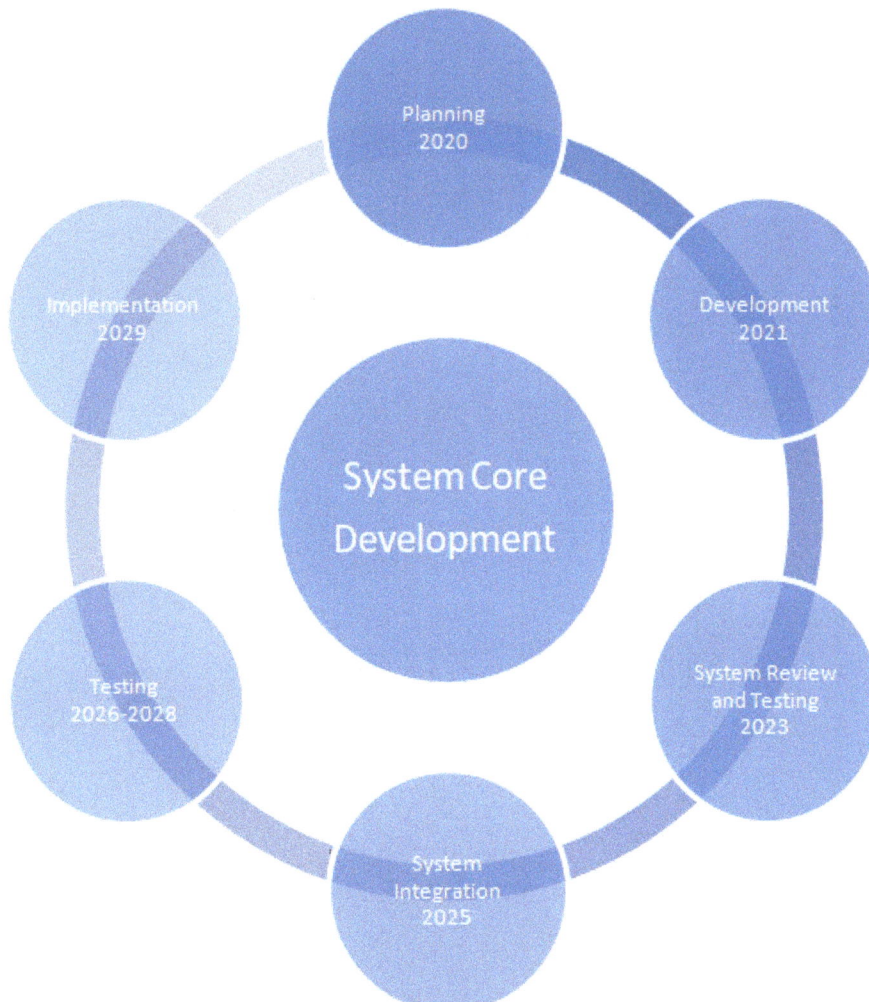

BUDGET SUMMARY

The following budget is an estimate of the costs from Phase I – Planning, to Phase V - Review, for the System Core.

Budget updates can be viewed at: **Advancian.org/budget**

Phase IV – System Integration and Phase V – Testing, have an estimated increase of four percent for the development team. Each nation's integration process will vary and will be compiled by and funded by each nation after system integration requirements are established.

Summary Budget for 2020 through 2029 (see the enlargement and budget details on the following pages):

System Core Planning and Development Budget	2019	2020	2020	2021	2022	2023	2024	2025	Summary Total	Annual Average (over 7 years)
Expenses			Planning	Development	Development	Public Review Development	Development	Integration		
OPERATIONS			26,863,226	27,937,755	29,055,265	30,217,476	31,426,175	32,683,222	$178,183,120	$29,697,187
MARKETING AND AWARENESS			2,865,552	5,307,360	5,517,476	8,235,355	8,564,769	8,907,360	$ 39,397,871	$ 6,566,312
*Community Festivals **		281,727	281,727	563,454	585,992	609,432	633,809	659,161	$ 3,615,305	$ 516,472
*Literature Distribution ***		2,144,025	2,144,025	4,288,050	4,459,572	4,637,955	4,823,473	5,016,412	$ 27,513,512	$ 3,930,502
Conferences, Expos, World Peace Fair		489,800	455,856	471,912	2,500,000	3,107,487	3,231,786	$ 10,206,841	$ 1,701,140
PERSONNEL		5,008,980	20,035,920	20,837,357	21,670,851	22,537,685	23,439,193	24,376,760	$137,906,746	$19,700,964
Consultants			14,600,000	15,184,000	15,791,360	16,423,014	17,079,935	17,763,132	$ 96,841,442	$16,140,240
STARTUP/ONE TIME EXPENSES		1,527,150	3,054,300	0	0	0	0	0	$ 4,581,450	$ 654,493
TECHNOLOGY AND R&D			11,022,355	15,487,794	15,648,541	4,346,590	0		$ 46,505,280	
CONTINGENCY (24%)			18,825,925	20,341,024	21,044,038	19,622,429	20,407,326	21,223,619	$121,464,361	$20,244,060
	Startup	Startup								
Expense Total:	$0	$8,961,882	$97,267,278	$105,095,290	$108,727,532	$101,382,549	$100,917,398	$104,954,093	$627,306,022	$89,615,146
Revenue (Required SC Foundation Members)										
Foundation Member Average Annual Gift		545	545	545	545	545	545	545		
Monthly Donation		52	52	52	52	52	52	52		
No. of Foundation Members Needed		16,444	178,472	192,835	199,500	186,023	185,170	192,576	1,151,020	164,431
Income Total	$0	$8,961,882	$97,267,278	$105,095,290	$108,727,532	$101,382,549	$100,917,398	$104,954,093	$627,306,022	$89,615,146
Plan 360 Book Distribution (also online)		585,000	585,000	1,170,000	1,216,800	1,265,472	1,316,091	1,368,735	7,507,097	1,072,442
Book Cost		$12.00	$12.48	$12.98	$13.50	$14.04	$14.60	$15.18		
Total Book Distribution Cost:	$7,020,000	$7,300,800	$15,185,664	$16,424,814	$17,765,079	$19,214,709	$20,782,630	$103,693,696	$14,813,385

Membership and Rate Requirement					
Total Seven Year Budget (2016 - 2022)		$627,306,022			
Annual Rate Per Foundation Member	Foundation Members:	144,000			
Based on seven year budget	Annual Rate: $622	Monthly Rate: $51.86	Daily Rate:	$1.73	

* Annual increase rate of 4 percent

** Attendance of 22 community festivals throughout the world - May to September

*** Distribution of 26,000 booklets weekly (22.5 weeks from May to September Total of 585,000 per festival season)

System Core Planning and Development Budget

Expenses	2019 Startup	2020 Startup	2020 Planning	2021 Development	2022 Development	2023 Public Review Development	2024 Development	2025 Integration	Summary Total	Annual Average (over 7 years)
OPERATIONS			26,863,226	27,937,755	29,055,265	30,217,476	31,426,175	32,683,222	$178,183,120	$29,697,187
MARKETING AND AWARENESS			2,865,552	5,307,360	5,517,476	8,235,355	8,564,769	8,907,360	$ 39,397,871	$ 6,566,312
Community Festivals **		281,727	281,727	563,454	585,992	609,432	633,809	659,161	$ 3,615,303	$ 516,472
Literature Distribution ***		2,144,025	2,144,025	4,288,050	4,459,572	4,637,955	4,823,473	5,016,412	$ 27,513,512	$ 3,930,502
Conferences, Expos, World Peace Fair			439,800	455,856	471,912	2,500,000	3,107,487	3,231,786	$ 10,206,841	$ 1,701,140
PERSONNEL		5,008,980	20,035,920	20,837,357	21,670,851	22,537,685	23,439,193	24,376,760	$137,906,746	$19,700,964
Consultants			14,600,000	15,184,000	15,791,360	16,423,014	17,079,935	17,763,132	$ 96,841,442	$16,140,240
STARTUP/ONE TIME EXPENSES		1,527,150	3,054,300	0	0	0	0	0	$ 4,581,450	$ 654,493
TECHNOLOGY AND R&D			11,022,355	15,487,794	15,648,541	4,346,590	0	0	▲ 46,505,280	
CONTINGENCY (24%)			18,825,925	20,341,024	21,044,038	19,622,429	20,407,326	21,223,619	$121,464,361	$20,244,060
Expense Total:	$0	$8,961,882	$97,267,278	$105,095,290	$108,727,532	$101,382,549	$100,917,398	$104,954,093	$627,306,022	$89,615,146

Revenue (Required SC Foundation Members)

	2019 Startup	2020 Startup	2020 Planning	2021 Development	2022 Development	2023 Public Review Development	2024 Development	2025 Integration	Summary Total	Annual Average
Foundation Member Average Annual Gift		545	545	545	545	545	545	545		
Monthly Donation		52	52	52	52	52	52	52		
No. of Foundation Members Needed		16,444	178,472	192,835	199,500	186,023	185,170	192,576	1,151,020	164,431
Income Total	$0	$8,961,882	$97,267,278	$105,095,290	$108,727,532	$101,382,549	$100,917,398	$104,954,093	$627,306,022	$89,615,146
Plan 360 Book Distribution (also online)		585,000	585,000	1,170,000	1,216,800	1,265,472	1,316,091	1,368,735	7,507,097	1,072,442
Book Cost		$12.00	$12.48	$12.98	$13.50	$14.04	$14.60	$15.18		
Total Book Distribution Cost		$7,020,000	$7,300,800	$15,185,664	$16,424,814	$17,765,079	$19,214,709	$20,782,630	$103,693,696	$14,813,385

Membership and Rate Requirement

Total Seven Year Budget (2016 - 2022): $627,306,022

Foundation Members: 144,000

Annual Rate Per Foundation Member

Based on seven year budget — Annual Rate: $622 | Monthly Rate: $51.86 | Daily Rate: $1.73

---

* Annual increase rate of 4 percent

** Attendance of 22 community festivals throughout the world - May to September

*** Distribution of 26,000 booklets weekly (22.5 weeks from May to September Total of 585,000 per festival season)

System Core

INITIATIVE EXPENSES

Administration

	Months/Qty		Rates		Total - Year One	Year Two	Year Three	Year Four	Four Year Total
				2020	2020	2021	2022	2023	
					Total - Year One	Year Two	Year Three	Year Four	Four Year Total
						Four percent increase per year			
Office Building / Rental	12				1,482,492		17,789,900	18,501,496	19,241,556	20,011,218	75,544,170
Number of Employees/People	262								0.00
Min. Space Requirement per persons	200								0.00
Min. Sq. Footage Requirements	52,400								0.00
Percentage Increase	45%								0.00
Servers and Additional Space Requirements	23,580								0.00
Communication Center and Conference	10,800								0.00
Actual Square Footage	86,780								0.00
Average Price Per Square Foot	$17.08								0.00
Annual Cost per Square foot	$205.00								
Utilities	12	% of Real-estate	5	74,125	889,495	925,075	962,078	1,000,561	3,777,208
Insurance	12		6,000	72,000	74,880	77,875	80,990	305,745
Internet Access	12		3,000	36,000	37,440	38,938	40,495	152,873
Web Hosting	12		800	9,600	9,984	10,383	10,799	40,766
				0	0	0	0	
Water and Trash Removal/Recycling Services	12	% of Real-estate	0.05	74,125	889,495	925,075	962,078	1,000,561	3,777,208
Banking	12		800	9,600	9,984	10,383	10,799	40,766
Credit Card Processing - Variable	12	varies	Not Accounted for				0
Office Supplies	12		5,141	61,696	64,164	66,731	69,400	261,991
Monthly Personnel Motivation Events	12	262	60	188,640	196,186	204,033	212,194	801,053
Health Care Insurance	12	262	2,200	6,916,800	7,193,472	7,481,211	7,780,459	29,371,942
								0

See Notes:

Sub-Total Annual Administration/Office	26,863,226.20				26,863,226	27,937,755	29,055,265	30,217,476	140,936,949
				2020	2021	2022	2023	

Marketing and Awareness

	qty	Cost	2020	2021	2022	2023	Total
Marketing and Outreach							
Literature Distribution	22.5	3.665	2,144,025	4,288,050	4,459,572	4,637,955	
Exhibition Expenses	26000					2,500,000	
Festivals and Community Events	23	$ 12,249.00	281,727	563,454	585,992	609,432	
SMS Texting Clickatell (100,000 monthly)	12	5,500	66,000	68,640	71,280	73,920	279,840

Conferences	Participants	Days		Cost	2020	2021	2022	2023	Total
Conferences Fees	6	4		3,000	72,000	74,880	77,760	80,640	305,280
Travel	6	4		1,100	26,400	27,456	28,512	29,568	111,936
Hotel	6	4	5	600	72,000	74,880	77,760	80,640	305,280
Meals and Entertainment	6	4	5	240	28,800	29,952	31,104	32,256	122,112
Miscellaneous	6			300	1,800	1,872	1,944	2,016	7,632
Travel - Local Reimbursements	12	16		700	134,400	139,776	145,152	150,528	569,856
Travel - Chapters	12	4		800	38,400	38,400	38,400	38,400	153,600
						0	0	0	0
						0	0	0	0
Sub-Total Conferences				373,800					

	2020	2021	2022	2023	Total
Sub-Total Marketing And Awareness	2,865,552	5,307,360	5,517,476	8,235,355	21,925,743

One Time Expenses	Qty	2020	2021	2022	2023	One Time Expenses
Office Design	1	100,000	100,000			100,000
Office Design Construction	1	300,000	300,000			300,000
Furnishing and Fixtures						
Desks	96	800	76,800			76,800
Chairs	96	350	33,600			33,600
Cubical and Office	96	600	57,600			57,600
Computer and Servers						
Computer Software	262	1,100	288,200			288,200
Computers	96	1,400	134,400			134,400
Programmer/Graphic Designer Computers	7	3,600	25,200			25,200
Servers and Technology	1					
AdvanCN	1	35,000	35,000			35,000
Phone System	1	35,000	35,000			35,000
Phones	278	500	139,000			139,000
Copier/Scanner	4	10,000	40,000			40,000
Fax unit	4	300	1,200			1,200
Security Systems						
Entry System	1	50,000	50,000			50,000
Camera System	1	150,000	150,000			150,000
Audio/Video/Editing Equipment	1	260,000	260,000			260,000
SYSTEM CORE						
Desks	182	800	145,600			145,600
Chairs	182	350	63,700			63,700
Computer and Servers						
Computers	182	4,500	819,000			819,000
Servers and Technology	2					
Communication Centers	1					
Community Kiosk	1	300,000	300,000			300,000
		Hold				
Sub-Total One Time Expenses	3,054,300.00					
Sub-Total System CORE	1,328,300.00					
Total One Time Expenses		$3,054,300	$0	$0	$0	$3,054,300

Personnel
Rates include employer taxes and insurances

Initiative Personnel	Qty	Onsite CR	Wage	Year One 2020 Annual Wages	Year Two 2021	Year Three 2022	Year Four 2023	Four Year Total
					Four percent increase per year			
President	1	1	1	124,000	128,960	134,118	139,483	526,562
Chief Board of Directors	1	1	1	124,000	128,960	134,118	139,483	526,562
Assistant to the Board	1	1	1	80,000	83,200	86,528	89,989	339,717
Board of Directors	12			100,000	1,200,000	1,248,000	1,297,920	1,349,837	5,095,757
Legal Council	4			100,000	400,000	416,000	432,640	449,946	1,698,586
Director of Marketing	1	1	1	95,000	95,000	98,800	102,752	106,862	403,414
Marketing Managers	4	4	4	55,000	220,000	228,800	237,952	247,470	934,222
Media Relations Coordinator	1	1	1	95,000	95,000	98,800	102,752	106,862	403,414
Media Unit - Audio, Video, Editing (see Equipment)	5	5	5	75,000	375,000	390,000	405,600	421,824	1,592,424
Director of Accounting	1	1	1	95,000	95,000	98,800	102,752	106,862	403,414
Accountants	3	3	3	65,000	195,000	202,800	210,912	219,348	828,060
Human Resource Director	1	1	1	95,000	95,000	98,800	102,752	106,862	403,414
HR - Assistants	2	2	2	65,000	130,000	135,200	140,608	146,232	552,040
Programmers for InDivisibe Website/Com Network	2	2	2	85,000	170,000	176,800	183,872	191,227	721,899
Tech Helpers - Phone Agents - Customer Service	40	40	40	55,000	2,200,000	2,288,000	2,379,520	2,474,701	9,342,221
Office Manager	1	1	1	65,000	65,000	67,600	70,304	73,116	276,020
Administrative Assistant	8	8	8	55,000	440,000	457,600	475,904	494,940	1,868,444
Director of Security	1	1	1	95,000	95,000	98,800	102,752	106,862	403,414
Security Officers	15	15	15	65,000	975,000	1,014,000	1,054,560	1,096,742	4,140,302
Media Communications Director	1	1	1	95,000	95,000	98,800	102,752	106,862	403,414
Media Presenters	3	3	3	75,000	225,000	234,000	243,360	253,094	955,454
Total Global Systems Alliance Employees	96	92	77					0
								0
The System CORE Personnel								
CORE Project Lead Developer	8	8	8	150,000	1,200,000	1,248,000	1,297,920	1,349,837	5,095,757
Directors of Infrastructure and Technology	2	2	2	135,000	270,000	280,800	292,032	303,713	1,146,545
CORE Directors	9	9	9	135,000	1,215,000	1,263,600	1,314,144	1,366,710	5,159,454
Programmers	51	51	51	100,000	5,100,000	5,304,000	5,516,160	5,736,806	21,656,966
Assistants	16	16	16	55,000	880,000	915,200	951,808	989,880	3,736,888
Total CORE Employees	182	178	163					
Total AdvanCN and System CORE Employees	262							
Sub-Total AdvanCN Personal Cost	7,493,000							
Sub-Total System CORE Personnel Cost	8,665,000							
Sub-Total Personnel	16,158,000			16,158,000	16,804,320	17,476,493	18,175,553	68,614,365
Personnel Taxes			24%	3,877,920	4,033,037	4,194,358	4,362,133	16,467,448
Total Personnel	4382631			$20,035,920	$20,837,357	$21,670,851	$22,537,685	$85,081,813

Technology and R&D		Qty	Wage/Rate	Annual Wages 2020	Year Two 2021	Year Three 2022	Year Four 2023	Four Year Total
Initiative Personnel						Four percent increase per year		
	R&D Personnel	8	150,000	0	1,200,000	1,248,000	1,297,920	3,745,920
	Assistants	16	72,000	0	1,152,000	1,198,080	1,246,003	3,596,083
	R&D Expenditures	1	10,000,000		1,666,667	1,733,333	1,802,667	5,202,667
Testing Phase	Tier IV Data Center		11,022,355	0	11,022,355	11,469,128	11,469,128	34,407,383
System Integration	Multi-Tier International Data Center System Infrastructure	International Expense		0	n/a	n/a	n/a	0
Full Implementation	Global Neurological Core System and Infrastructure	International Expense		0	n/a	n/a	n/a	
	Tier XII Data Center Network			0 Applicable 2022				
Total Technology and R&D		36699257 187		$11,022,355	$15,487,794	$15,648,541	$4,346,590	$46,505,280
Non Employees Consultants / Auditors				2020	2021	2022	2023	
	Auditors - Accounting Services	4 Quarterly Audit	75,000	300,000	312,000	324,480	337,459	1,273,939
	Consultants (Major Industry)	260	55,000	14,300,000	14,872,000	15,466,880	16,085,555	60,724,435
Sub-Total AdvanCN Personnel Cost		7,493,000						
Sub-Total System CORE Personnel Cost		8,665,000						
Sub-Total Non Employees Consultants/Auditors		14,600,000						
Total Non Employee Expense		88		$14,600,000	$15,184,000	$15,791,360	$16,423,014	$61,998,374
Total Annual Expenses				$78,441,353	$84,754,266	$87,683,494	$81,760,120	$332,639,233
Estimated: Annual Budget With Contingency Rate: 24%				$97,267,278	$105,095,290	$108,727,532	$101,382,549	$412,472,649

OTHER AND FUTURE FUNDING

PHASE I. TO PHASE IV. FUNDING

Date	Phase	Planning
2020	Phase I	Planning
2021	Phase II	Development
2023	Phase III	System Review
2025	Phase IV	Testing
5	Total Years	

Commitments by numerous funders will be required for the planning and development of the System Core. Phase one – planning; phase two – development; and phase three – public review, will not commence until phases one, two and three are fully funded.

We are seeking your funding commitment for a duration and amount you feel comfortable with. Once commitments are secured for phase one through phase three, donation fulfillment letters will be forwarded.

FUTURE FUNDING

Date	Phase	Planning
2020	Phase I	Planning
2021	Phase II	Development
2023	Phase III	System Review
2025	Phase IV	Testing
2027	Phase V	Testing
2029	Phase VI	Full Implementation
9	Total Years	

During the System Review Phase, AdvanCN will attempt to procure integration consensus from our partner nations. Each nation will be responsible for the initial cost of system integration, and nations that require integration assistance may be required to submit resource bonds, which AdvanCN will utilize for integration cost.

Additional funding for the System Core project will be required until the System Core is fully implemented, for which AdvanCN will request funds from all national partners. Once the System Core is implemented, no further funds will be needed and all outstanding debt reconciled with resource apportionments based on the 60/30/10 Resource Partition Plan.

CLOSING STATEMENT

Advancian is focused on constructing social economic systems to define our future with advanced social-economic theories and logic.

If we do not change our social and economic systems, we will not survive -- nothing that is wrong, that does not function perfectly with its environment has. What does not advance becomes obsolete. What violates original, universal, and divine Laws, exits space and time. What does not exist, is forgotten.

We cannot escape the effects of our actions, there are Laws, and we are out of compliance. The needs and pain throughout the world are proof.

If we are to prevent our own self-induced extinction, we must advance.

What remains hidden has the power to frame opinions, change minds, and to deceive.

Man can gauge if they are right by acknowledgment of effects.
Effects not measured are diminished and ignored.

But, a system that details every need and every effect cannot be denied.
The System Core displays, makes real, and will allow us to prevent pain.
The System Core will be the tool to accurately calculate cause and effects, and give those we refer to as "they," names.

AdvanCN's intent is to help humanity achieve the next step of our evolution as a social species.

We thank you for your attention and your assistance.

AdvanCN

THE NEXT STEP | GET INVOLVED

Once the System Core is developed, we will have a choice, our current system, or one that leads to global peace.

We hope you will join us in bringing peace to the world, not through violence, but by ensuring the people have a truly democratic social-economic system.

Now that you are informed about the System Core and Willit ideology, what will you do?

ACTION STEPS

STEP 1

Discover AdvanCN and learn about our mission, goals, and objectives

AdvanCN is a nondenominational Cooperative Faith Religious Order established to help facilitate international collaboration for the development of the System Core.

- Review AdvanCN's Mission Statements and Bylaws: http://AdvanCN.org
- Review AdvanCN's Manifesto

You are entitled to full disclosure regarding AdvanCN's mission and beliefs prior to your commitment of support.

STEP 2 – PARTICIPATE AND STAY INFORMED:

- Help design the System Core
- Join us at SoAct.org - FREE Online Community
- Participate in the Community Forums and Discussion Groups
  Post your opinions and tell us what you need to ensure the System Core works for you
- Stay informed, and attend Advancian events
- Sign up for Newsletters and RSS Feeds

STEP 3 - SPREAD THE WORD

There are many ways to help spread the word:

- Create a Local Alliance Chapter
- Email and Door to Door Campaigns; Social Networks – send a support message to your friends about the System Core
- Distribute Advancian brochures
- Submit the System Core proposal to your foundation's board and request their support.

- Support the planning and development of the System Core by becoming a Donor, Foundational Member, or a Foundation Angel
  Donate at: donate.Advancian.org

To support the planning and development of the System Core, you can also submit a personal commitment letter to: BoardofDirectors@AdvanCN.org

Your letters of support are also appreciated and can be forwarded to us at: supportletter@AdvanCN.org

To ensure full disclosure regarding funds usage, a real-time accounting system is available online. **SoAct.org** is the central communication and project management portal for Advancian.

Donation Transparency

a NFP Initiative

Donate with confidence and the assurance your donation will be used for the purpose intended.
1) Select an Initiative 2) Review the mission, goals, and budget to see how your donation will be used 3) Donate
View all payment requests, purchases, and services received by the nonprofit and the vendors who received the funds.

Donors	NonProfits	Payees
Donate - Sponsor an Initiative	Submit Project & Budget	List Products Services & Contracts
NFP Wishlists	Submit Payable	Confirm Work or Delivery
Volunteer	Project Management Access	Confirm Payment
View Payable Request	Post an Opportunity	Search for Opportunities
Subscribe to Payable Request	Contract Payee	Become a Vendor

Penbyte.com Registration Required - SoAct.org transactions incur no commission fees

General Ledger   Payment Ledger

NFP Initiatives (501 c.3)   Members' Communication Site

APPENDIX - A

TECHNOLOGICAL REQUIREMENTS

The System Core will require entry and communication systems for administrators and the public, and will be composed of inter-tier level systems.

System levels are outline based on a hierarchal system ranging from level 0 to level 8: community district level (L1) will be a tier one level system; City level (L2) will be a tier two level system, State level (L3), National level access (L4), Regional level (L5), a central data storage infrastructure (L6); and a global neurological core processing network (L7) that feeds from all System Hierarchal Networks for analysis and reporting based on a standardized field assignment dictionary for all data, and a standardized record categorization system, and segmented by the individual, business units, and administrations.

The following are the technology cost estimates for each system phase

PHASE I TO III

Software and application development and server network

Estimated Cost: $425,799,531

PHASE IV - TESTING PHASE

Mass Community System Testing Tier IV Data Center for first system testing, which will be accessible at the World Peace Expo – Estimated rollout date 2021 to 2022)

Estimated Cost: $201,506,491

PHASE V - SYSTEM INTEGRATION

Global Multi-Tier Level System Infrastructure

Estimated Cost: International Expense

FULL IMPLEMENTATION

Global Central and Redundancy System Network Infrastructure

Estimated Cost: International Expense

TECHNOLOGICAL RESEARCH AND DEVELOPMENT

Mass data storage and instantaneous recall processing systems

Estimated Cost: $46,505,280 from years 2020 Phase II to Phase IV, 2025 (5-years R&D)

System Core Development Contract

PURPOSE

All donations for the planning, development, and implementation of the System Core will be used for the purposes outlined within the Systemic Reform Solutions proposal dated January 2020. All software developed through your donation will be for the exclusive use of the People and the administrative bodies, corporations, organizations, and individuals designated by the people.

The System Core or any of its component parts may not be sold to any third party.

CONTRACT

This Software Development Agreement states the terms and conditions that govern the contractual agreement between **Advancian,** a Subsidiary of AdvanCN, having its principal place of business in Chicago, IL, (the "Developer"), and **the People and Donors** (the "Client") who agree to be bound by this Agreement.

WHEREAS, the Developer has conceptualized *The System Core* (the "Software"), which is described in detail within the proposal named and date *Systemic Reform Solutions of January 2020* and the Developer is a contractor with whom the Client has come to an agreement to develop the Software.

NOW, THEREFORE, In consideration of the mutual covenants and promises made by the parties to this Software Development Agreement, the Developer and the Client (individually, each a "Party" and collectively, the "Parties") covenant and agree as follows:

1. DEVELOPER'S DUTIES

The Client hereby engages the Developer and the Developer hereby agrees to be engaged by the Client to develop the Software in accordance with the specifications within the Systemic Reform Solutions plan (the "Specifications").

The Developer shall complete the development of the Software according to the milestones that will be confirmed by the people. In accordance with such milestones, the final product shall be delivered to the Client within nine years, after all funds have been raised (the "Delivery Date").

For a period of the life of the Software, the Developer shall provide the Client with answers to any questions or assist in solving any problems with regard to the operation of the Software and bill the Client at the Developers' Willit Rate for any assistance thereafter. The Developer agrees to respond to any reasonable request for assistance made by the Client regarding the Software within [the time frame designated by the people] of the request.

Except as expressly provided in the Software Development Plan approved and enacted by the People, the Client shall provide Willit compensation for support or assistance, to the Developer after the Software is integrated and enacted.

2. DELIVERY

The Software shall function in accordance with the Specifications on or before the Delivery Date.

If the Software, as delivered, does not conform with the Specifications, the Client shall notify the Developer in writing of the ways in which it does not conform with the Specifications. The Developer agrees that upon receiving such notice, it shall make reasonable efforts to correct any non-conformity.

The Client shall provide to the Developer written notice of its finding that the Software conforms to the Specifications within [90] days of the Delivery Date (the "Acceptance Date") unless it finds that the Software does not conform to the Specifications.

3. COMPENSATION

In consideration for the Service, the Client shall pay the Developer at the Willit Rate per person (the "Willit Rate"). Fees billed under the Willit Rate after the completion and implementation of the Software shall be due and payable upon the Developer's submission of an invoice. Invoices will be provided for work completed by the developer once every week.

4. INTELLECTUAL PROPERTY RIGHTS IN THE SOFTWARE

The Parties acknowledge and agree that the Developer will hold all rights in the Software including, but not limited to, copyright and trademark rights.

5. CHANGE IN SPECIFICATIONS

The Client may request that reasonable changes be made to the Specifications and tasks associated with the implementation of the Specifications. If the Client requests such a change, the Developer will use its best efforts to implement the requested change without delaying delivery of the Software. In the event that the proposed change will, in the sole discretion of the Developer, require a delay in the delivery of the Software or would result in additional expense to the Client, then the Client and the Developer shall confer and the Client may either withdraw the proposed change or require the Developer to deliver the Software with the proposed change and subject to the delay and/or additional expense. The Client agrees and acknowledges that the judgment as to if there will be any delay or additional expense shall be made solely by the Developer.

6. CONFIDENTIALITY

The Developer shall disclose all information regarding the (i) Software, including, without limitation any information regarding the Software's code, and the Specifications.

7. DEVELOPER WARRANTIES

The Developer represents and warrants to the Client the following:

Development and delivery of the Software under this Agreement are not in violation of any other agreement that the Developer has with another party.

The Software shall operate according to the Specifications. If the Software malfunctions or in any way does not operate according to the Specifications, then the Developer shall take any reasonably necessary steps to fix the issue and ensure the Software operates according to the Specifications.

8. INDEMNIFICATION

The Developer agrees to indemnify, defend, and protect the Client from and against all lawsuits and costs of every kind pertaining to the software including reasonable legal fees due to the Developer's infringement of the intellectual rights of any third party.

9. NO MODIFICATION UNLESS IN WRITING

No modification of this Agreement shall be valid unless in writing and agreed upon by both Parties.

10. APPLICABLE LAW

This Software Development Agreement and the interpretation of its terms shall be governed by and construed in accordance with the laws agreed to by the People.

IN WITNESS WHEREOF, each of the Parties has executed this Software Development Agreement, both Parties by its duly authorized officer, as of the day and year set below by the Developer, and in the Donation Form for the Client.

Agreement Date: January 2020

Wrina Iamwe

Wrina Iamwe

HELP SPREAD AWARENESS

You can help right our world by joining the Systemic Reform Movement. Join us, login to SoAct.org and register.

Help spread awareness about the Systemic Reform Movement purchase a t-shirt, distribute brochures, become a coder, or donate to support planning, development, and implementation.

You can download or purchase brochures at SoAct.org

Together, we can right the world.

DONATION FORM

Your donation helps spread awareness and helps with the planning development and implementation of Systemic Reform Solutions.

Donate online at http://donate.Advancian.org or mail your donation to Advancian

Make Checks Payable to:

Advancian - or - **NFP Initiatives** (501c.3.)

332 South Michigan Ave., Lower Level - A67
Chicago, IL 60604

Phone Number: (312) 274-5055

DONATION DESIGNATION

☐ Systemic Reform Solutions—the System Core

Donation Amount ($ USD): _____

Donor Name: _____

Address: _____

City: _____   State: _____   Zip: _____

Phone: (_____) _____ - _____

Email: _____

Systemic Reform Movement Membership

Foundation Member	☐ $60 Monthly	☐ $720 Annual
Foundation Hero	☐ $200 Monthly	☐ $2,600 Annual
Foundation Angel	☐ $435 Monthly	☐ $5,200 Annual
Major Foundation Donor	$ _____	

Advancian T-shirt - $40.00   ☐ Small   ☐ Large   ☐ XX Large

DONATE ONLINE AT DONATE.ADVANCN.ORG

www.ingramcontent.com/pod-product-compliance
Lightning Source LLC
Chambersburg PA
CBHW042353030426

42336CB00029B/3461

9 781733 774031